Learning Language

Learning Language

A Revision of *Learning English*

Philip G. Penner
Ruth E. McConnell
University of British Columbia

Macmillan of Canada

Canadian Cataloguing in Publication Data
Penner, Philip G., date.
Learning language
First ed. published in 1963 under title: Learning
English.
Includes index.
ISBN 0-7705-1397-2
1. English language — Grammar — 1950-
2. English language — Rhetoric. I. McConnell,
Ruth E., date. II. Title.
PE1112.P4   1977   428'.2   C76-017188-2

Printed in Canada

Cover photos: upper left, Marian Bancroft; two lower
left, Marian Bancroft; lower centre, reproduced by
permission of the Art Gallery of Ontario — Woman
Holding a Fish and an Ulu, 1954, by Pinnie Nuktialuk, Canadian, 1934-1969; serpentine and ivory,
26.7 cm high; gift from the fund of the T. Eaton Co.
Ltd. for Canadian works of art, 1954.

Acknowledgments

For permission to reprint copyrighted material grateful acknowledgment is made to the following:

The Associated Press for "French bury English: 'Flashback' becomes 'Retrospectif'" from the Vancouver *Sun*, January 17, 1973.

The Beaver for the short text by Malvina Bolus accompanying the frost photograph by Lillian Allen, from *The Beaver*, Winter 1971.

Burns & MacEachern Limited for the excerpts from *God Bless Our Home: Domestic Life in Nineteenth Century Canada* by Una Abrahamson, copyright 1966 Burns & MacEachern Limited.

Cambridge University Press for excerpts taken from the *New English Bible*, 2nd edition ©1970 by permission of Oxford and Cambridge University Presses.

The Canadian Press for "Eskimos — Language Problem", as it appeared in the Vancouver *Sun*, August 21, 1972.

The Literary Trustees of Walter de la Mare, and The Society of Authors as their representative, for "The Picture" from *The Complete Poems of Walter de la Mare*.

Andre Deutsch Limited for "Letter From a Bricklayer to the Firm for Whom He Works" taken from *The Ring Around the World* edited by Jean L'Anselme, translated by Michael Benedikt, published 1967 by Rapp & Carroll Ltd. Reprinted by permission of Andre Deutsch Limited acting on behalf of Rapp & Carroll Ltd.

Doubleday & Company, Inc., for the excerpt from the letter from Albert Einstein to the President, taken from *The Drama of Albert Einstein* by Antonina Vallentin, copyright 1954 by Antonina Vallentin. Reprinted by permission of Doubleday & Company, Inc.

Faber and Faber Ltd. for "The Animals" from *Collected Poems 1921-1958* by Edwin Muir, reprinted by permission of Faber and Faber Ltd.; "He Was" from *Poems 1943-1956* by Richard Wilbur, reprinted by permission of Faber and Faber Ltd.

Gage Publishing for excerpts from *A Dictionary of Canadianisms*. ©1967 Gage Educational Publishing Limited. Used by permission.

Dr. Rena V. Grant for "Wood Odors" by Walt Whitman, © by Harper Brothers, December 1960. Reprinted by permission of Dr. Rena V. Grant.

Harcourt Brace Jovanovich, Inc., for "To Look at Any Thing" by John Moffitt, ©1961 by John Moffitt. Reprinted from his volume, *The Living Seed*, by permission of Harcourt Brace Jovanovich, Inc.; "Languages" by Carl Sandburg from *Chicago Poems* by Carl Sandburg, copyright, 1916, by Holt, Rinehart and Winston, Inc.; copyright, 1944, by Carl Sandburg. Reprinted by permission of Harcourt Brace Jovanovich, Inc.

Harper & Row, Publishers, Inc., for "Knob" from *The Carpentered Hen and Other Tame Creatures* by John Updike. Copyright ©1958 by John Updike. Reprinted by permission of Harper & Row, Publishers, Inc.

D. C. Heath and Company for adaptation of "The Fourteen Words" from *Efficient Reading* by James I. Brown, copyright 1962 D. C. Heath and Company.

William Heinemann Ltd., London, for the facsimile of Winston Churchill's first letter taken from *Winston S. Churchill*, Volume 1.

The Hogarth Press Ltd. and the author for the excerpt from *Cider with Rosie* by Laurie Lee.

McClelland and Stewart Limited for "The Grass" from *Rocky Mountain Foot* by George Bowering, reprinted by permission of The Canadian Publishers, McClelland and Stewart Limited, Toronto.

McGraw-Hill Ryerson Limited for "De-noised" by Eric Nicol. Reprinted by permission of the author and McGraw-Hill Ryerson Limited.

National Council of Teachers of English for "Letter from a Triple-Threat Grammarian" by George W. Feinstein, from *College English*, April 1960. Copyright ©1960 by the National Council of Teachers of English. Reprinted with permission.

Government of Newfoundland and Labrador Department of Tourism for excerpt taken from *Historic Newfoundland* by L. E. F. English.

The New Yorker for "The Naughty Preposition", by Morris Bishop. Reprinted by permission. ©1947, 1975 The New Yorker Magazine Inc.

W. W. Norton & Company, Inc., for excerpt from *"Where Did You Go?" "Out." "What Did You Do?" "Nothing."* by Robert Paul Smith. By permission of W. W. Norton & Company, Inc. Copyright ©1957 by Robert Paul Smith.

Owen Sound Sun-Times Limited for "Tribute on a Tombstone" taken from *The Sun-Times*, July 17, 1972.

Oxford University Press Canada for "Sea Cliff" taken from *Collected Poems* by A. J. M. Smith.

The Province, Vancouver, for "On the buses" by Olivia Ward, photographs by Peter Hulbert, taken from *The Province*, October 19, 1972.

Rothco Cartoons Inc. for the excerpt from "Spit and Sawdust" by Hardcastle, taken from *Punch*, December 2, 1970. ©1970 Punch (Rothco).

Scholastic Magazines, Inc., for "Tom Smith". Reprinted by permission from *Scholastic Scope*, copyright ©1965 by Scholastic Magazines, Inc.

Simon & Schuster, Inc., for excerpt from Introduction by Edmund Carpenter from *I Breathe a New Song*, edited by Richard Lewis. Introduction copyright ©1971 by Edmund Carpenter. Reprinted by permission of Simon & Schuster, Inc., Children's Book Division.

"Southbound on the Freeway" and "Ornamental Sketch with Verbs" (both of which first appeared in *The New Yorker*) from *To Mix With Time* by May Swenson are used by permission of the author, copyright ©1963 by May Swenson, published by Charles Scribner's Sons, New York.

The University of New Brunswick Library for permission to reproduce the facsimile of the letter to Prime Minister R. B. Bennett (No. 396174 of the Bennett Papers).

Wesleyan University Press for "Two Friends" from *Figures of the Human* by David Ignatow. Copyright ©1963 by David Ignatow. Reprinted by permission of Wesleyan University Press.

Xerox Education Publications for "Foul Shot" by Edwin A. Hoey. Special permission granted by *READ* Magazine, published by Xerox Educational Publications, © Xerox Corp. 1962.

Illustrations

page 20 Emma Hesse

page 25 Universitetets Oldsaksamling, Oslo

page 29 French Government Tourist Office

page 35 Transworld Feature Syndicate Inc.

page 47 The Montreal Amateur Athletic Association (photo presently on loan to the Public Archives of Canada)

page 52 John Ross Robertson Collection, Toronto Public Libraries

page 53 Emma Hesse

page 68 Reproduced by permission of the Art Gallery of Ontario — Woman Holding a Fish and an Ulu, 1954, by Pinnie Nuktialuk, Canadian, 1934-1969; serpentine and ivory, 26.7 cm high; gift from the fund of the T. Eaton Co. Ltd. for Canadian works of art, 1954.

page 89 Reproduced by permission of the Art Gallery of Ontario — *The West Wind*, 1916-17, by Tom Thomson, Canadian, 1877-1917, oil on canvas, 120.6 x 137.5 cm; gift of the Canadian Club of Toronto, 1926.

page 110 Don Fernley

page 158 Don Fernley

page 160 Stedelijk Museum, Amsterdam

page 197 Canada Post

page 224 Gordon Watt

Preface

Language is the means by which we see ourselves and our connections with the world around us. This central place of language in our lives is eloquently expressed in the following words:

> In spite of all the wonders produced by modern technology, language remains the most marvelous instrument ever devised by man. It is impossible to exaggerate our debt to the nameless prehistoric ancestors who somehow, over long ages, evolved this elaborate system of verbal symbols, or complicated noises. Without it man could never have developed his brainpower, carried on his distinctive activities, transmitted all the lore he was accumulating, ordered his complex social life. Quite simply, he could never have realized his humanity. And now language has become all the more important because of the wonders of modern technology. Communication is infinitely more rapid, far-flung, and busy than ever before. Day and night, language is constantly at work ordering the manifold affairs of our society.*

Yet this world of language, so important, so familiar, and so quickly learned by any child, remains largely unknown. Although the recent dramatic increase of knowledge about the operations of language has given us new insights, it has also deepened our sense of the mystery that surrounds language. Furthermore, this new information has robbed teachers of the over-simplifications that in the past gave their teaching the blessed assurance of what was thought to be certain knowledge. They must now chart a course using a map which at best can represent the terrain in only tentative outlines.

For the writers of textbooks, the task is also difficult. What principles should govern their selection of materials for a year's study? What aspects of language and language learning should be given priority? In short, what language experiences, planned and unplanned, will best serve our common purpose—to help students to love and respect language, and strengthen their skills in its use?

These difficulties, however, must not stop us from seeing that new knowledge and theories about language and language learning have given us new opportunities to make our teaching more effective. We now know for sure where we should begin. The starting point is not, as in the past, with a prepackaged set of language items to be imposed upon students from without, and often isolated from the world of language around them and within them. A modern text must start with and build on the students' *human* need for language, their unique and inherent linguistic ability, and their natural curiosity about language, rather than with the language that we think they need.

For these reasons, the choice of materials in *Learning Language* was directed by a twofold purpose: to give students a deeper understanding of human language that will help them realize how much their growing mastery of language can affect the quality of their lives; and to provide opportunities to develop their language potential (referred to as "competence" by some linguists) into increasingly more effective and satisfying performance.

It may seem that a concentration on practical skills is all we have time for, and that the inclusion of anything not primarily utilitarian diverts us from this task. But it can also be argued that a preoccupation with narrow isolated "skills" has rarely resulted in an increased sensitivity to the variety within English or allowed the rich oral experience that leads to independent reading and in turn to better writing. The combination of too little knowledge about why the language is what it is with too much repetitive drill can kill the interest and positive attitudes upon which improvement in skills is based. Such negative approaches can make students fearful and timid in their use of language rather than curious about the language around them and eager to exploit the richness that English offers.

---

*H. J. Muller, *The Children of Frankenstein* (Bloomington: Indiana University Press, 1970), p. 191. (Canadian distributor: Fitzhenry & Whiteside Limited, Don Mills, Ontario.)

To the authors, therefore, "getting back to basics" is not a return to a narrowly defined literacy which confuses means with ends. A truly literate person has the necessary skills, but knows more than "correctness"; he has at least some understanding of the language connection in human affairs.

The authors believe that the historical perspective used in this text provides one way of moving towards the achievement of this wider literacy. *Learning Language*, by focussing upon the language around students and providing information about the rich background of the language and its varieties, can help students make sound judgments and choices, and can arouse and feed their curiosity about language. Such an approach can lead students towards an appreciation of their linguistic inheritance, and towards a lifelong interest in the workings of language, with a desire to use it well.

Our special thanks go to Judith Penner, who worked with us for a period of two years, and often alone, finding material and writing the first drafts from which we could work, and adding her own touches of imagination.

We also thank Maria MacKay and Dorothy Palmarche who, as teachers of English, responded to the manuscript with constructive criticism.

PHILIP PENNER

RUTH McCONNELL

Contents

Chapter 6

Chapter 7

Chapter 8

Language in Use: Varieties of English   296

Learning
Language

Marian Bancroft

This Book Is About

LANGUAGE IS

—made by people, not by grammarians.

—Something arising out of the work, needs, ties, joys, affections, tastes, of long generations of humanity and has its bases broad and low, close to the ground.

— Walt Whitman

—Closer...than breathing, and nearer than hands and feet.

— Tennyson

Eleven languages together account for over one half of the world's speakers.

Can you guess what the eleven are?

Marian Bancroft

LANGUAGE IS UNIQUELY HUMAN; THAT IS, BELONGING ONLY TO MAN

Language...

Read the following sentence aloud several times. Each time you read it stress a different word. Start with **John**.

John had two big dogs.

What difference does it make to the meaning of the sentence to stress one word rather than another?

There are between 4000 and 7000 languages in the world today; 4000 to 7000 ways in which language has been organized.

Writing a language down came very late in man's development.

LANGUAGE IS ORGANIZED NOISE

THIS IS A LUZ.

NOW THERE IS ANOTHER ONE.

THERE ARE TWO OF THEM.

THERE ARE TWO_____ .

Why do you speak English rather than some other language?

Do you feel you know the **whole** English language?

We are all born with language-learning ability, but we learn a language in stages, and we learn the language we are exposed to.

LANGUAGE IS LEARNED

This Book Is About

Marian Bancroft

Can you have a society without language?

"Ever'body says words different," said Ivy. "Arkansas folks says 'em different, and Oklahomy folks says 'em different. And we seen a lady from Massachusetts, an' she said 'em differentest of all. Couldn' hardly make out what she was sayin'."

— John Steinbeck: *The Grapes of Wrath*

Every language has many varieties, called **dialects**, within it. There is really no **one** "English language", but many "Englishes".

What other varieties of English do you know of besides your own?

Experiment: When you go home from school try not to speak unless you absolutely have to. Afterwards discuss what happened.

LANGUAGE IS A SOCIAL ACTIVITY

Language...

DOG
CHIEN
PERRO
HUND
CANIS

Try to think of a dog without
thinking of the word.

What sound does a dog make?
The following language-groups would answer the
question this way:

French	ouâ-ouâ
German	wau-wau
Japanese	wung-wung

LANGUAGE IS ARBITRARY; THAT IS, 'DEPENDENT UPON THE AGREED OPINION
OF A GROUP'

Spring Day

The spring day closes,
Lingering
Where there is water.

— Issa (a Japanese Haiku)

Reading a poem in translation is like smelling a flower through a blanket.

The Inuit (Eskimo) have many words for different kinds of snow, but only one word for all summer flowers. Why?

Some Indian tribes use the same word for working and dancing. Why do you think we differentiate?

"The person who . . . has never lifted the 'language curtain' behind which other people move and talk and think and feel in a way which is peculiar to them, may not even suspect that there *is* a way of living which is distinct from his own, let alone understand it."

— UNESCO: *Problems in Education X*, Paris, 1955

LANGUAGE IS RELATED TO THE WHOLE SYSTEM OF THE HABITS, IDEAS, BELIEFS, SKILLS, ARTS, AND INSTITUTIONS OF A GIVEN PEOPLE; THAT IS, TO CULTURE

To have squeezed the universe into a ball
To roll it towards some important question.

— T. S. Eliot: *The Love Song of J. Alfred Prufrock*

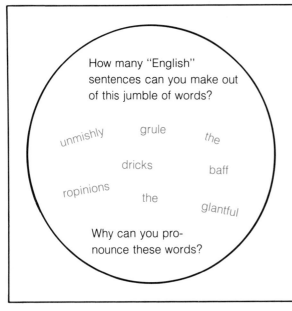

How many "English" sentences can you make out of this jumble of words?

unmishly   grule   the

dricks   baff

ropinions   the   glantful

Why can you pronounce these words?

How do you know this surname is not English?

DRDLA

There is a **pattern** to the way we make words and a **pattern** to the way we put words together to make meaningful sentences.

There is no limit to the number of sentences that can be made in any one language. How is it that we can understand sentences we have never seen or heard before?

How did English-speaking people deal with the pronunciation of the written word **Xerox**?

LANGUAGE IS SYSTEMATIC

Is this English?

Give we ilkan þare langage,
Me think we do þam non outrage.
To laud and Inglish man i spell
Þat understandes þat i tell. . . .

Zest is the ground rind of lemon. What additional meaning does **zest** now have? Do you see a connection between the original and the later meaning?

Language changes because it is made by people — who change, who encounter new experiences. With new experiences come new words and new meanings for old words.

"*Look, Pop! Environment!*"

—drawing by B. Tobey; © 1974 The New Yorker Magazine, Inc.

LANGUAGE CHANGES

Of course, you won't be able to answer all these questions now, but you can think about them. Come back and discuss them again as you progress through the book. Remember that the very obvious questions are sometimes the deepest, and the most difficult to answer. For example, when Isaac Newton asked, "Why does the apple fall?" it led him to discover the theory of gravity. By asking the right question, which to some people would seem silly, he changed our knowledge of the universe.

????

DOES

A PARROT

TALK

OR DOES IT

JUST

PARROT TALK

????

Using the sign language of the deaf, psychologists at two U.S. universities ... have trained a six-year-old female chimp named Washoe to communicate with extraordinary effectiveness by means of some 150 of the American Sign Language (ASL) hand gestures.... She can string as many as four or five of these gestures together to form the equivalent of meaningful human sentences.... Will Washoe set about teaching her offspring the sign language gestures she has mastered so that they in turn pass them on to successive generations?

—*Newsweek*

Can gestures work in the dark?

Man's capacity to articulate a future tense ... his ability and need to "dream forward", to hope, make him unique.

—George Steiner: "The Language Animal"

Many animals have fascinating communication systems. Bees, for instance, dance to inform one another of the location of food. Dolphins use a variety of clicks, whistles, and squeaks to communicate with one another. Yet most scientists and linguists would call these automatic code signals rather than true languages.

Language is only one, and probably the most recent, of a great sum of expressive codes.

—George Steiner: "The Language Animal"

Add to this list:

With language we hope // sing // dream // plan // imagine // worship // tell lies // remember // organize ...

A POEM FOR DISCUSSION AND TO BE READ FROM TIME TO TIME AS YOU STUDY THIS BOOK

THE ANIMALS

They do not live in the world,
Are not in time and space.
From birth to death hurled
No word do they have, not one
To plant a foot upon,
Were never in any place.

For with names the world was called
Out of the empty air,
With names was built and walled,
Line and circle and square,
Dust and emerald;
Snatched from deceiving death
By the articulate breath.

But these have never trod
Twice the familiar track,
Never never turned back
Into the memoried day.
All is new and near
In the unchanging Here
Of the fifth great day of God,
That shall remain the same,
Never shall pass away.

On the sixth day we came.

—Edwin Muir: *Collected Poems 1921–1958*

NAMING OUR WORLD

The beginning of all instruction is the study of names.

—Antisthenes (c. 400 B.C.)

WHAT'S IN A NAME?

Surnames are made in four general ways:

a. Local surnames: for example, **Brooker** 'dweller by the brook'
                                     Fleming 'from Flanders'
b. Surnames of relationship: for example, **Richardson** 'son of Richard'
c. Surnames of occupation or office: for example, **Smith** 'blacksmith, farrier'
                                     Colter 'man in charge
                                                 of colts'
d. Nicknames: for example, **Hawkeye** from 'hawk's eye'
                           Fairweather, probably 'one with a bright and
                                            sunny disposition'

—P. H. Reaney: from *A Dictionary of British Surnames*

FIRST NAMES
ACTIVITY

Get into small groups and discuss your preferences for names. If you had the responsibility of naming a baby, what name would you choose? for a boy? for a girl?

What is your name?
Why is that your name?
Where did it come from?
What is the use of having
   a name?

ACTIVITY

Find the equivalent of your own name (first or surname) in at least two or three languages.

NICKNAMES ARE

—names added to or substituted for the proper name of a person, place, or thing, for example, **Hairspray, Mad Dog, Little Guy,** and **Lumpy** are the nicknames of a close group of boys.
—abbreviations or familiar forms of first names, for example, **Elizabeth** to **Betty, Bett, Liz, Liza, Bess, Beth,** etc. List some nicknames and see if you can discover any **patterns** by which they are created.

The Eskimo language doesn't simply name things which already exist. Rather, it brings things-actions (nouns-verbs) into being as it goes along. This idea is reflected in the practice of naming a child at birth. When the mother is in labor, an old woman stands around and says as many different eligible names as she can think of. The child comes out of the womb when its name is called. Thus the naming and the giving birth to the new thing are inextricably bound together.

—from the introduction by Edmund Carpenter to *I Breathe a New Song: Poems of the Eskimo*, ed. by Richard Lewis.

The **Inuit** have been called the **Eskimo** for many years ('eaters of raw flesh', a name given them by outsiders). In recent years they have preferred to be called **Inuit** 'human being', rather than **Eskimo**.

How important are the associations that names carry?

NAMES AND MAGIC

It is a primitive tendency in man to assume that only one true language exists: his own.... This notion ... is linked to the concept of language as magic. A name is a manifestation of the person himself: for instance, in Australia the name of a dead child must not be used again. It is also a means of exerting power: in ancient Egypt, when the gods refused to let a dead man pass, he threatened to reveal their names to the demons. Lastly, to name things is to create them. In Gilgamesh's Mesopotamia, things appeared as fast as they were named by Apsu, the god of creation; a thing without a name had no existence.

—Philippe Wolff, *Western Languages A.D. 100–1500*

—WIZARD OF ID by permission of John Hart and Field Enterprises, Inc.

MORE PATTERNS IN NAMING

Make a list of names given to cars, boats, housing developments, houses, summer cottages, etc. What patterns do you see here? What are some of the impressions these names are intended to convey?

BY LANGUAGE WE CHANGE THE NATURAL WORLD INTO OUR HUMAN WORLD

As We Change

This representation of the world was painted by Richard of Haldingham about 1275. He shows east at the top, west at the bottom, and Jerusalem, "the holy city", as the centre of the world.

—reproduced by permission of the Dean and Chapter of Hereford Cathedral (photo: F. C. Morgan)

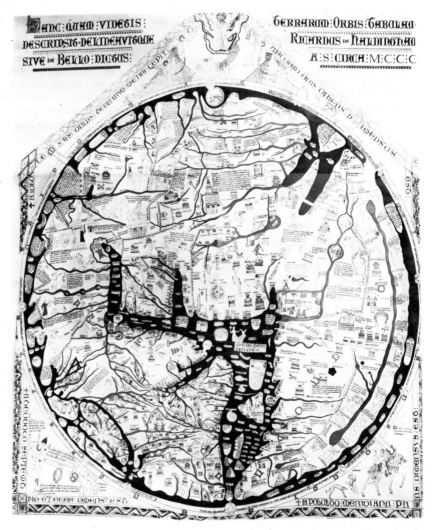

WE CREATE NEW WORDS TO DESCRIBE DIFFERENT WAYS OF SEEING THE WORLD

From EARD-FÆST, an Old English word (before A.D. 1000) meaning 'fixed to the ground', ——

Our Language Changes

—NASA

Above: The earth rising, taken from Apollo II during the 1969 voyage to the moon.

What existing words or roots of words did we use to make the words **astronaut** and **lunain**?

Many of the new words of the Space Age are borrowed from the vocabulary of the sea, for example, **spaceship, cosmonaut, moon voyage.** Can you think of some others?

How long has the word **astronaut** been in the dictionary? Check in several new dictionaries and in several older ones and see if you can find out.

The words **ecology** and **pollution** have been in the language for a long time, though few people were familiar with these words and their meanings. Why do you think these words have recently become part of the common vocabulary of a great number of people?

WE MAKE NEW WORDS ACCORDING TO OLD PATTERNS

to EARTHRISE, a twentieth-century word which came about when astronauts saw the earth from a new perspective—the moon. It is now possible for us to see our world from a distance. **Our world view has changed.**

LANGUAGES

There are no handles upon a language
Whereby men take hold of it
And mark it with signs for its remembrance.
It is a river, this language,
Once in a thousand years
Breaking a new course
Changing its way to the ocean.
It is mountain effluvia
Moving to valleys
And from nation to nation
Crossing borders and mixing.
Languages die like rivers.
Words wrapped round your tongue today
And broken to shape of thought
Between your teeth and lips speaking
Now and today
Shall be faded hieroglyphics
Ten thousand years from now.
Sing—and singing—remember
Your song dies and changes
And is not here tomorrow
Any more than the wind
Blowing ten thousand years ago.

—Carl Sandburg

Chapter 1

"In the Beginning"

History of the English Language

A fifteenth-century painting of the Tower of Babel

Museum Boymans — van Beuningen Rotterdam, 16th century

The Tower of Babel. Pieter Bruegel de Oude

Why do you think Western man has been so intrigued by the Biblical story of the Tower of Babel?

Where Did Human Language Come From?

It is plain that my native tongue had a share in begetting me, and thus is, in a sense, the cause of my being.

— Dante

Nobody knows how language began, though we think man may have begun to speak during the last Ice Age, about 100 000 years ago. But why human beings have language unlike the language of other animals, and whether language developed suddenly or evolved gradually over thousands of years, are still unanswered questions.

Nearly every culture, however, has myths about language. These myths are not always about its origins, but often explanations of why man speaks so many different languages. The best known in Western civilization is the story of the Tower of Babel.

Once upon a time all the world spoke a single language and used the same words. As men journeyed in the east, they came upon a plain in the land of Shinar and settled there. They said to one another, "Come, let us make bricks and bake them hard"; they used bricks for stone and bitumen for mortar. "Come," they said, "let us build ourselves a city and a tower with its top in the heavens, and make a name for ourselves; or we shall be dispersed all over the earth." Then the LORD came down to see the city and tower which mortal men had built, and he said, "Here they are, one people with a single language, and now they have started to do this; henceforward nothing they have a mind to do will be beyond their reach. Come, let us go down there and confuse their speech, so that they will not understand what they say to one another." So the LORD dispersed them from there all over the earth, and they left off building the city. That is why it is called Babel, because the LORD there made a babble of the language of all the world; from that place the LORD scattered men all over the face of the earth.

— Genesis 11: 1-9

The following legend comes from west-coast North American Indians.

Right after the Stone Age, the Indians had only one name and language, and one tribe covered the whole continent. . . .

They died off the face of the earth from a sickness that was a punishment from the Creator. It was worse than the white man's small-pox. You will find the bones piled together where they died.

After the sickness came a winter that lasted seven years, with nothing to eat. It seems that the Creator made people that got too smart—he wanted to be master of the world.

Then came a great flood from the north that buried the ones that had died. . . .

Only those with big canoes and strong cedar rope could save themselves. This rope that they used was so strong that you can still find some of it where it was left, on the sides of Mount Garibaldi and Mount Baker.

After the flood, everyone started speaking different languages — like it is now.

Very few people know the old language now. Today it is used only by Indian witch doctors and medicine men— and the language works, because it was the first language and the language of God.

— recited by Chief Mathias Joe

All such stories view the break-up of one language into many as a tragedy for man. Why?

Where Did English Come From?

Many languages resemble one another so much that we consider them to be members of a language "family". In 1786, Sir William Jones, who worked for the East India Company, startled scholars by suggesting that English was related to such exotic languages as ancient Sanskrit, Persian, and the modern languages of India, and also to Greek, Russian, Welsh, and other European and Western Asian languages. He based his theory on the fact that these languages seemed to follow certain similar patterns in sounds, grammar, and basic vocabulary.

Here are some modern examples. What patterns do you see?

ENGLISH	DUTCH	GERMAN	FRENCH	LATIN	GREEK	SANSKRIT
father	vader	Vater	père	pater	patēr	pitar
brother	broeder	Bruder	frère	frater	phrāter	bhrātar
me	mij	mich	moi	me	me	me
three	drie	drei	trois	tres	treis	tri
seven	zeven	sieben	sept	septem	hepta	sapta

> We recognize a pattern when we see a repetition of similarities. When we look at an oak leaf and a maple leaf how do we know that both are leaves? How do we know that they are different kinds of leaves?

—Thelwell — ©1964 *Punch* (Rothco)

Once scholars realized that many apparently different languages might be related, they began to search for similarities, tracing them back through many languages to establish connections. They pieced together a "family tree" for these Western languages, and called this language group **Indo-European.**

We have no written records of the "parent" language, Indo-European. The oldest records we have are some religious writings, dating from about 1500 B.C., written in Sanskrit (the ancestor of many of the languages of modern India) and carefully copied through the centuries. But there is little doubt that about 4000 or 3000 B.C. certain tribes spoke one language, and that when these tribes migrated, their language slowly changed into different languages — yet recognizable as descendants of the original.

The following map shows nine main languages of the Indo-European family. From these most of the modern languages of Europe and Western Asia gradually developed.

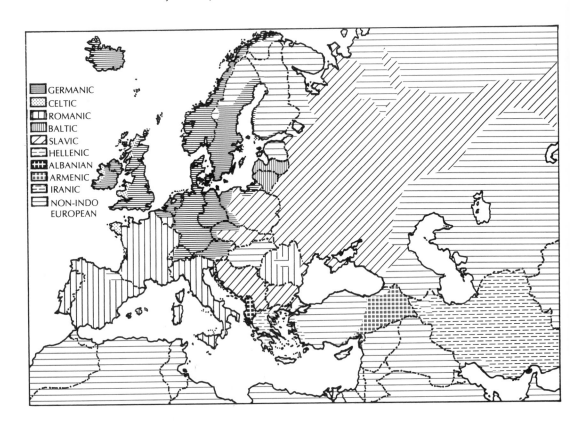

GERMANIC
CELTIC
ROMANIC
BALTIC
SLAVIC
HELLENIC
ALBANIAN
ARMENIC
IRANIC
NON-INDO
EUROPEAN

THE INDO-EUROPEAN LANGUAGES IN PRESENT-DAY EUROPE

A SIMPLIFIED TABLE TO SHOW THE MAIN INDO-EUROPEAN LANGUAGES

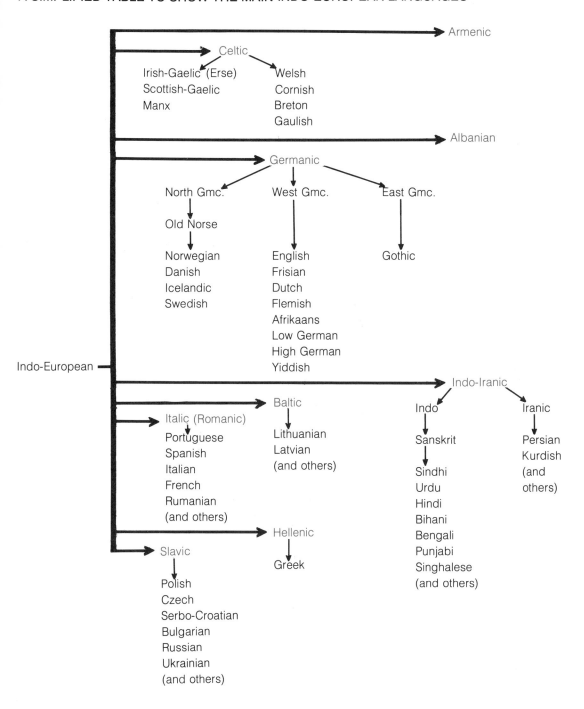

Now let us look closely at one branch of this large Indo-European family—the branch from which English evolved.

Looking at English

Have you ever examined our language closely? Have you ever wondered about its patterns, its odd pronunciations and sometimes illogical spellings, and its vast storehouse of words?

Why, for example, do we find in the Bible and other old books words that we no longer use, words such as **Thou shalt** and **verily**?

Why do we say **two big dogs** and not **two dogs big**? or **big dogs two** or **dogs big two**?

Why do we have so many pronunciations of the **ough** letter-group, as in **rough, though, through, bough,** and **bought**?

Why do we use **sing, sang, have sung,** and **ring, rang, have rung,** but not **bring, brang, have brung**?

Why do we use apostrophes to show possessives of nouns, as in "The book is **John's**", but not of pronouns, as in "The book is **his**", or in "The book is **yours**", or in "The book is **theirs**"?

Why do we have so many Latin words and prefixes such as **pro-** and **con-** and **anti-**, and Latin and Greek plurals such as **larvae, phenomena,** and **oases**?

A knowledge of the history of the language—its origin, growth, and changes—can help us to understand present-day English. This chapter explores the beginnings of English:
—the way it is related to other languages
—and the reasons for the continual changes in its

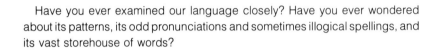

vocabulary,
pronunciations,
spelling, and
grammar.

Celtic:
The Earliest Known Language in Britain

The earliest known language spoken in Britain was not English, or any form of Germanic, but another branch of Indo-European—**Celtic**. This was the language that Julius Caesar heard when his Roman troops invaded Britain in 55–54 B.C. Caesar's army, threatened by revolts in Gaul (another Celtic region), merely established its victory over the Celts, took slaves, exacted annual tribute money, and then withdrew. But almost one hundred years later, the Emperor Claudius raided Britain and established a firm Roman rule that lasted for over three hundred years. Although Latin was the language of these new rulers, Celtic remained the language of the people.

When the Roman legions left Britain about A.D. 410, the Celts (or Britons, as the Romans called them) had to struggle against raids by other Celtic tribes from the northern and western parts of the British Isles. Because of this continual harassment, the Britons welcomed the arrival of various Germanic tribes from the continent to strengthen their own forces. After these Germanic tribes (Angles, Saxons, Jutes, and Frisians) defeated the enemy Celts, they decided to stay in this attractive land, and gradually they and other Germanic invaders pushed the Britons back into the mountainous parts of Wales and North Scotland.

In these two regions, the Isle of Man, and Ireland, the Celtic language has survived in the forms of **Welsh, Scottish-Gaelic, Manx,** and **Erse (Irish-Gaelic)**, though of course with many changes.

We still have a few Celtic words in the language. Early ones include **torr** 'peak'; **cumb** or **combe** 'valley' — as in **coomb** and place-names, for example, **Cumberland**; and thousands of place-names, for example, **London, Thames, Avon,** and **Devon**. This borrowing has continued through the centuries. Some more recent borrowings from Celtic areas are **bog, brogue, clan, slogan,** and **whisky** 'water of life'.

Why have place-names survived, whereas other words have disappeared?

About two-thirds of the river-names in Modern England are Celtic in origin. Why have so many survived?

If you look at the chart on page 21, you will see that Celtic and Germanic belong to different branches of the Indo-European family. The word **Welsh** itself is not Celtic, but a Germanic word meaning 'foreigner'.

Wales — 'land of the Wealas'; in Old English, **wealh** 'stranger, foreigner'

Cornwall — Old English **Cornwealas** from **corn** 'a horn, headland' and **wealas**, thus 'the headland Welsh'

What do you think **walnut** originally meant?

English: The Language That Took Over

Gradually, from A.D. 449 to about 700, the Germanic invaders took over most of what is now called England. The smallest group, the Jutes, claimed Kent and the Isle of Wight. The Saxons took the area just north and east of the River Thames (Middlesex and Essex), and all that land south and west of the Thames (Sussex and Wessex), with the exception of Cornwall. The rest of the country, including Lowland Scotland, was settled by the largest of the three tribes, the Angles, from whose name eventually came the term **English**.

The language as it developed from the time of these settlements (beginning about A.D. 450) until just after the Norman invasion (approx. A.D. 1100) is usually referred to as **Anglo-Saxon** or **Old English**.

INFORMING IDEA

English belongs to the Germanic branch of the Indo-European language family. If you look at the diagram of this "family" you can see that English is closely related to modern German, Dutch, and Scandinavian languages.

CELTS (Gaelic)

Firth of Forth

ANGLES

Humber River

CELTS
(Welsh)

ANGLES

Thames
River

SAXONS
(Essex)

LONDON

JUTES

SAXONS

(Wessex)

(Sussex)

CELTS (Cornish)

English Channel

—map adapted from Nist: *A Structural History of English*

The Peoples of England, A.D. 550

The Coming of Christianity

Unlike the Celts, the Anglo-Saxon invaders were not Christians. Indeed, we still use the names of four of their Germanic gods to name the days **Tuesday** (the day of Tiw), **Wednesday** (Woden), **Thursday** (Thunor or Thor), and **Friday** (the goddess Frig). But after the arrival of St. Augustine and missionaries in 597, all England became Christianized. Churches, monasteries, and schools flourished, and with several centuries of relative peace, England became a

centre of learning and art. Scholars produced many works of poetry and prose written in **Anglo-Saxon** (or **Old English**), some of which have survived the centuries. We have manuscripts of the hymns of Caedmon (the first English poet we know by name); translations of the Bible; poems about wars and battles; old riddles and magic spells; and the great epic poem about the hero Beowulf. King Alfred the Great himself translated many important Latin works into the language that his people spoke.

The Attacks from the Danes

[Year] 787 [789]. In this year Beorhtric took to wife Eadburh, daughter of king Offa. And in his days came first three ships of Norwegians from Hörthaland [around Hardanger Fjord]: and then the reeve rode thither and tried to compel them to go to the royal manor, for he did not know what they were: and then they slew him. These were the first ships of the Danes to come to England.

—*The Anglo-Saxon Chronicle*, translated from Anglo-Saxon by G.N. Garmonsway

Much of the art and writing of the Anglo-Saxons was destroyed by the ordinary processes of time and by new Germanic invaders — people from the areas that are now Sweden, Denmark, and Norway. Known as the Vikings — but also as Scandinavians, Norsemen, Danes, and the "heathen"—these tribes in the eighth to eleventh centuries became pirates and raiders all over Western Europe, ranging as far as Russia, Arabia, the Mediterranean, and west to the British Isles, Greenland, and North America. In 787 the pirates began to raid England, pillaging towns and monasteries, stealing treasure, and burning manuscripts. By the 800s these Danes wanted the land itself, and they began to occupy most of England, Scotland, and Ireland. Only the Kingdom of Wessex held out, and even there King Alfred was forced at times to go into hiding. Eventually, after a victory over a large Danish force, King Alfred managed to make a treaty with the newcomers; the Danes took the land to the north and east—an area called "the Danelaw" — and the Anglo-Saxons kept the south and west. Many present-day differences in speech within England are survivals from this early division of settlement.

In time the Danes became Christianized and assimilated with the Anglo-Saxons, and by the tenth century England was one kingdom. Because the Danes also spoke a Germanic language (Old Norse), their speech was very similar to English, a fact which made easier the mixture of the two peoples. A **kirk** in Scotland, for example, is merely the Scandinavian form of what is **church** in the speech of southern England. Many of our everyday words, for example, **get, give, are, they, cut, sky, sister, take,** and **call,** are Scandinavian in origin — evidence of how readily the two languages blended to make a richer Old English. Often, as with **kirk** and **church,** both forms have remained in the language, and sometimes the Scandinavian word has replaced the Anglo-Saxon word. The scholar Mario Pei suggests that if Anglo-Saxon had developed without Danish influence we would probably say not:

Take the knife and cut the steak.

but: Nim the metter and sned the oxflesh.

The superb technical skill and craftsmanship that went into the building of this Viking ship demonstrate the human need to give permanent shape to experience which is constantly changing. The Vikings expressed this need in making beautiful objects of gold and ivory and beautiful ships. But, unlike the Irish Celts and the settled English, the Norsemen did not make books. Such development, suggests Kenneth Clark, needs settled conditions.

Civilisation means something more than energy and will and creative power: . . . [It needs] a sense of permanence. The wanderers and the invaders were in a continual state of flux. They didn't feel the need to look forward beyond the next March or the next voyage or the next battle. And for that reason it didn't occur to them to build stone houses, or to write books. . . . Civilised man . . . must feel that he belongs somewhere in space and time; that he consciously looks forward and looks back. And for this purpose it is a great convenience to be able to read and write.

—Kenneth Clark: *Civilisation: A Personal View*

Gokstad Ship, Oslo

What Was Anglo-Saxon (Old English) Like?

Old English was so different from Modern English that it seems almost a foreign language. We can, however, recognize some of the words.

BEOWULF

lines 739—45

Ne thæt se aglæca   yldan thohte,
ac he gefeng hrathe   forman sithe
slæpendne rinc,   slat unwearnum,
that ban-locan,   blod edrum dranc,
synsnædum swealh;   sona hæfde
unlyfigendes   eal gefeormod,
fet ond forma.

Nor did the monster   think to delay that [his killing]
but he seized suddenly   in the first rush
a sleeping warrior,   slit [him] without hindrance
bit into [his] bone-locks [or bone-locker],   drank the
  blood from [his] veins,
gulped [him] down in huge chunks;   soon he had
of the unliving one   all devoured,
[even] feet and hands.

These above lines from the Anglo-Saxon (Old English) poem *Beowulf* (changed into modern print and punctuation) describe how the monster Grendel devours a sleeping warrior at the great hall of Hrothgar. With the help of the closely literal translation, see how many of the Old English words you can recognize.

What words in the Old English do you think might be related to the following words of Modern English:

fang (for example, a dog's fangs)
former and **foremost**
rash (meaning 'hasty, impetuous in action')
swallow (as of food)

The lines also illustrate a characteristic of Old English — the making of colourful compounds. These compounds are often more descriptive and picturesque than their modern English counterparts. From the context, what do you think the compound **ban-locan** 'bone-locks' or 'bone-locker' describes?

—reproduced by permission of the British Library Board — Cotton MS. Vitellius A XV, f. 133

Above: A page from the only surviving manuscript of the Anglo-Saxon poem *Beowulf*. The manuscript dates from about A.D. 1000, but the poem was oral for centuries before this.

Old English was a highly inflected language, that is, its grammar system relied heavily on changing the forms of the words rather than on word order.

Here is the Lord's Prayer, in Old English, in Modern English (two versions), and in German. Compare them carefully. (Note that Ð and Þ equal modern **th**.)

OLD ENGLISH

FÆDER URE,
ÞU ÞE EART ON HEOFENUM,
SI ÞIN NAMA GEHALGOD.
TO-BECUME ÞIN RICE.
GEWURÐE ÞIN WILLA ON EORÞAN,
 SWA SWA ON HEOFENUM.
URNE DÆGHWAMLICAN HLAF
 SYLE US TO DÆG.
AND FORGYF US URE GYLTAS,
 SWA SWA WE FORGIFAÐ URUM GYLTENDUM.
AND NE GELÆDDE ÞU US ON COSTNUNGE,
AC ALYS US OF YFELE. SOÞLICE.

GERMAN

Unser Vater der du bist im Himmel,
Dein Name werde geheiliget,
Dein Reich komme,
Dein Wille geschehe auf Erden wie im Himmel.
Unser täglich Brot gib uns heute,
Und vergib uns unsere Schulden,
Wie wir unsern Schuldigern vergeben.
Und führe uns nicht in Versuchung, sondern er-
 löse uns von dem Übel
(Denn dein ist das Reich und die Kraft und die
 Herrlichkeit in Ewigkeit.)
Amen.
(Luther's Version)

MODERN ENGLISH

Our Father,
Which art in heaven,
Hallowed be thy name.
Thy kingdom come.
Thy will be done in earth, as it is in heaven.
Give us this day our daily bread.
And forgive us our debts, as we forgive our debtors.
And lead us not into temptation,
But deliver us from evil.
For thine is the kingdom, and the power, and the
 glory, for ever.
Amen.
(King James Version, 1611)

Our Father in heaven,
thy name be hallowed;
thy kingdom come,
thy will be done,
on earth as in heaven.
Give us today our daily bread.
Forgive us the wrong we have done,
as we have forgiven those who have wronged us.
And do not bring us to the test,
but save us from the evil one.
Amen.
(New English Bible)

Can you see similarities between the Modern English words and the Anglo-Saxon and German words?

Modern English	name	earth	heaven	evil	kingdom
Old English	nama	eorþan	heofenum	yfele	rice
Modern German	Name	Erden	Himmel	Übel	Reich

Modern English has been simplified as a result of inflections having been dropped. For example, the gift in present-day English remains unchanged whether it is used as a subject or an object of the verb. In Old English the gift is seo giefu when sub-ject, but tha giefe when object. In this respect Old English is much like Modern German.

In a highly inflected language such as Old English, the endings are clues to word relationships, and word order is therefore not very important. For example, all three of the following sentences would mean the same thing because the words would have endings as markers to indicate their function.

The gift the man on the table put.
On the table the gift put the man.
The gift put the man on the table.

But in modern English, because most of the inflections have disappeared, the word order must be more rigid. To avoid nonsense, we must use a pattern close to:

The man put the gift on the table.

INFORMING IDEA

In Modern English **word order**, not **inflection**, is the main clue that tells us which is the subject, and which is the object. Compare these:

The boy bit the dog.
The dog bit the boy.

The Maple Leafs beat the Canadiens.
The Canadiens beat the Maple Leafs.

In a humorous article from *Punch*, the English writer Paul Jennings imagines that, if the English language had gone on developing without outside interruption, it might have sounded like this today:

Wel may the bells outclangen, wel may the folk and their childer be blithe and merry on a folkwide holyday, on this nine-hundredth yearday when we make wassail for our goodenlich offpushing of William the Conquered. For many a moon the Anglish have taken as granted and godspel truth, as a foregift and bottom-thing of our folkbeing, that never an outlander, from east ne west ne any other gau of the lodestone, has made conquest of this snugfast eyot.

Glossary

childer — compare German **Kinder** 'children', as in our **kindergarten**

goodendlich — 'fortunate' (literally 'good ending like')

gau — Gau in Modern German means 'district, region'

godspel — literally 'good message, good tidings'
foregift — 'first gift, primary gift'
eyot — 'island'
lodestone — 'way- or direction-stone' (our **compass**)

But a great event changed the course of the "Englisc" language.

"1066 and All That"

It is a river, this language,
Once in a thousand years
Breaking a new course
Changing its way to the ocean.

— Carl Sandburg

The greatest changes in English occurred after 1066, following the conquest of England by the Normans — known as the Norman-French because, although Scandinavian in origin, they had lived in the north of France for five generations and spoke French. (Look on the chart on page 21 and you will see that French is a Romance language, evolved from Latin.)

French became the official language because the Normans were the rulers and the English the ruled. French, not English, literature was read and written by those who aspired to culture. Therefore a great many of our words relating to law, government, and leisure came to us from French. Some examples are **parliament, duchess, armour, justice, money, pleasure, castle,** and **chivalry.**

Because the conquered Anglo-Saxon people became the serfs and labourers of the Norman lords, the Anglo-Saxon words that have remained are the everyday words of house and home, such as **stone, man, day, drink, home, fish, hunting, love, light, sleep,** and **water.**

Separated by language and class, the Normans and English had little contact, so that the country remained bilingual for almost three hundred years — indeed, strictly speaking, England was trilingual, because Latin was the language of the Church, of scholarship, and of much literature.

A section of the Bayeux tapestry, woven to commemorate the conquest of England in 1066, and preserved at Bayeux, France

FOR DISCUSSION

ENGLAND WAS BILINGUAL; CANADA IS BILINGUAL

I — What is the difference between **a multi-lingual** country and **a bilingual** country?

— What is meant by an **official** language?

— Name some modern countries where more than one language is spoken. Discuss the attitudes in these countries to the different languages spoken. Do the languages have equal status legally? Does one language have more prestige than another? Why does a language gain prestige?

II — Imagine that Canada was suddenly invaded by another language-speaking group, and that these outsiders managed to conquer Canada, taking over all the influential positions in government, in law, and in business. Canadian English would still be the language of the majority of the people, but not the language of those who controlled the country. What do you think would happen to our two languages in this situation?

— In bilingual countries one language is usually dominant. Why? What is the situation in Canada? Why?

— What is "Franglais"?

— In Canada, English and French are the official languages. Why did this happen? What is the place of other languages spoken by Canadians, for example, Polish, Ukrainian, Chinese, Italian, etc.?

English Makes a Comeback

By the mid thirteenth century, the descendants of the Normans began to think of themselves as Englishmen. Though they still spoke French, they found it convenient to learn English as well. By this century, too, an important new middle class of English-speakers emerged — artisans, craftsmen, and merchants. Gradually, English became the language of instruction in the schools and replaced French as the official language.

INFORMING IDEA

Notice that when one group began willingly to learn the language of the other, neither language was lost, and a new, enriched English emerged.

English also became once again a written language and the language of literature. One of our first great English poets, Geoffrey Chaucer (1340? – 1400), wrote in a form of English so changed from Old English that we now call it **Middle English**. His *Canterbury Tales*, a series of stories told by pilgrims on their way to Canterbury Cathedral, gives us a lively picture of fourteenth-century England. Here is an example of Chaucer's English:

> At nyght was come into that hostelrye
> Wel nyne and twenty in a compaignye,
> Of sondry folk, by aventure yfalle
> In felaweshipe, and pilgrimes were they alle

The fox who nearly catches Chauntecleer, the rooster, is described:

> His colour was bitwixe yelow and reed,
> And tipped was his tayl and bothe his eeris
> With blak, unlyk the remenant of his heeris;

Chaucer's decision to write, not in French and not in Latin, but in the English of London shows his confidence in English as a language that would last.

How was it that English became the nation's major language when the ruling class spoke French? It survived because, for over three hundred years, it was primarily the **oral** language of the people, open to change and quick to reflect the experiences of its speakers. When the two languages (Old English and French) gradually fused into Middle English, the basic structure remained English, but the vocabulary was enriched by thousands of French words. The highly inflected grammatical system of Old English changed to one of few inflections and a strict word order.

If a man who speaks only English finds himself for a period of time alone with a man who speaks only French, what could be the effect upon the English and French spoken?

Here is the first part of the Lord's Prayer in Wyclif's translation of the Bible, written about 1380. Compare this Middle English version with the Old English.

OLD ENGLISH

(The **th** has here been modernized.)

Faeder ūre, thū the eart on heofenum.
sī thīn nama gehālgod.
Tō-become thīn rīce.
Gewurthe thīn willa on eorthan, swā swā on heofenum.

MIDDLE ENGLISH 1380

(The letter **u** was used for **v**.)

Oure fadir that art in heuenes,
halwid be thi name;
thi kyngdom cumm to;
be thi wille don as in heuen and in earthe.

1. What do you notice about the word order in the first line?
2. Although Middle English kept a few noun endings, such as **e** and **en**, that are now dropped, most endings (except plurals and possessives) disappeared. What endings have disappeared in line 4?

—reproduced by permission of the British Library Board—Royal MS. 18 D II, f. 148

Early sixteenth-century representation of Chaucer's Canterbury pilgrims

Changes in Vocabulary

The fusing of the two languages has given English a large and varied vocabulary—probably the largest of any language in the world—and many synonyms with subtle differences in meaning.

In the early stages, speakers and writers often used both the French and the Anglo-Saxon word to make sure of being understood. Some of such pairs are still used together; examples are **nook and cranny, grief and sorrow, meet and proper**, and many legal terms such as **goods and chattels.**

Here are some pairs of Anglo-Saxon and French words. Examine each pair carefully and discuss in class the slight differences in meaning.

FROM ANGLO-SAXON	FROM OLD FRENCH	
help	aid	Would you call out "Aid! Aid!" if you were drowning?
begin	commence	Which do you use more commonly?
love	adore	Which is the more fundamental word?
gift	donation	What is the difference in meaning?
freedom	liberty	Which is stronger?
sad	melancholy	Which is stronger emotionally?
answer	reply	Which is more common? Which more literary?

Can you add to this list?

" O.K., MOM, I'VE DONE ALL THE 'NOOKS'—
NOW WHAT'S A 'CRANNY'?!"

—Copyright © 1974. Reprinted by permission of *Saturday Review* and Al Johns

Look up the original meanings of **nook** and **cranny**. Why do you think the two words have become a unified phrase?

ACTIVITY

Decide whether the following words are derived from Old English (Germanic) or from French. Then check your decisions with a dictionary that gives the **etymology** (origins) of words, for example, *Dictionary of Canadian English: The Senior Dictionary.*

Use the abbreviations in the dictionary you consult. Sometimes you will find AF, meaning Anglo-French, or OF, meaning Old French, and OE, meaning Old English.

house; residence
observe; watch
deluge; flood
feeble; weak
ancient; old
eat; dine
ask; question
flame; fire
bought; purchased

The Sound of the Language Changes

During the hundred years after Chaucer (after 1400), the language continued to change rapidly, particularly in the pronunciation, producing many regional variations in both speech and writing. Why do you suppose that William Caxton, our first printer, chose to use the variety of English spoken in London?

Below is an excerpt from one of William Caxton's first prefaces. Aside from the spelling, does it seem very different from modern English?

And certaynly our langage now vsed varyeth ferre from that. whiche was vsed and spoken whan I was borne/For we englysshe men/ben borne vnder the domynacyon of the mone. whiche is neuer stedfaste/but euer wauerynge/wexynge one season/and waneth & dyscreaseth another season/And that comyn englysshe that is spoken in one shyre varyeth from a nother. In so moche that in my dayes happened that certayn marchauntes were in a shippe in tamyse for to haue sayled ouer the see into zelande/and for lacke of wynde thei taryed atte forlond. and wente to lande for to refreshe them And one of theym named sheffelde a mercer cam in to an hows and axed for mete. and specyally he axyd after eggys And the good wyf answerde. that she coude speke no frenshe. And the marchaunt was angry. for he also coude speke no frenshe. but wold haue hadde egges/and she vnderstode hym not/And thenne at laste a nother sayd that he wolde haue eyren/then the good wyf sayd that she vnderstod hym wel/Loo what sholde a man in thyse dayes now wryte. egges or eyren/certaynly it is harde to playse euery man/by cause of dyuersite & chaunge of langage.

Glossary

mone: moon
tamyse: Thames
zelande: 'Zeland, land of the sea'
mercer: a cloth merchant
mete: food (the meaning has since narrowed to one kind of food)
eyren: eggs (closer to the Modern German **Eier**)
playse: please

ACTIVITY

Transcribe Caxton's piece into contemporary English. Discuss the changes you must make.

New Discoveries — New Ideas — New Words

LANGUAGE —

> It is mountain effluvia
> Moving to valleys
> And from nation to nation
> Crossing borders and mixing.
>
> —Carl Sandburg

Writing tends to slow down grammatical changes within a language. Therefore, the most noticeable changes in English since Caxton's time have been, not in grammar, but in the vocabulary. The borrowing of new words increased at a tremendous rate during the Renaissance, when the English people came in contact with new ideas, new experiences, and other languages. By Shakespeare's time at least a third of the people could read, so that new words that were written down quickly became current.

By 1600 the English language contained words from over fifty countries. How do you think this influx of words might have happened?

FOR ORAL DISCUSSION

What kind of contacts with the English does each group of words suggest? All were borrowed into English before 1700.

bouillon	tableau	galleon
cauliflower	burlesque	armada
champagne	scene	desperado

madrigal	deck	zero
violin	dock	algebra
stanza	yacht	zenith
allegro	cruise	
	skipper	

diagnosis	calico	azure
pneumonia	bungalow	shawl
clinic	chintz	tulip
thermometer	curry	jasmine

A fifteenth-century Dutch trader

INFORMING IDEA

I'll have them fly to India for gold,
Ransack the ocean for orient pearl,
And search all corners of the new-found world
For pleasant fruits and princely delicates.

—Christopher Marlowe: *Dr. Faustus* (1588)

The Renaissance ('rebirth') was the great age of discovery, an age that really began with Marco Polo's journeys to the East in the thirteenth century and the opening up of land routes between Europe and Asia. When these land routes were cut off as a result of war, Europeans set out to find sea routes to the treasures of the East—the spices and textiles of Persia, India, and China. In the process they discovered that the world consisted of more lands and oceans than they had imagined. Though the world didn't change, people's vision of it did, and this change in world view was reflected in their languages.

Because the Renaissance came later to England than to Italy, France, and Spain, the English language borrowed from these languages words which expressed the new world view. From the French theatre, for example, came words such as **ballet** and **vogue**, and from the Italians were adopted hundreds of words concerning music, opera, and poetry.

An even greater number of new words came from Latin and Greek, still the languages of learning and also of the new Science. Hundreds of these, such as **adminiculation** 'aid', were never in common use and have long since disappeared from English. Others, such as **democracy, education, appropriate,** and **anonymous,** are still current. This process of borrowing from Latin and Greek words and elements, particularly for present-day science and technology, still goes on. For example, words like **telecast** and **videotape** have come into the language within your lifetime. What other recent words of science and technology can you think of?

BORROWED WORDS

MEANINGS THEN AND NOW

CHAUFFEURS
ORIGINALLY A 'FRENCH' MEDIEVAL BAND OF BRIGANDS WHO FORCED THEIR VICTIMS TO RUN OVER RED HOT COALS. FORTUNATELY OUR 'CHAUFFEURS' NOW HAVE A MORE SEDATE WAY OF DRIVING THEIR 'VICTIM'.

FANATIC
DERIVED FROM THE 'LATIN' WORD 'FANUM' MEANING A TEMPLE. SOMEONE WHO WAS CONSTANTLY IN THE TEMPLE WAS CALLED A FANATIC & HENCE THE WORD'S IMPLICATION OF EXCESSIVE ENTHUSIASM.

POODLE
THIS IS DERIVED FROM THE GERMAN PUDEL-HUND FROM PUDELN (TO SPLASH). EXACTLY WHY THEY WERE KNOWN AS SPLASH-HOUNDS IS UNCERTAIN.

EASEL
THIS HAS BEEN ADOPTED IN A SIMILAR MANNER TO THE 'CLOTHES HORSE'. IT IS DERIVED FROM THE DUTCH WORD FOR A DONKEY 'EZEL'.

DANDELION
FROM THE NORMAN DENTS-DE-LION (TEETH OF A LION).

ASSASSIN
FROM HASHSHASHIN WHICH WAS THE ARABIC NAME FOR A GROUP OF MUSLIM FANATICS WHO USED THE DRUG HASHISH. THEY FLOURISHED AT THE TIME OF THE CRUSADES & CHARACTERISTICALLY KILLED THEIR POLITICAL ENEMIES BY STEALTH.

HUSBAND
THIS ORIGINATED FROM TWO DANISH WORDS: HUS-HOUSE & BONDI = PERSON. THEY CAME TO MEAN A MAN WHO HAD A WIFE BECAUSE A PEASANT WHO HAD A HOUSE WAS ALMOST INVARIABLY MARRIED.

PUPIL
PUPIL ORIGINALLY MEANT A SMALL CHILD OR DOLL. IT WAS ADOPTED TO MEAN THE CENTRE PART OF THE EYE BECAUSE IF YOU LOOK INTO SOMEONE'S PUPIL YOU SEE A SMALL 'DOLL-LIKE' REFLECTION OF YOURSELF.

ACTIVITY

Use a dictionary of word origins, and try making some cartoons yourself. Your class may wish to do a display of illustrated word origins.

TWO LITERARY EVENTS THAT HELPED TO SHAPE OUR LANGUAGE: SHAKESPEARE AND THE 1611 BIBLE

Of the many literary works produced during the English Renaissance, the works of William Shakespeare (1564 – 1616) and the 1611 translation of the Bible, authorized by King James, have had the most effect upon the language. Because people heard and read these books, certain phrases and sayings have become part of our everyday language. Here are a few examples. Do you recognize them?

FROM THE 1611 BIBLE:

my brother's keeper
stranger in a strange land
man shall not live by bread alone
grind the faces of the poor
set thine house in order
thirty pieces of silver
be of good cheer
one pearl of great price
heap coals of fire on his head

FROM SHAKESPEARE'S WRITINGS:

thereby hangs a tale
a heart as sound as a bell
the naked truth
Lord, what fools these mortals be!
out of the jaws of death
all the world's a stage
uneasy lies the head that wears a crown
A plague o' both your houses!
forget and forgive
the game is up

ACTIVITY

Here is Psalm 23 as it looked in the original 1611 version of the Bible:

> The Lord is my shepheard, I shall not want. He maketh me to lie downe in greene pastures: he leadeth mee beside the still waters. He restoreth my soule: he leadeth me in the pathes of righteousnes, for his names sake. Yea though I walke through the valley of the shadowe of death, I will feare no euill: for thou art with me, thy rod and thy staffe, they comfort me. Thou preparest a table before me, in the presence of mine enemies: thou anointest my head with oyle, my cuppe runneth ouer. Surely goodnes and mercie shall followe me all the daies of my life: and I will dwell in the house of the Lord for euer.

Practise reading the above passage aloud. Aside from the spelling, how does the language seem different from today's English?

ACTIVITY

Practise reading any short, well-known excerpt from a play by Shakespeare, and read it aloud to the class or a group.

English Beyond England

And who, in time, knows whither we may vent
The treasure of our tongue, to what strange shores
This gain of our best glory shall be sent,
T'enrich unknowing nations with our stores?

—Samuel Daniel: *Musophilus* (1599)

While the language was absorbing terms borrowed from many countries, it also began to spread, carried first by traders and explorers to other parts of the world, and eventually by the colonists who settled in the territories claimed by England. In each new colony established by speakers of English, the language developed in its own way as the settlers adapted to their new surroundings and tried to find ways to describe the many unfamiliar things they encountered. They gave new meanings to old words, borrowed words from the native populations, or coined new words.

Therefore, many varieties of English exist today beyond the British Isles. Canadians, Americans, Australians, New Zealanders, South Africans, and Englishmen all speak the same language, but in slightly different ways.

A major difference lies in vocabulary. Many words found in one variety of English, but not in another, reflect the natural life peculiar to that country: the animals, the trees, and the type of land. Australians speak of the **outback** 'hinterland', Canadians of the **bush**, and South Africans of the **veld** or **veldt** (from Dutch).

If, by the time England was establishing her colonies, her language had not become a national language, and if printing had not helped to standardize and spread the written word, the "Englishes" of the colonies would likely have diverged much more than they did, and may even have become different languages. But while the spoken language in each region still continues to change, the written language gives all these Englishes a common ground.

Changing Attitudes to English

The widening of English from the language of a small island to an increasingly important world language resulted in changing attitudes to English. Scholars began to view the English language as important enough to be studied in its own right, just as Latin and Greek had been studied. They began to write dictionaries and to make systematic descriptions of English grammar and usage.

Unfortunately, some influential scholars had the mistaken notion that somewhere there existed a "pure", perfectly "correct", and "logical" English, and that any additions to, variations in, or changes in the language, unless approved by the best minds, were corruptions of the way the language ought to be. The following statement by Alexander Gill in the 1600s is typical of this attitude to new words — one that has persisted through the centuries:

O harsh lips, I now hear all around me such words as *common, vice, envy, malice;* even *virtue, study, justice, mercy, compassion, profit, commodity, colour, grace, favor, acceptance.* But whither, I pray in all the world, have you banished those words which our forefathers used for these new-fangled ones? Is the new barbaric invasion to extirpate the English tongue?

Think of some words that we use today that people call "new-fangled". How many of them do you think will stay in the English language?

Today, however, scholars recognize that a language is a growing thing that changes because the world changes and because all who use the language change. This attitude does not mean that one word is as good as another. The arguments for and against "newness" are never absolute, and the choice of the right word is never simple. Judgments about change must be controlled by the speaker's or writer's sensitivity.

Some of us, through imaginative speech or writing or through holding positions of prestige, affect the language more than others. But, because we think, because we do things, because we are alive, we are **all** makers and changers of language.

English Becomes a World Language

When Boy Scouts have a World Jamboree, how do they communicate?

At the Olympic Games, what languages are used?

How does the United Nations Assembly cope with the various languages represented?

What happens in a Canadian courtroom if the accused or accuser does not speak either English or French?

Read the following newspaper item:

ESKIMOS

Language problem

PANGNIRTUNG, N.W.T. (CP) — Eskimos in the eastern and western regions of the Arctic speak dialects so different they have trouble understanding one another.

The situation created a language problem when delegates arrived in this Baffin Island settlement for the first annual meeting of the Eskimo Brotherhood of Canada.

Conference organizers had planned to hold all sessions of 10-day meeting in the Eskimo language but found shortly after it started Thursday that they had a communications gap on their hands.

By the weekend, the comments of every speaker were being translated into English, which nearly all delegates can speak to some degree.

The combination of the two languages filled in most of the gaps created by the two dialects.

About 60 delegates from all parts of the Arctic are attending the conference.

1. Why might the delegates to the conference be reluctant to use English?
2. In what other situations or places is English used as the Interlingua, and yet is done so reluctantly?

Almost since the time of myths such as the Tower of Babel story, man has dreamed of a universal language, one that would help wipe out the barriers created when one group speaks differently from another. For centuries, Latin seemed to fill this role, especially amongst scholars of the Western world. In the eighteenth and nineteenth centuries, German was the international language of science, and French the international language of cultured society and of diplomacy.

Since then, various enthusiasts have tried to promote artificial languages such as Esperanto, Volapük, and Ido in the hope that one of these would become the interlingua of the world. A language works adequately, however, only if it is the native language of a particular society, able to express the deepest thoughts and hopes of those who use it and to change as the society changes. An artificially created language can never have the richness and vitality of a natural language, and the dream of a truly universal language is probably unrealizable.

In spite of the fact that there are thousands of languages in the world, only a few attain the status of a "world" language. Today English has emerged as the most important world language, the one learned by millions of people whose native tongue is not English. But we have no guarantee that English will remain the dominant language. Its ascendance is based on the political and cultural power of those who speak it. And no civilization or language has ever been granted immortality.

Cities and Thrones and Powers,
Stand in Time's eye,
Almost as long as flowers,
Which daily die.

—Rudyard Kipling

Your song dies and changes
And is not here tomorrow
Any more than the wind
Blowing ten thousand years ago.

—Carl Sandburg

INFORMING IDEAS

We are **inheritors** of a language.
We are **created** by language.
We are **creators** of language.

FOR DISCUSSION

What makes Canada linguistically unique? Read the following and discuss both the problems and blessings of bilingualism in Canada.

Compared to other bilingual states — among them Finland, South Africa, and Belgium ... — Canada is fortunate that her official languages both have international status. English is today the mother tongue of more than 250 000 000 people. To this figure should be added some 200 000 000 who speak English as their second language or who have a good working knowledge of it. French, for its part, is the mother tongue of around 65 000 000 people and is constantly used by another 150 000 000 throughout the world. These two languages thus have world-wide prestige.

—*Report of the Royal Commission on Bilingualism and Biculturalism*

Summary

About one-fourth of our present words are Anglo-Saxon; the rest are newly coined, borrowed, or adapted from foreign words. For instance, think of new words brought into English by such events as: the First World War and the Second World War; the advances of science in space exploration; nuclear warfare; medicine; changes in world politics; new products. You can find traces of the history of the speakers of English in the following examples of foreign words in our language.

A Few Examples of Borrowings

EARLY BRITONS (CELTS)

Very few words: perhaps **ass, bin, cairn**
Many place-names: **pen** 'hilltop' (Pendleton, Penrith), **derva** 'oak' (Derwent, Derwin)

ROMAN (LATIN)

Church words: **bishop, candle, mass, priest**
Place-names: **castra** 'camp' (Lancaster, Manchester, Chester), **vicus** 'village' (Greenwich, Sandwich, Warwick), **stratum** 'paved road' (Stratford, Streatham)

Others: **wine, cheese, mile, purple**

SCANDINAVIAN

Extensive influence, though hard to trace because so closely related to Anglo-Saxon.
New words: **law, die, fellow, low**
Check a dictionary and see if you can make a list of ten words beginning with sk- or sc- (pronounced sk-) borrowed from Old Norse. (Not all were Scandinavian!)
Place-names: usually ending in **-thorpe, -beck, -by** 'village' (**Derby, Newby; by-law** 'town-law'), **-thwaite** 'meadowland', and others

NORMAN FRENCH

Words related to government, law, the Church, the arts, cooking, etc.: **power, baron, armour, prison, attorney, sermon, sauce.**

LATIN

About one-fourth to one-half of the English vocabulary comes from Latin, either directly or through French.
Words: **simile, exit, apparatus, via, ego**
Prefixes, suffixes, roots: **ad-, ex-, -ite, -tion, ten-** 'hold', **dic-** 'speak'

GREEK

Science (often international): **botany, physics, physiology**
Theatre: **drama, comedy, tragedy, episode**
Roots: **phos-** or **phot-** 'light'; **tele-** 'far'

ARABIC

Some were brought back by the Crusaders, so entered English early: **sugar, minaret, mosque, sultan, cotton, cipher**

ITALIAN

Many words of the arts: **opera, piano, fresco, sonnet**

DUTCH

From trade rivalry in the 1500s and 1600s: **buoy, skipper, splice**
From the wool and weaving trades: **pack, spool**

SPAIN

From the sea and from American colonies: **mosquito, cigar, canyon**

AMERICAN INDIAN

New things: **toboggan, muskeg, sockeye, moose, squash**

INDIA

nabob, sahib, chutney, curry

MODERN FRENCH

Culture and food: **café, soufflé, matinée**
Phrases: **Cherchez la femme, bon mot, tête-à-tête, enfant terrible**
Wars: **garage, fuselage, hangar, communiqué**

MALAYAN

sago, amok (or **amuck**), **bamboo, gingham**

CHINESE

tea, pekoe, shantung, pongee

GERMAN

From names of scientists and inventors: **bunsen, diesel, fahrenheit**
War and other sources: **wanderlust, ersatz, flak, blitz** (**blitzkrieg** 'lightning war')

RUSSIAN

Many political words: **bolshevik, soviet, troika** — also **sputnik**
(How do you think the word **beatnik** arose?)

ACTIVITY

Make an "educated guess" as to where the following English words came from. Then check with a dictionary that gives the etymology of words.

1. lariat	7. giraffe
2. scherzo	8. ski
3. etiquette	9. jackal
4. crag	10. barbecue
5. booze	11. marmalade
6. ether	12. checkmate (in chess)

WHAT LANGUAGE DO READERS OF THIS BOOK PROBABLY SPEAK?

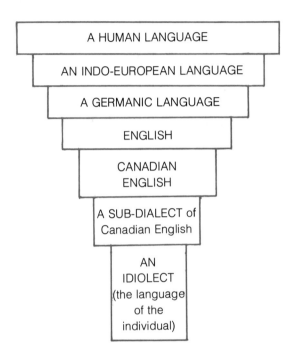

A HUMAN LANGUAGE

AN INDO-EUROPEAN LANGUAGE

A GERMANIC LANGUAGE

ENGLISH

CANADIAN ENGLISH

A SUB-DIALECT of Canadian English

AN IDIOLECT (the language of the individual)

ACTIVITY

Many place-names or elements in place-names in England are Anglo-Saxon in origin. Often place-names became surnames of families who lived there. Here are some common Anglo-Saxon elements:

burgh or **bury** 'fortified place' — as in **Edinburgh, Cadbury**

ham 'village' (our **home**) — as in **Grantham, Birmingham**

ton 'enclosure, village' (our **town**) — as in **Moncton, Newton**

-ing 'the dwellers at, the people of' — as in **Hastings, Buckingham**

Can you think of places in Canada, named after places in the British Isles, that use these elements? You may wish to do some research on place-names or street-names in your own area, or on surnames.

FOR DISCUSSION

Of what regional varieties of English are you aware? Can you give some examples? Are they equally acceptable? What seems to determine people's attitudes to regional variations?

ACTIVITY

Sir Walter Scott in his novel *Ivanhoe*, a fictionalized account of the social tensions between the conquered Anglo-Saxons and the conqueror Normans in the late 1100s, points out that, whereas the words for farm animals—**pig, swine, cow, ox**, etc. —are Anglo-Saxon words, yet those for the meat on the table — **pork, beef,** etc. — are French.

Why do you think this is so?

List eight foods that interest you and can be grouped under some category (fruit, vegetables, grains, spices, desserts, etc.) and find out the origins of the words. Then write a sentence or so summarizing your findings.

"Once in a thousand years
Breaking a new course."

Chapter 2

"Words . . . of Ourselves and of Our Origins"

North American English

"What on earth kept you?"

"It's a long story—just when I entered the last roundabout out of Basingstoke, a large estate car cut in in front of me. I swerved to the left and stopped on the verge, narrowly missing a prang from behind by an articulated lorry."

"Thank Heaven, you're safe. But all this could only have taken a few minutes. What makes you over an hour late for your tea?"

"I said it was a long story. The sudden stop stalled the motor. My hysterical attempts to get the thing started wore down the accumulator. Finally, I walked to the nearest call-box in a lay-by just over a fly-over leading to the motorway—about a fifth of a mile, I should think. I dialled your number repeatedly but the line was always engaged. Fortunately, a panda stopped to investigate, and helped me start the car."

"Well, you've missed the mixed grill, but there's Scotch egg in the fridge, and plenty of trifle for afters."

British English is different from North American English.
What variety of English is being used here?
Try rewriting the above dialogue in the English **you** use.

English Comes to North America

The English people who went to new homes in North America in the early 1600s took with them their language—the varieties of English spoken in different parts of Elizabethan England. Later the Scotch and Irish added their varieties. As the colonies grew along the Atlantic coast of what is now the United States, the language in the new area developed in its own way, and by the mid-1700s visitors from the "home country" were commenting upon the new kind of English being spoken in the North American colonies.

DO YOU USE THESE?

I guess so.
bug meaning 'insect'
fall meaning 'autumn'
druggist (British **chemist**)
have gotten
"**Loan** me a dime."

Old Words Kept

Many of these differences arose because the colonies, separated from the homeland by an ocean, kept some words and meanings that in England disappeared or changed. Visitors have often commented, for example, upon the North American use of **I guess**, meaning 'I suppose so'; this phrase and meaning were used in Chaucer's time, but have long gone from British usage. The older use of **fall** for 'autumn' has generally died out in the home country, and **druggist**, though still used in Scotland, has been replaced in England by **chemist**. In England, although the word **bug** is used, it now means 'bedbug', but North Americans have kept its older and wider meaning.

Many North American usages are found in British regional dialects only, for example, Somerset **drool**, and Surrey **pond** (which in other parts of England

refers to an artificial pool). In Newfoundland today **pond** can mean a 'lake', and in the Maritimes a 'salt lagoon'. Such regional forms probably came to America with one group of speakers, then spread.

The colonists also kept some older verb forms. A noticeable example is the American **have gotten**, meaning 'have obtained'—though all varieties may use **have forgotten**, and British English uses the older form in the phrase **ill-gotten gains**. The use of **loan** as a verb, as in "Will you loan me some money?", also has a long history. But today in formal writing and general Canadian usage **lend** is preferred.

INFORMING IDEA

The language of a colony tends to keep older forms brought from the mother country.

Older Pronunciations in North America: England's English Changes

---

How do you pronounce the following words? How does an English or Australian speaker pronounce them?

    dance   romance (Do they rhyme?)
    star   far   farm
    carved   calved (Are they homophones?)
    aunt   ant (Are they homophones?)

The main forms of British speech (not Scotch, Irish, or some provincial dialects) underwent certain sound changes during and after the late 1700s. Except for speakers in places close to the Atlantic seaboard, North Americans did not share in some of these changes. These sound differences in the home country are still the chief markers that set North American speech apart from all other dialects of English. Other British colonies, for example, those in Australia, New Zealand, and South Africa, were formed **after** these British changes in pronunciation, and thus share the changes with England.

THE MAJOR CHANGES

The most noticeable differences in pronunciation between North American and British English are in:

(1) **the "r" sound in certain positions within a word**. Most of North America uses the older pronunciation and pronounces the "r" before consonants, for example, **barn** and **farm**, and at the end of such words as **bar** and **far**. Southern British English has dropped this "r".

(2) **the "a"**. Most North Americans have kept the older "flat a", as in **cat**, whereas Southern British has changed the vowel sound to a "broad a", as in **father**, in about 150 common words, for example, **dance, ask, aunt, path**. The pronunciation of **romance**, unlike that of **dance**, did not change — as many British "pop" singers have discovered when using North American lyrics.

(3) **stress**. Most North American English tends to use an older secondary stress on the third syllable of certain words, especially those ending in -ary (díctionàry), -ery (cémetèry), and -ory (explánatòry), whereas the British say díction'ry, cémet'ry, explanat'ry. How do you pronounce library? secretary? primary?

IN ALL OF THE ABOVE EXAMPLES, THE PRESENT NORTH AMERICAN PRONUNCIATION IS CLOSER TO SEVENTEENTH-CENTURY ENGLISH THAN TO MODERN BRITISH ENGLISH.

One must also keep in mind that both British and North American English have within them variant pronunciations.

ACTIVITY

How do you pronounce the following words? What other acceptable variations exist? (Use dictionaries.)

futile   juvenile   roof   hoof   soot
controversy   rations   leisure

North Americans as Innovators and Creators of Language

Not everything in North American English that is different from British English is an older form. It is not surprising that the colonists, faced with new conditions, should have to make some new words.

1. Probably the easiest way in which an English speaker creates new terms is to **change the meaning of an old word**. Here are some North American examples.

barn — in England **barn** is 'a building for storing grain'.
　　　 — Why do you think its meaning came to be extended on this continent to include the livestock?

store — in England people go to the **shops** for goods. (What verb do North Americans use to mean 'to go to the store'?) The word **store** or **stores** in England generally refers to a storehouse.
　　　 — How did this word probably acquire its new meaning in the new country?

Sometimes separate areas adapt different "old" words for new inventions. Examples of old transportation words used in new ways are **carriage** and **coach**, transferred to trains, and **horsepower** to mechanical energy.

See if you can name the British equivalents for these words pertaining to cars:

hood—	wrench—	spark plug—
gas—	gear shift—	windshield—
fender—	muffler—	generator—

2. Borrowing

The North American colonists also adopted words from the people they met. Often, in making the words "English", they distorted the original sounds. This is particularly true of words and place-names borrowed from Indian languages.

(a) Indian words:

The Indians of North America assisted the early settlers to cope with their new and harsh environment by teaching them much about food, transportation, and survival. As North Americans, we therefore have hundreds of words in our vocabulary which reflect the skills, knowledge, and cultures of the different Indian tribes.

Why do you think these sets of words were borrowed very early by the colonists?

moose raccoon opossum skunk

pow-wow wigwam tomahawk teepee

squash hickory pecan succotash

(b) French words:

Have you seen a **lacrosse** game?
— eaten **chowder**?
— travelled across the **prairies**?

What relationships do you see between these English words and the corresponding French words: la crosse 'hooked stick'
chaudière 'pot'
prairie 'meadow'?

Why do you think English speakers on this continent borrowed these French words:

caribou gopher	portage depot

prairie coulee	cache carry-all

Explore this kind of borrowing further. Using the *Dictionary of Canadianisms* (Gage, 1967), make a list of other words borrowed from the French speakers of Canada.

Lacrosse poster, 1876

(c) **Spanish words**:

> Do you sit on a **patio**?
> —eat in a **cafeteria**?
> —like to watch a **rodeo**?

Where would the English meet Spanish cultures? What aspect of Spanish-American life spread the following set of terms to all the North American West:

corral lariat lasso ranch stampede bronco?

The Mexican-Spanish suffix **-teria**, as in **cafeteria**, has given rise to dozens of North American terms, for example, **washeteria**, **snacketeria**, yet only two— **cafeteria** and **groceteria** — seem to have survived long in the language.

Can you explain why this is so?

(d) **Dutch words**:

> Do you eat **cookies**?
> —ride **sleighs**?

By 1664 Dutch settlers were well established in New York and up the Hudson River Valley to Albany. Some borrowings from these Dutch traders and settlers are:

caboose scow stoop ('porch')
boss dumb ('stupid') **waffle**
Santa Claus poppycock cole-slaw

> In the 1830s, an English immigrant to Canada explains in a letter home to England what a "stoup" is:
>
> Dinner was laid out in the *stoup*,… a sort of wide verandah. … These stoups are of Dutch origin, and were introduced, I have been told, by the first Dutch settlers in the states, since which they have found their way all over the colonies.
>
> —Catherine Parr Traill: *The Backwoods of Canada*

(e) **German words**:

> Can you imagine North America without **hamburgers**?

A large number of German-speaking settlers came to Pennsylvania before 1700, to be followed later by many more immigrants. There were also early German settlements in Canada.

Why do you think these words have been borrowed from German into North American English?

delicatessen frankfurters sauerkraut wiener noodle dunk pretzel

ACTIVITY

Make a list of words using the German elements **-burger** and **-fest** (as in **songfest**).

> Why only **western** Ontario?
>
> **bank barn** or **banked barn** a two-storey barn built into a hill so as to permit entry to the bottom level from one side and to the top level from the other side.
> **1906** CONNOR *Doctor* 26: For many summers the big boulders were gathered from the fields and piled in a long heap at the bottom of the lane on their way to their ultimate destination, the foundation of the bank-barn.
> **1952** PUTNAM *Cdn Regions* 237/2: In western Ontario, the bank barn is common with a basement stable for the animals. In eastern Ontario bank barns are a rarity.
> **1961** *Ontario Hist.* Mar. 11: In all areas except where Pennsylvania Dutch settled with their huge banked barns, the usual outbuildings or "offices" were generally one two-bay centre-door log barn.
>
>
>
> A bank barn, seen from back and front

(f) Borrowings from other languages:

> Do you like to eat **pizza?**
> **chop suey?**
> **smorgasbord** style?

A few words have filtered into the North American language — some into the whole English language — from other cultures. Can you identify the languages from which these come? Can you add to the list?

**kibitz gumbo juke-box schmaltz
chow mein nix schnozzle**

3. Coining a word or phrase

Although speakers of a language seldom coin a completely new word, North Americans have been particularly creative. Some, such as **vaseline**, **kleenex, nylon**, and **kodak**, are trade names that have become common nouns. In others, the sound or the imagery echoes the meaning and gives rise to new words, for example:

**gobbledygook honky-tonk glad-hander
rat race**

Discuss the comparisons and images that probably inspired these North American terms:

**rubber cheque stuffed shirt egghead
tightwad ghost writer bushwhacker
a bromide rubberneck to strike it rich
to get to first base to sidetrack**

ACTIVITY

Look through ads in magazines, etc. for interesting trade names. Can you organize them by how they were coined?

SUMMARY: INFORMING IDEAS

1. Early in the seventeenth century, the English language was taken to North America, where it developed in its own way.

2. The main sound differences between North American English and other varieties of English (but not Scottish, Irish, and some sub-dialects in Great Britain) are:
   (a) retention of **r** in certain positions, where most other varieties have lost it
   (b) retention of the older "flat a" (as in **cat**) where most other varieties have changed to a "broad a" (as in **father**) in many common words
   (c) differences in stress, for example, **medicine, garage**

3. The language of a colony tends to be conservative, keeping older forms brought from the mother country.
   At the same time, the language of a colony is hospitable to change in vocabulary, adopting words from all sources to meet new situations.

4. Each large variety of English has sub-dialects within it—regional and social.

5. No regional variety of speech (for example, Canadian English, Australian English, South American English) is inherently better than another. Each reflects the history and experiences of its speakers.

6. The written form of English is the "interlingua", the form shared by all English-speaking areas.

'*Blimey! Beef must be pricey.*'

—from *The Listener*, June 15, 1972. Reprinted by permission of Barry Fantoni

The ultimate test of knowing a language is to be able to share the linguistic jokes made in the language. How many Canadians or Americans would "get the point" of this British cartoon? They would have to know that the British term for 'a roast of meat' is **joint**, and that **pricey**, as one might guess, is colloquial in Britain for 'expensive, dear'.

ACTIVITY

Make an experiment about attitudes to other varieties of English. Tape (from people if you can, but if this is impossible, use TV, radio, recordings, etc.) a short piece of language from various dialects (for example, Scottish, Southern British, Cockney, New York Eastside, Newfoundland Canadian, midwest Canadian, Bostonian, Southern United States, etc.). Play them back to your class or to any group. See how many they can identify. Have them put beside each (use numbers as a code) the attitudes they have towards each kind of speech. Gather and organize your results and discuss them.

You may wish to make a tape-presentation of your material, using your own voices to introduce and comment upon the varieties of language.

English Comes to Canada

"And from nation to nation
Crossing borders and mixing."

The English language in Canada has had a separate existence for about two hundred years. In this time it has developed in its own way, especially in vocabulary. Do you know, for instance, what the following words mean? Do you use them? All are **Canadianisms**, that is, words or phrases that originated in Canada or have developed special meanings in Canada. What would an American or Britisher make of them?

to sit on a **chesterfield**	to be a **Mountie**
to run in a **riding**	to be a **bush pilot**
to play **broomball**	to be a **Bluenose**
to wear a **tuque**	to play **lacrosse**
to go into **muskeg** country	to wear **mukluks**

Where Did Canadian English Come From?

In 1763 the speakers of English in what are now the provinces of Ontario and Quebec were limited to a few merchants and soldiers. In the Atlantic provinces (excluding Newfoundland) there were only about 17 000 people, most of them from New England.

This English-speaking population was dramatically increased by the influx of thousands of settlers during and after the American War of Independence (1775–83). The first groups, known as the United Empire Loyalists, came to the Maritimes by ship and to "Canada" by land. After the war these were followed by disbanded soldiers and many settlers from the former Thirteen Colonies, so that by 1791, when Upper Canada was separated from Lower Canada, at least 10 000 people were settled in the area now called Ontario and about 40 000 in the Maritimes.

In Upper Canada the flood of immigrants, mainly from the United States, continued for about thirty years, and it has been estimated that in 1814 eighty per cent of the 94 000 people there were American in origin.

These forty years from the beginning of the American Revolution thus saw established in both the St. Lawrence and the Atlantic areas an English-speaking population, largely North American in origin.

The English of "Canada" Then

What language did these settlers speak? Some, of course, spoke German, Dutch, or Gaelic, and some spoke British English or Scottish English. But most of the newcomers had lived in North America for generations and spoke the varieties of North American English of the time.

Here is a comment by a British observer about Ontario speech in the early 1800s. What terms do you think he found strange? What terms do you find strange?

We were struck, as every new comer is, by the new meanings put by Canadians on words, the new connections in which they used them, and the extraordinary way in which some were pronounced. Of course, we heard people "guessing" at every turn, and whatever any one intended doing, he spoke of as "fixing". You would hear a man say, that his wagon, or his chimney, or his gun, must be "fixed"; a girl would be ready to take a walk with you, as soon as she had "fixed herself"; and the baby was always "fixed" in the morning, when washed and dressed for the day. "Catherine," said a husband one day to his wife, in my hearing pronouncing the last syllable of her name, so as to rhyme with line, "I calculate that them apples'll want regulatin'," referring to some that were drying in the sun. They "reckon" at every third sentence. A well-informed man is said to be "well posted up" in some particular subject. . . . A pony was praised to me as being "as fat as mud". . . . Any log, or trunk of a tree, or other single piece of timber, is invariably a "stick", even if it be long enough for a mast. All the stock of a timber-yard is alike, "lumber". An ewer is "a pitcher"; a tin-pail is "a kettle"; a servant is "a help"; an employer is "a boss"; a church pew is "a slip"; a platform at a meeting is "a stage"; children are "juveniles"; and a baby is "a babe".

—John C. Geikie: *Adventures in Canada*.

Watercolour by James Peachey, done between 1774 and 1797. Encampment of the Loyalists at Johnston, a new settlement, on the banks of the St. Lawrence in Canada. Johnston, named after the great land-owner around Schenectady, New York, later became Cornwall, Ontario.

SUGGESTED ACTIVITY

Find some books on Canada, especially your own part of Canada, which describe the early days. List all the words and terms strange to you and make a dictionary of them. You may also enjoy making up and presenting a play or filmstrip with commentary about the information you gather. The *Dictionary of Canadianisms* will help with definitions of words strange to you.

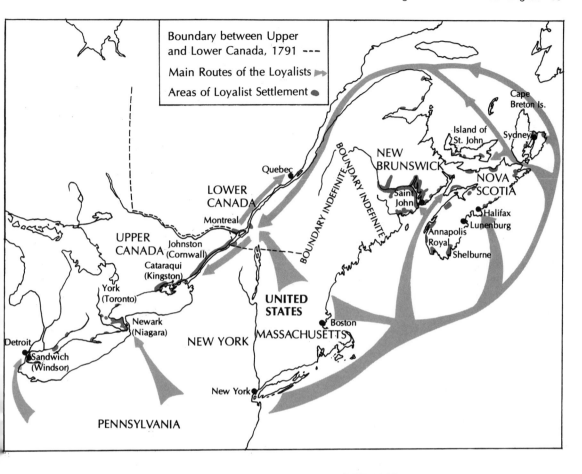

Boundary between Upper and Lower Canada, 1791 - - -

Main Routes of the Loyalists ▶

Areas of Loyalist Settlement ●

Cape Breton Is.

Island of St. John

Sydney

NEW BRUNSWICK

NOVA SCOTIA

Quebec

BOUNDARY INDEFINITE

BOUNDARY INDEFINITE

Saint John

Halifax

Lunenburg

LOWER CANADA

Montreal

Annapolis Royal

Shelburne

UPPER CANADA   Johnston (Cornwall)

Cataraqui (Kingston)

York (Toronto)

UNITED STATES

Newark (Niagara)

Boston

Detroit

Sandwich (Windsor)

NEW YORK   MASSACHUSETTS

PENNSYLVANIA

New York

LOYALIST SETTLEMENTS BEFORE 1800

The English of Canada, though "North American" in its base, nevertheless has features that distinguish it from "American". In the 1830s about 300 000 Britishers came to Canada — Scots (who influenced education), many Irish (especially during the potato famines of the 1840s), Scotch-Irish from Ulster, and Welsh, as well as English. This second wave of immigrants and later ones helped to make Canada different from "the States", the British varieties of speech adding much to Canadian language. The Canadian community also began to develop in its own way, and English-speaking Canadians have continued to shape their language to meet their new experiences.

Canadian English is, therefore, not just a blend of eighteenth-century North American and British English, but a particular development from that blend — a form of English more "North American" than "British" but distinctly different from both these large varieties.

Canadian English Goes West

The English-speaking people who, in the latter half of the nineteenth century, settled western Canada were mainly from Ontario and other parts of eastern Canada. Rapid transportation by boat and rail allowed these settlers to maintain their speech connections with their former home. Consequently, the distinct speech differences that isolation brings did not appear. The children of non-English-speaking immigrants to the West learned the English of the people around them, which was largely Ontario English. For a country so large, Canadian English is remarkably homogeneous.

Of course, pockets of different speech and some interesting regional differences in vocabulary do exist — differences coming from original settlement and then from special experiences and contacts with other people. We find, for example, touches from Gaelic in Cape Breton and places in Ontario and Quebec; phrases and sounds from New England in parts of Nova Scotia; from Scotch and Irish in the Ottawa Valley; from Pennsylvania "Dutch" (meaning **Deutsch** 'German') in western Ontario; from late-nineteenth-century British in Vancouver Island; from American in southern Alberta; and from Canadian French in settlements near Edmonton. Such differences are more apparent in the older, and often more isolated, areas of the Atlantic region —and it is astonishing how long some old forms can linger, especially in one's "home" speech. But we do not find in Canada the great differences of speech heard in Britain—as, for instance, between a Yorkshireman and a Londoner, or between a Cockney and a "university man" from London; or in the United States between a speaker from Chicago and one from Louisiana. A Torontonian visiting in Vancouver, Edmonton, Winnipeg, or Halifax does not find the English spoken in these places very different from his own.

—Public Archives of Canada

"Colonists on the Red River in North America" c. 1822

Pen drawing by Peter Rindisbacher (1806–34), who at fifteen emigrated with his family from Switzerland to Canada. His sketch shows an immigrant from Switzerland with his wife and children, a disbanded German soldier, an immigrant from Scotland, and a settler from French Canada. Can you identify them?

—Public Archives of Canada

—Poster in Dutch — Lees Dit! — published by the Canadian Pacific Railway and advertising the Manitoba 1971 Prairie Exhibit. The poster was originally advertising to bring immigrants to the Canadian West.

This poster is typical of the literature distributed in Europe during the nineteenth century to advertise the advantages of emigrating to the new wheat lands of western Canada.

FOR DISCUSSION

1. In England, a Canadian is usually taken to be an "American"; in the United States, either his speech is not noticed as being different or he is asked if he is from England; occasionally, in either area he has the pleasure of being recognized as a Canadian.

    (a) What characteristic features in your speech suggest to Britishers that you are Canadian?

    (b) What features in your language suggest to people in the United States that you are not "American"?

    (c) One characteristic of Canadian speech is an older **ou** sound in such words as **house**, **out**, **about**, and **mouth** (noun). Listen to Canadian speakers and American speakers (tape them if you can) and see if you can detect the difference.

2. There are three main sub-dialects of speech in the United States:

    Northern: New England and Hudson Valley areas, and the settlements that spread west from them

    Midland: most of Pennsylvania, to South Carolina, Indiana, and central Illinois

    Southern: Maryland, Virginia south, and the Mississippi basin

    Which of these do you think Canadian English would be most like? Why?

How does your speech match these items typical of these three areas:

	Northern	Midland	Southern	Mine
The **s** in "to grease a wheel" and in grea**s**y is pronounced like	s	s	z (also S. Midland)	
A small stream is regularly called a	brook	run (N. Midland)	branch (in many areas)	
A paper container is a	bag	poke	sack	
A frying pan is called a	spider	skillet	skillet or spider	
11 45 on the clock is a quarter ____ to twelve.	to or of	till	till or to	
You say you are sick ____ your stomach. (Note: "at one's stomach" is common everywhere.)	to	on or in		
To get water, you turn on the	faucet	spigot	spigot or spicket	

Were there any items for which you did not match any of the three United States dialects? Do you, for instance, turn on a **tap** to get water? If so, you are using the British word.

3. Sometimes Canadians use a British form (or one from a British dialect), sometimes the American form, and sometimes they go their own way. Many words have variant pronunciations in **all** regions.

How do you pronounce these words?

	usual Br.	usual U.S.	mine
ate	et (rhymes with **let**)	ate (rhymes with **late**)	
lieutenant	begins like **left**	begins like **loot**	
schedule	begins like **shed**	begins like the **sch-** of **school**	
the letter **z**	zed (rhymes with **bed**)	zee (rhymes with **bee**)	
missile	ends with the **-ile** of **mile**	rhymes with **thistle**	
i of **semi**	rhymes with **me** (usually)	rhymes with **my** (usually)	
the **o** in **progress**	like the **o** in **go**	like the **o** in **got**	

One form is not "right" and the other "wrong". They are just different. And behind such differences may lie hundreds of years of history.

4. Here are a few words for which Canadians have variant pronunciations. Look these up in a **Canadian** dictionary, and discover the different ways in which Canadians pronounce these words. You may wish to work in teams of three: one using a British dictionary, one an American (not an "International" one), and one a Canadian. Then compare results.
khaki bade been drought leisure program quinine sterile economics

A Reminder:

It is important to bear in mind when discussing variants within speech that such variants are often relics of older speech. A change can occur in one area and spread out, but may not reach all regions. The everyday speech of many Canadians contains older forms such as **back of** ('behind'), **he clumb**, **he be**, and pronunciations such as **hum** for **home**, **yelk** for **yolk**, and the vowel of **book** and

hook for **roof**. All these are found in other dialects of English. Knowledge of the history of one's own language can make such variations interesting—evidence that we all **inherit** certain forms of speech.

FOR DISCUSSION

What are the influences that can move Canadian English closer to United States English? What influences counteract these? What do you think will happen to Canadian English in the future?

Tuning in to Canadian Speech

See if you can develop a "good ear" for the sounds that various speakers of English use. A tape-recorder will be a useful tool.

Some Sounds to Listen For:

1. **ou**   One characteristic of Canadian speech frequently noticed by Americans is an older **ou** sound in words such as **out**, **about**, **house**, **louse**, **mouse**, and **lout**.

Canadians have systematized this sound; it appears before certain consonants, especially -s, -t, -ch, but not before the others, nor in the final position. Try saying the following pairs until you hear the difference:

lout: loud   house: houses (the **s** is a z sound)
about: abound   out: owl   couch: cow
Ouch!: Ow!   **mouth** (noun): **mouth** (verb)

Most Americans and Britishers use the second kind of **ou** (or something like it) for all the words. Because this change is automatic to most Canadians — part of their language system — they are generally unaware that they use two **ou** sounds.

2. **"long" i**   This sound, too, is an automatic switch for most Canadians, and follows a pattern similar to the **ou** sound. Try these pairs, and see if you hear the difference in the vowel sounds (this is a little harder to hear):

rite: ride   rite: rye   fife: five   life: lie   light: lied

Most Britishers and Americans use the second vowel sound only.

With your tape-recorder, tape non-Canadian voices (from records, TV, etc.), and see if (a) your classmates can distinguish Canadians from non-Canadians, and (b) you can analyse some of the different speech sounds.

The Canadian Word Hoard

In 1967 some Canadian scholars published *A Dictionary of Canadianisms on Historical Principles*. It was the first attempt to record as many **Canadianisms** as they could find in print (words that either originated in Canada or are used in Canada in a special way), with quotations and references showing their uses and any changes in meaning or spelling.

Examine each group of words, and discuss what experiences, activities, or contacts with other languages gave rise to these Canadianisms.

Set 1
half-section
grid road
colonist car
harvest special
saskatoons
correction line

Set 2
habitant
lacrosse
lateer
cariole
levee
mush!
tuque

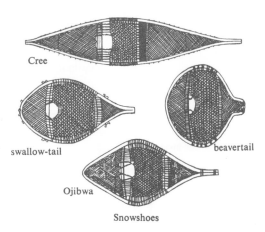

Cree

swallow-tail

beavertail

Ojibwa

Snowshoes

Set 3
Manitou
toboggan
shaganappi
kokanee
kinnikinik
tamarack
wapiti
caribou

Set 4
portage
Nor'Wester
Here-Before-Christer
voyageur
boat song
York boat
point-blanket coat
Long Traverse

Set 6
sugar bush
sugaring-off
robin run
frog run
bud run
sap weather
rock maple

Set 5
blueline
dressing-shack
drop pass
rink rat
elbowing
face-off
poke-check

Set 7
chimo
atigi
oomiak
Inuit
husky
kayak
mukluk
Ookpik

Set 8
Metro
Expo
B and B
Hydro
Medicare
NDPer
Socred
separatist

Travois

ACTIVITY

1. Here is how the *Dictionary of Canadianisms* traces the history of the words **larrigan** and **bombardier**. The meaning of the word **larrigan** has remained narrow and denotes only one kind of waterproof, laced boot; but notice how the meaning of the word **bombardier** has widened to indicate a variety of vehicles used for travelling over the snow.

larigan *n*. See **larrigan**.

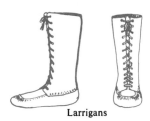

Larrigans

larrigan ['lærəgən] *n*. [origin unknown] a type of moccasin of oil-tanned cowhide having uppers reaching almost to the knee and, usually, flexible soles. See also **shoepack** (def. 1). Also spelled *laragan, larigan*.
1898 *Hints for Intending Klondikers* 12: For clothing, then, take . . . 1 pair Canadian laragans or shoe-packs; 3 pairs seamless felt ankle moccasins. . . . **1905** WALLACE *Labrador Wild* 266: The snow clogged in all that was left of my cowhide mocassins (larigans) and I took them off. . . . **1950** BIRD *This is N.S.* 99: The cook said after, it was lucky they had been cold enough to leave their larrigans on, else they'd run in their sock feet. **1961** *Sat. Night* 23 Dec. 18/1: After breakfast that day I rode to school on the rear runner of a fishmonger's sleigh wearing a pair of cowhide larrigans greasy with linseed oil.

larriganed *adj*. shod with larrigans.
1904 ROBERTS *Watchers of Trails* 287: Then turning on his larriganed heels, he strode up the trail. . . .

Do **you** wear larrigans in certain kinds of weather? If not, what kind of outdoor boots, comparable to larrigans, do you or your friends own? Look up the name of these boots in the *Dictionary of Canadianisms*, and discover the origin and history of this word.

bombardier [ˌbɑmbɚ'dir] *n*. [< Armand *Bombardier*, of Valcourt, Quebec, the inventor] a vehicle used for travelling over snow and ice, equipped with caterpillar tracks at the rear and a set of skis at the front. See also **skimobile**. Cp. **snowmobile**. Also spelled *Bombardier* (originally a trademark).
1949 *Report of DME Test Team* III 2: DRB Bombardier snowmobile had two snags drive through [the] bottom of the vehicle. **1958** *Edmonton Jnl* 24 June 4 16/4: The Bombardier has the edge from the standpoint of most drivers . . . because it steers by forward skis, rather than by its wide tracks. **1962** *Globe and Mail* (Toronto) 23 Mar. 23/8: We traveled to our fishing hole in a conveyance known as a bombardier. . . . **1964** *Calgary Herald* 21 Feb. 19/2: Heated bombardiers drive their cargo into the packing plants where it is unloaded and weighed. . . .

A bombardier

bombardier trail *North* a road used by bombardiers.
1957 *Aklavik Jnl* Feb. 5/2: On the second day he hit deep snow on the old bombardier trail and was forced to take snowshoes ahead of his team.

Can you up-date this illustration? Collect as many terms as you can find for vehicles used to travel over snow. Check to see:

(a) if the word is a Canadianism,
(b) how the word was coined.

Watch catalogues and Canadian advertisements for new names, and try to discover how the new words came into being.

2. Look in the *Dictionary of Canadianisms* to see how it traces the history of the word **mackinaw**.

An Example of Canadian Regionalisms from Newfoundland

Newfoundland, England's oldest colony, has been relatively isolated geographically and politically for centuries, and within the island itself the people have often lived in small isolated communities. Therefore the language developed many local variations. Also found are many features of Elizabethan or older English and of the original speech of the settlers, who came mainly from Ireland and southwest England.

The place-names, derived from a dozen languages, reveal the mixture of people who, for centuries, went to the fishing grounds every year: French, Portuguese, Spanish, Bretons, Basques, Channel Islanders — there is even a Turk's Island! Other place-names suggest the hardships and the sense of humour of these early newcomers. Here are a few. Can you imagine the circumstances in which they could have been coined?

> Blow-me down
> Nick's Nose Cove
> Breakheart Point
> Safe Harbour
> Confusion Bay
> Bleak Joke Cove
> Famish Gut
> Bay D'Espoir
> Comfort Cove

The vocabulary of Newfoundlanders is so rich in regional terms that scholars are now compiling a Newfoundland regional dictionary. If you feel that you have run out of insults to hurl at someone, you might try using some of the following Newfoundland phrases. It is important to note that, with the possible exception of two or three, all the words listed below are not used everywhere in Newfoundland today.

Words familiar in one locality may be strange in another. Most of these terms are as much of a curiosity to an average Newfoundlander as they are to people outside the province. Some of the words are from Irish, Scottish, and other British dialects.

> **bostoon** 'an ignorant person'
> **gilderoy** 'a proud person'
> **jackeen** 'a rascally boy'
> **ral** 'a disorderly fellow'
> **shooneen** 'a coward'
> **binicky** 'ill-tempered'
> **oonshick** 'a person of low intelligence'
> **gommil** 'a moron, a half fool'

Special conditions and special activities—the fishery, in particular—have given Newfoundlanders many terms and expressions, some of which are shared with the Maritimes. An example is, "That's some hot in there" ('really hot', 'very hot').

Can you match these words and their meanings?

1. brewis
2. tickle
3. gansey
4. screech
5. jinkers
6. flake
7. callibogus
8. bawn

a. heavy sweater
b. rum and spruce beer
c. beach or rocks on which fish are hung to dry
d. stew with ship's biscuit, codfish, etc.
e. a black rum
f. unlucky people—or gremlins
g. narrow strait
h. wooden platform to dry fish

What changes in Newfoundland since the Second World War have affected the regional varieties of Newfoundland speech?

Other Regional Terms in Canada

ACTIVITY

Each group is a set of terms confined mainly to a certain region of Canada. Can you identify the area? Discuss how you think the terms arose, and consult the *Dictionary of Canadianisms* to check your ideas.

Set 1—**droke** (or **drogue**) **grayback** **shiretown**
     sloven **cradle-hill**

Set 2—**poplar bluff** **black blizzard** **chinook wind**
     nuisance grounds **Métis** **goldeye**

Set 3—**laker** **bulker** **Aurora trout**

Set 4—**klahowya** **skookum** **salt-chuck**
     tillicum **tyee** **salal** **oolichan**

Set 5—**pingo** **Kabloona** **tupek** **permafrost**
     coast sledge **cooney** **cat-train**

ACTIVITY

French-Canadian explorers, missionaries, and fur-traders, were the first Europeans to see many parts of North America. North American English has thus adopted many French-Canadian geographical terms. Some — **plateau, rapids, prairie, portage**— have entered the general English language. Others are limited to certain regions or to place-names.

Can you match each French-Canadian word in the list below to its meaning in the following list? (The *Dictionary of Canadianisms* can give you much more information about each word.)

1. aboiteau (Maritimes)
2. anse (mainly in place-names)
3. barachois, barrasway (Atlantic Pr.)
4. brulé
5. butte (U.S. and Cdn. West)
6. chute (Ont. and Que.)
7. coulee (Prairies and West)
8. coteau
9. côte (mainly place-names)
10. sault, saut
11. snye (Ottawa Valley, Northwest)

a. cove, bay
b. deep ravine, with sloping sides, sometimes with creek
c. swift flowing water (where lumbermen had to be careful)
d. coast, side or district on the slope of a hill
e. side-channel, often bypassing falls
f. small bay at sea-level, with bar at end
g. waterfall, rapids
h. 'small hill', usually isolated, often with a flat top
i. burnt-over land or forest
j. dam, with sluice gate to control flow
k. slope, hillside

Now see if you can find place-names that use these words.

What did **Detroit** once mean? What did **depot** mean originally?

Using the *Dictionary of Canadianisms*, make your own matching test of Canadian words derived from French Canadian, and try tests on one another.

SOME SUGGESTIONS FOR ACTIVITIES

1. Write your own "linguistic autobiography", showing the backgrounds (family, neighbourhood, reading, etc.) which contributed to your **idiolect** (from **idio** 'peculiar to oneself' and **lect** 'language', thus 'one's own particular or individual language'). Or write about your family language.

2. Interview some "old-timers" in your family, neighbourhood, or area, and discuss their early experiences with them. If possible, find out what they used to call things, what school experiences they remember, how they spent holidays. Use old photographs, books, catalogues, etc. to help stimulate memories. Then make either an oral report or, with visual aids, a presentation of what you discover about the language and the experiences of these people. Listen especially to **how** they talk and see if you can detect differences, and perhaps some traces of other forms of English. Do they use or know a slang that you don't use? Develop the ear of a good dialectologist.

3. Find some recent immigrants to Canada and discuss with them their experiences with the Canadian language. Your informants may have come to Canada speaking another language or merely another dialect of English. It may take a lot of talking to find out what you want. For example, some people from certain parts of Europe find our personal names difficult because in their languages a girl's name always ends in a grammatical inflection (often **-a**, as in Marya, Carolina, Paula, etc.) marking "female". Our names have no such helpful identifying marker.

4. Discover as much as you can about the languages of the Indians or Eskimos (Inuit) of Canada, and prepare a report. (Canadian Government books contain some excellent material.) How many of these languages have or have had a written form?

5. Like Canadian English, but with an even longer history of separation from the "home" language, Canadian French has retained some older forms, made changes, and developed regional variations.

   Find out what you can about Canadian French and its differences from Parisian French.

Discuss what these lines now mean to you:

> Words . . . ,
> And of ourselves and of our origins.
>
> Wallace Stevens: from *The Idea of Order at Key West*

POLONIUS: What do you read, my lord?
HAMLET: Words, words, words.

—*Hamlet:* ii, ii, 190-91

"*Like I mean, man, you know,
the older generation, you
know like, they don't, you
know, communicate, like
man . . .*"

—Mahood—© 1972 *Punch* (Rothco)

Truth, or the attempt at truth, demands words to chip it out
of the head, words to scrape off the dross from the gold,
words to make it valid and useful to anyone else.
—Jill Tweedie

Chapter 3

Words, Words, Words

Becoming Aware of Words

1. Choose **one word** that best describes your closest friend.
2. What word do you most dislike?
3. What word do you use the most?
4. Write the title of your favourite song. What is the "key" word or phrase for you? Why?
5. List words that you have learned only recently.

ACTIVITY

Make a crossword of some of the hardest spelling words you know. Xerox copies, and see who in your group can solve it first.

—Reproduced with permission — New York News Inc.

Can You Imagine a World Without Words?

Try to express an idea without using words:
for example, Caution — truck crossing.
Good food served here.
What are you doing on Friday night?
What can a picture do that words can't do?
What can words do that a picture can't do?
In what way is the picture of seagulls on the facing page not worth a thousand words?

Make a list of words and phrases that come into your mind as you look at the picture. Then compare it with someone else's list. Can you see a pattern to your observations, to the kinds of words you have listed? Now, using some of your words and phrases, develop in sentence or short verse form an observation about the picture.

Marian Bancroft

The photograph of seagulls may convey many things; but there are many ideas that neither this photograph nor any other visual image can communicate. A photograph can make a fairly accurate visual representation of the statement "The white seagulls fly over the water", but how could it make the statement "These seagulls come here every day for food" or "This is my favourite seagull"?

There are various things that words can express and a painting or photograph can not. Words can deal with real, though invisible, things related to memory, anticipation, and emotion. Unlike the painter and photographer, the writer can go beyond the visual representation. How does Walter de la Mare convey this idea in the following poem?

THE PICTURE

Here is a sea-legged sailor,
Come to this tottering inn,
Just when the bronze on its signboard is fading,
And the black shades of evening begin.

With his head on his paws sleeps a sheepdog,
There stoops the shepherd, and see,
All follow-my-leader the ducks waddle homeward,
Under the sycamore tree.

Burned brown is the face of the sailor;
His bundle is crimson; and green
Are the thick leafy boughs that hang dense o'er
the tavern;
And blue the far meadows between.

But the crust, ale and cheese of the sailor,
His mug and his platter of Delf,
And the crescent to light home the shepherd
and sheepdog
The painter has kept to himself.

What is in the poem that cannot be in the painting described in the poem?

What does the actual carving have that is missing in this photograph?

Woman Holding a Fish and an Ulu, 1954, by Pinnie Nuktialuk

The images come from outside...But the judgments and the connections (what does it *mean*?) have to be made inside your head and they are made with words.

—Margaret Atwood

We Speak Our World

. . . our language emphasizes nouns, things already there, set apart from us, all clearly defined and easily seen. The Eskimo language, by contrast, makes little distinction between nouns and verbs; rather, all words are forms of the verb "to be", which itself is lacking in Eskimo. That is, all words proclaim in themselves their own existence. . . .

Eskimos have no real equivalents to our words "create" or "make". Their closest term means "to work on". The carver never attempts to force the ivory into uncharacteristic forms but responds to the material as it tries to be itself, and thus the carving is continually modified as the ivory has its say.

This is the Eskimo attitude toward not only ivory, but toward all things, especially people: parent toward child, husband toward wife.

It is also their attitude toward nature. Language is the principal tool with which the Eskimos make the natural world a human world. They use many words for "snow" which permit fine distinctions, not simply because they are much concerned with snow, but because snow takes its form from the actions in which it participates: sledding, falling, igloo-building. Different kinds of snow are brought into existence by the Eskimos as they experience their environment and speak; words do not label things already there. Words are like the knife of the carver: they free the idea, the thing, from the general formlessness of the outside. As a man speaks, not only is his language in a state of birth, but also the very thing about which he is talking.

—from the introduction by Edmund Carpenter to *I Breathe a New Song: Poems of the Eskimo*

Words: Old and New

What do these two words mean to you?

silly   resentment

Does your meaning of **resentment** make sense in the following sentence, written in 1651?

The Council taking notice of the many good services performed by Mr. John Milton . . . have thought fit to declare their *resentment* and good acceptance of the same, and that the thanks of the Council be returned to Mr. Milton.

What do you think **resentment** meant in 1651?

Does your meaning of **silly** fit the sixteenth century use of the word?

This Miles Forest and John Dighton, about midnight (the *silly* children lying in their beds) came into the chamber, and suddenly lapped them up among the clothes.

—Sir Thomas More: *History of King Richard III*

What do you think **silly** meant in the sixteenth century?

How long do you think these words have been in the language? Why have we made these new words?

communicaster	cartop	overkill
lunar module	splashdown	smog
ombudsman	skyjack	breathalyser
cablevision	biodegradable	bebop

As We Change Our Words Change

We organize our world by using words. When, as children, we learn to call some animals **cats** and other animals **dogs**, we are beginning to organize and classify what we see. Each time we add words to our vocabulary we are making finer and finer distinctions about the things that happen and exist around us. By doing so we begin to gain control over the chaos that surrounds us.

The human need to bring order to our world is made difficult because our world is constantly changing. To keep up with this change we make new words, drop others, or remake the meanings of old words. Until a few years ago, for example, **grass** was just the covering on the ground. The following cartoon illustrates how common one of its additional meanings has become.

"Man, you can't get away from the Drug Squad even in the park these days . . ."

—Toronto Sun Syndicate, 1972, Los Angeles Times Syndicate, 1975

Forgotten Words

Words survive in the language because they are needed. Although all of the following words can still be found in a comprehensive historical dictionary, none of them is commonly used today. Why do you think they have been forgotten?

varlet 'a knight's page; an attendant or servant'
younker 'youngster'
leechcraft 'the practice of bleeding someone with leeches'
juma 'warrior'
yclept 'named'

Because many of the words we use reflect our habits — the clothes we wear, the food we eat, the entertainments we choose—they are just as subject to the whims of fashion and custom as the things they name. Today, for example, we are more likely to speak of watching **a hockey game** than of **a jousting match**, of wearing a **scarf** rather than a **wimple**, of eating **toast** rather than **manchets**.

ACTIVITY

In a menu for a meal given to King Henry II on a visit to Canterbury in 1170, some of the dishes named were:

Cockyntryce   Buttered Worts   Garbage
Candle Ferry   Sugared Flawns   Tench with Sops

Why would **garbage** be listed as a dish on a king's menu? What do you think its earlier meaning might have been?

Ask your parents and grandparents (or other people older than yourself) if they remember eating foods that are no longer common today. Did they have different names for breakfast cereals or breakfast drinks, for example?

Words That Stay—Meanings That Change

As we have seen (p. 69), when the Council of State in 1651 used the word **resentment**, it meant 'gratitude' — a good feeling about what Milton had done. Obviously, the meaning of the word has changed to almost the opposite.

At one time these words, like many others in our language, also had different meanings:

villain 'farm hand'
uncouth 'unknown' and probably 'unknowing; ignorant'
smug 'trim and neat in appearance'

Do you see any connection between the older meanings and the present-day meanings of the above words?

How Fast Can A Language Change?

Suppose English changed as much in the next ten years as it has in the past five hundred (that is, from Anglo-Saxon times to the present). What would happen?

Many of our words, for example, **cow** and **house**, still mean what they did centuries ago. Many other words, however, have acquired entirely new meanings. Such change happens quite naturally with a language that is in constant use.

But if too many words change in meaning, or the meanings of words change too quickly, we lose the agreement necessary for understanding one another.

As the following example illustrates, we can usually find some connection between an earlier meaning (now lost) and the later meaning.

SHADOW AND SUBSTANCE

The first cartoon which appeared in *Punch* (1843)

Cartoons haven't always been funny. The original meaning of **cartoon** was 'a preliminary drawing for a painting or tapestry'. The present meaning of **cartoon**, 'the drawn joke', had its beginning a little over a hundred years ago in the English magazine *Punch*. Today the meaning of the word has widened to refer also to a political drawing that criticizes people or events.

Latin **charta** — 'paper'

French **carton**   (related to the English
Italian **cartone**   words **card**, **cartographer**,
                 chart, **charter**)

The **-oon** ending of **cartoon** is from French, and was generally used to "downgrade", for example, **balloon**, **buffoon**, **paltroon**, and **spittoon**.

"When *I* use a word...it means just what I choose it to mean — neither more nor less."

"The question is," said Alice, "whether you *can* make words mean so many different things."

"The question is," said Humpty Dumpty, "which is to be master — that's all."

— Lewis Carroll: *Through the Looking-Glass and What Alice Found There*

Is Humpty Dumpty right? Can one person change a language?

How Words Change

In general, a change in meaning occurs in these ways:

1. CHANGE IN THE RANGE OF MEANING —

how much or how little a word refers to.

(a) For example, these words have **widened** in meaning:

board — once meant only 'a piece of timber'. List the many ways in which we can use the word **board** today. How do you think these meanings developed from the earlier meaning?

navigate — from Latin **navis** 'ship' and **agere** 'to drive', once meant to guide ships only; what else can now be "navigated"?

Widening the meaning of a word is the most common way in which words with narrow, often technical, meanings have taken on general meanings. The computer terms **input** and **output** are typical. Can you think of others?

Other words **narrow** in meaning, to something more specific:

amateur — from Latin **amare** 'to love', once meant generally 'one who loves'. Gradually, it took on the more specific meaning of 'one who enjoys an activity without being paid'. Canadians sometimes use the word **shamateur**. What does it mean?

deer — once referred generally to any small four-footed animal. Shakespeare, for example, wrote: "Mice, and Rats, and such small Deare". Now it has narrowed to the specific meaning.

What wider meanings did the following words once have? Use dictionaries and other books dealing with the history of words.

diamond satellite carol piano
torpedo wife liquor stool

2. CHANGE IN THE REPUTATION OF A WORD — as a result of changing **attitudes** to what the word names. For example, these words have been **upgraded**:

lord, lady — at one time, these named people in charge of the household servants. In Old English **lord** was **hlaford** 'loaf-keeper'. Eventually, the words referred to people of noble rank, as in **Lord** and **Lady Hamilton**. Lady, however, also retains the general meaning, as in, "Are you the lady of the house?"

marshal — once merely 'the boy who holds the horses'.

knight — once 'boy, youth'; now someone honoured by his sovereign.

Find out the origins and changes in meaning of the word **chivalry**.

Rather than acquiring a higher status, English words more commonly change by being **downgraded** in status. Study these examples, and suggest how the change in meaning might have occurred.

censure—once meant 'to pass judgment on'; but now 'to judge unfavourably'.

retaliate—once meant 'to return in kind', whether good or evil; but now, 'to return evil for evil'.

ORAL ACTIVITY

These words once had more favourable meanings than they do today. What were they? Look up the words in class and then discuss your findings.

bribe   idiot   crafty   awful   cunning   officious

Some words undergo change both in range of meaning and in reputation. For example, the word **amateur**, as well as narrowing from 'one who is fond of' to 'a non-professional', has begun to take on negative overtones. In certain contexts, as in the statement "He's just an **amateur**", the word suggests incompetence, bumbling.

ACTIVITY

Find out the origins of the word **pioneer**. Can you relate the original word to **pawn** (in chess)? What processes of change are involved with the change to the modern meaning of **pioneer**?

ACTIVITY

Identify the kind or kinds of change in meaning that each of these words has undergone. Use dictionaries. Do four.

garble	cute	stink	bonfire
matinée	gopher	companion	blackguard
barbarian	doom	congress	pen

"Although every queen is a woman, not every woman is a queen."
queen—comes from the Anglo-Saxon **cwen** 'woman' and eventually came to mean 'the woman of the country'; thus, **queen** in its present-day sense.
What patterns of change in meaning does **queen** illustrate?

ACTIVITY

Sometimes the relationships that words have with other words have become hidden. Look at the following examples.

fire, focus, curfew

Focus was the Latin word for 'hearth' but in common speech also acquired the meaning 'fire'. This common meaning was adopted by the French in **feu** 'fire'. During the Middle Ages fires and lights had to be put out at a certain time every night. The French word for this, **couvre-feu** 'cover fire', was borrowed into Middle English as **curfu**, which became **courfew** and then **curfew**.

What is the relationship between these sets of words? First make a thoughtful guess, then look up the history of the words in historical dictionaries.

circus and **searchlight**
vagabond and **extravagant**
expedition, octopus, and **trapeze**
astonish and **thunder**
enthusiasm and **theology**
otter and **hydrangea**

WORD WATCHING

How do we recognize the meanings of so many of these words?

Chinatown spruce-up promoted once more

TELESHOP

Prancers. Very fashionable.

RESTO-BED

DIP DOT DESIGN BOOK

BANDORAMA

SUPP-hose for men . . .

Ladies' Cocktail Slipperettes

Elegant silver cocktail mules. Composition sole, stack heel. Five straps.

Plane hijackers slain

Trim-A-Home Shop

Stadium go-ahead blasted

Bylaw endorsed

How English Words Are Made

Here are some English words created or borrowed since 1900:

escalator (1900)
blurb (1907)
Borstal (1908)
biochemist (1913)
umpteen (First World War)
blimp (1916)
cellophane (1921)
gestalt (1924)
check-up (1924)
beautician (1926)
whodunit (1930)
cyclotron (1932)
G-man (1935)
microfilm (1938)
coolant (1939)
blitz (1940)
ascorbic (1940)
de-icer (1940)
aerostat (1940)
airgraph (1941)

jeep (1942)
electronics (1942)
Geiger (1943)
genocide (1944)
technicolor (1944)
existentialism (1944)
photo-finish (1944)
atomic age (1945)
blip (1945)
bebop (1946)
cybernetics (1947)
canasta (1948)
apartheid (1949)
bikini (1950)
cinerama (1952)
automation (1952)
Eurovision (1954)
psychedelic (1957)
Telstar (1962)
splashdown (1965)

"It broke. Now all I have is a yo."

—Reproduced with permission—The Register and Tribune Syndicate

Can you think of any possible explanation for words like
zigzag, **chit-chat**, etc.?

These two words were created by "admen". How do we know what they mean?

THE UNCOLA

**ANNOUNCING
THE UN-THROWAWAY
FIBRE-TIP**

In the past fifty years we have had to create new words at a greater rate than ever before. How do we create new words? And how do we make words that can be readily absorbed into the language?

Very few words are completely new, that is, invented without reference to words that already exist in the language. And all newly created words look "English".

Which word in each set of two looks un-English? Why?

brillig	flookism	ableswiffun
gbillr	ismflook	unswiffable

We recognize what seems English and what does not seem English because we unconsciously know the patterns allowed by the language system.

Look at the underlined words. Why do they seem English? What do you think the poem is about? Do the nonsense words remind you of any other words in the language? Have any of Carroll's inventions become accepted English words?

He took his <u>vorpal</u> sword in hand:
   Long time the <u>manxome</u> foe he sought —
So rested he by the <u>Tumtum</u> tree,
   And stood awhile in thought.

And as in <u>uffish</u> thought he stood,
   The <u>Jabberwock</u>, with eyes of flame,
Came whiffling through the <u>tulgey</u> wood,
   And burbled as it came!

One, two! One, two! And through and through
   The <u>vorpal</u> blade went snicker-snack!
He left it dead, and with its head
   He went <u>galumphing</u> back.

—Lewis Carroll: *Through the Looking-Glass and What Alice Found There*

INFORMING IDEA

There is almost no limit to the number of English words we can make, but the ways in which we make them are restricted to a few recognizable patterns.

Look again at the new words listed at the beginning of the chapter:

communicaster	cartop	overkill
lunar module	splashdown	smog
ombudsman	skyjack	breathalyser
cablevision	biodegradable	bebop

Who could imagine creating the phrase **lunar module** before anyone thought of space travel, or the word **cablevision** before television was invented? Did anyone speak of **biodegradable** detergents before pollution was a major worry? Yet both **lunar** and **module** are words that have been in the language for some time; it is the combination that is new. So is the combination of the older words **cable** and **vision**, of **over** and **kill**, of **sky** and **jack**, of **splash** and **down**, and of **tour** and the suffix **-ism**. Communicaster is a combination of **communicate** and **caster** (as in **broadcaster** and **newscaster**). How do you think **smog** and **breathalyser** were made? The word **biodegradable** was made by adding the prefix **bio-** 'life' (Greek) and the suffix **-able** to the word **degrade**, which has among its meanings 'to decompose in stages'. We borrowed the Swedish word **ombudsman** about 1962.

Though words are sometimes pulled "out of the air" or borrowed, most new words use the resources present in the language. In this way the language is both **stable** and **dynamic**. Instead of inventing a whole new language, we use the old language in new ways.

A language must be *stable* to provide a reliable means of precise communication yet *dynamic* in order to accommodate itself to change.

—W. Earl Britton

An understanding of the patterns of English word-making can help us to decipher new and unfamiliar words, even those that are scientific or technical. This knowledge can also increase our enjoyment of words, and the delight in word play. Even the dullest-looking words may have fascinating histories that tell us a great deal about the people who created and used them.

Common Patterns of Word-Making

How We Make Words 1: Compounding

How were these words made?

overpass	ceasefire	water-tight	fibreglass
highway	splashdown	breakneck	dry cleaners
scarecrow	high school	railroad	super-tanker

Compounding is the putting together of two or more words to make a new word. Some of these compounds are "open", for example, **high school**; some are hyphenated, for example, **make-up**; and some are written as one word, for example, **blackbird**. All of them, however, are made up of words that can stand by themselves.

Does it make any difference to the meaning whether the word is written in its "open" form or its closed form? Is there a pattern of difference in the pronunciation? For example,

a red cap	and	a redcap
a black bird	and	a blackbird
a green house	and	a greenhouse
a hot plate	and	a hotplate

The meanings of **ceasefire** and **breakneck** are fairly obvious provided we know the meanings of **cease** and **fire**, of **break** and **neck**. With other compounds, for example, **breakfast** and **highway**, the meaning is not so obviously related to the component words.

Sometimes two words become so common as a unit that the spelling changes. For example,

day's eye became **daisy**
holy day became **holiday**
Woden's day became **Wednesday**

WORD WATCHING

Compounding

Make your own montage of recent compound words.

ORAL ACTIVITY

Create as many compound words as you can by adding other words to each of those listed below: for example, **tree** — **treetop, tree house, tree frog, tree line**

black	day	up	hot
out	life	time	cold

A great number of compounds arise when capsule descriptions are valuable. Here are examples.

a. Science

New technical terms are often made by combining non-technical words, for example, **feedback, countdown, airtight**. Notice that the use of these words has widened beyond their narrow scientific meaning.

b. Advertising

Advertising has created words such as **warm-up** pants, **snowfunstylemobiling, split-suede fur-trims, outperformers**, and **knee-highs**.

Why might **snowfunstylemobiling** be effective in an advertisement?

ACTIVITY

Skim through newspapers and magazines to find more examples of compounds. Look especially for words you haven't seen before. When you have a good collection, discuss in class which of these compound words are likely to catch on, and which ones seem to serve an immediate purpose only.

c. Poetry

Poets sometimes make their own compound words in order to create vivid, memorable images. Here are some examples from *Crow*, a book of poems by Ted Hughes:

Seeing the *clawtrack* of star
Hearing the *wingbeat* of rock.

His *temple-veins* gnarl, each like the pulsing head of a month-old baby.

The spark that *flash-thumped* fused his watch of all things.

So he took his *lavender-bag* ancestors under one arm.

Some such invented words may pass into common use, but most will not.

Did you notice that some of the examples from poetry are hyphenated? Why might that be?

ACTIVITY

Look for other compounds in poetry and then discuss their effectiveness.

In English, when compound words are made from a modifier and a noun, for example, **blackbird**, the modifier usually comes first. However, some legal and government terms linger in our language that follow French order, with the modifier after the noun. Some examples are:

notary public	fee simple
governor general	court-martial
attorney-general	aide-de-camp

Can you add to the list? How are the plurals made?

Sometimes, French order is used to make a phrase sound impressive or sophisticated, for example, **house beautiful**. Why do we use **Lake Superior, Air Canada**?

The Hyphen in Compounds

In an article about the new Supplement to the *Oxford English Dictionary*, Terry Coleman makes the following comments about hyphens:

Nothing disappears more quickly than a hyphen. The Supplement likes hyphens, and gives **air-line** and **flyover** (as in motorways). Perhaps by now these have become **airline** and **flyover**, since ... the life-span (lifespan?) of a hyphen can be as little as five years. Many disappear leaving one word, as in **flyover**. Others disappear leaving two separate words, as in **bath salts**. With hyphens . . . all is anarchy, and after the brief life-span (lifespan?) of a hyphen, there is no way of knowing which way the construction may go.

—from "Gazumping Old Onions" in *The Guardian*, October 21, 1972

ACTIVITY

Look in magazines and newspapers to see what is happening to the hyphen in these words:

air-line make-up life-span fall-out black-out

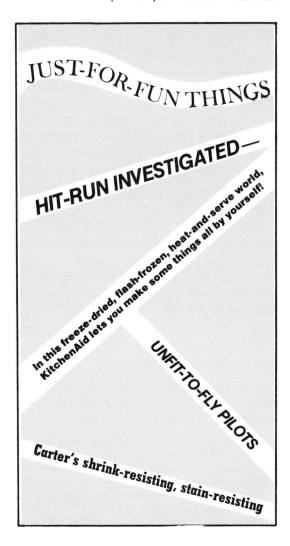

How We Make Words 2: Clippings

How did we make these words?

fridge	mike	lunch	women's lib
gas	lab	bike	deb
photo	plane	gym	champ

It is common to shorten or **clip** words for the sake of speed and economy, for example, to say **fridge** instead of **refrigerator**, **plane** instead of **airplane**.

Think about the language you use at school. Do you normally say **Home Economics** or **Home Ec**? **Physical Education** or **Phys Ed**? **examination** or **exam**? Why are such words shortened?

What other clipped words do you use with your friends?

Although many clippings are confined to oral speech, for example, **prof** for **professor**, and **sax** for **saxophone**, some eventually come to be used as often as their longer forms and thus move into written English, for example, **gas** for **gasoline**, and **photo** for **photograph**.

Occasionally, we drop the longer form altogether, as with these older words:

wig from **periwig**	**mob** from **mobile vulgus**
cab from **cabriolet**	**cello** from **violoncello**

and in these fairly recent ones:

lead(ing) **singer**	**cook**(ing) **book**
bank(ing) **account**	**spark**(ing) **plug**

Some clippings have been in the language for so many years that they now have meanings which differ from their longer forms, though the meanings are often connected. How do we differentiate, for example, between these pairs? (Use your dictionary.)

alone and **lone** **amend** and **mend**
defence and **fence** **omnibus** and **bus**

Is there any point in retaining both words? Why?

ACTIVITY

Check with an etymological dictionary (one which explains the origin and history of words) to find the longer forms of these clippings.

sport   spite   stain   size   tend

How do they differ in meaning from their original forms?

Clipping is also a common way of making nicknames. For example,

Patricia becomes **Pat, Patty,** or **Patsy**
Edward becomes **Ed, Eddie, Ted,** or **Teddy**
Joseph (or **Josephine**) becomes **Jo, Joe, Joey** (or **Josie**)

Notice that with some clippings the spelling changes, for example, **mike** and **bike** for **microphone** and **bicycle.** Can you think of a reason for the changes you notice?

ACTIVITY

Your own names may illustrate this pattern of word-making. List the nicknames of those in your class. How many are examples of clipping?

How We Make Words 3: Blends

What words were put together to make these new words?

cinemaddict	shamateur	swingles
sexational	oilionaire	alcoholiday
sexigration	recreology	

Blends are telescoped words or, as Lewis Carroll said, "two meanings packed up into one word". Carroll invented many blends, for example, **chortle**, a blend of chuckle and snort, and **galumphing**, which suggests both galloping and triumph.

Some blends are now so common that we rarely think of their origins. For example,

motel — motor and hotel
brunch — breakfast and lunch
motorcade — motorcar and cavalcade
dumfound — struck dumb and confounded

Science has also contributed many blends. For example,

transistor — transfer and resistor
positron — positive and electron (What is a negative electron called?)
bit — binary and digit (a computer term)

Where did **quasar** come from?

Some Blends

they'd better
Canuckle under

How to create a Manwich

Chocolasses cake

The Megapopulist Multiversity

BREATHALYSER

DUTCH TOT CARNAPPED

your threadaches are over

ACTIVITY

Look for blends in magazines, newspapers, signs, and advertisements. Make a list or montage of them, and three or four months later see if any of them become commonly used.

Here are some interesting blends:

Franglais — a mixture of the two French words **Français** and **Anglais**.

Spanglish — a similar blend of the English words **Spanish** and **English**.

moped — first used in Germany to describe a motorized pedal bicycle.

ACTIVITY

How creative are you in making up your own blends? For example,

pompetent (To describe someone who is competent but pompous about it.)

bumpbed (This word was coined by a three-year-old to describe the bunk bed on which she always bumped her head.)

vidiot (A blend of **video** and **idiot** — 'television addict'.)

What would you call, for example,
   a sunny day with clouds (a_____day)
   a mixture of Japanese and English
   a mixture of being flustered and frustrated
   a politician mainly concerned about ecology
   a person who is glibly articulate
   a movement for the liberation of adolescents (or children, etc.)
   a movement for the cessation of liberation movements
   someone who is both perplexed and expectant
   an expert on chess (or checkers)

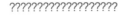

Try making up some of your own, especially humorous ones.

How We Make Words 4: Functional Shift

Aside from the fact that they are verbs, what do the underlined words in the following account have in common? On what pattern are they coined?

In Vancouver we <u>booked</u> passage on the Northern Prince for Prince Rupert. From there we <u>bussed</u> to Prince George, where we <u>lunched,</u> and then <u>motored</u> to Kamloops with friends. We <u>breakfasted</u> early, then <u>golfed</u> all day. We <u>dinnered</u> late and then <u>aired</u> back to Vancouver. Next year we plan to <u>vacation</u> in Eastern Canada. Friends of ours, who have <u>holidayed</u> in P.E.I. and <u>package-toured</u> the Gaspé Peninsula, are urging us to do the same. If we can <u>leisure</u> our way, we'll be happy. We don't like to <u>deadline</u> a holiday and to <u>wolf</u> our food in order to catch the next bus.

Changing the function of words (that is, changing one part of speech into another, for example, nouns into verbs, verbs into nouns) is one of the most common ways in which we make new words. Although these shifts are recognizably English and understood, some achieve acceptable status but others do not. Which of the underlined words in the above passage do you find unacceptable? Can you give any reason?

ACTIVITY

Use each of the following words as a noun and as a verb. For example,

We have a roomy **tent** for our vacation. We **tented** for two weeks.

   bar   service   golf   pipe   ticket

ACTIVITY

Use each of the following as an adjective and as a verb. For example,

It was a very **dull** day. He hit a rock and **dulled** the edge of his axe.

   yellow   brown   best   slow   black

ORAL ACTIVITY

What happens when these words shift function? Use each of these words in two sentences, first as a noun, then as a verb. Say the sentences aloud.

Pattern 1: permit   suspect   object
            subject   content   protest

            rebel
            contract

Pattern 2: house   abuse
            mouth   use

            wreath (watch spelling)
            loath   "   "
            breath   "   "

What patterns can you see? Can you think of other words that fit these patterns?

What happens to these words? Mark the stress patterns.

to break down   a breakdown
to get away   a getaway
to hold up   a hold up
to fall out   fall-out
to sit in   a sit-in

With some words, not only the pronunciation but also the written form of the word changes. The noun is usually written as one word or hyphenated, for example, **breakdown**, **fall-out**, to show that it is a unit.

ACTIVITY

Look for examples of functional shift, particularly ones you haven't heard before, for example, the following cartoon:

"Cheer up, sir. My friend here thinks we've bottomed out."

Drawing by Stan Hunt; © 1970 The New Yorker Magazine, Inc.

Here are two examples from Shakespeare:

Cleopatra: "He words me, girls, he words me."

—*Antony and Cleopatra*: v, ii, 191

Hamlet: " . . . you shall nose him as you go up the stairs."

—*Hamlet*: IV, iii, 38-39

The following are examples from the newspaper:

ACTIVITY

a. Combine the following words in as many ways as you can, first as nouns, then as verbs:

break	up
back	down
off	put
take	get
in	out

b. Mae West is credited with the remark: "It is better to be **looked over** than **overlooked**." Make up some of your own sayings using a similar pattern.

How We Make Words 5: Acronyms

An acronym of **Ca**nadian **Y**ellow **P**ages **S**ervice

A special form of clipping is one in which the first letters of several words form a pronounceable word. The resulting word is called an **acronym**. For example,

NATO from **N**orth **A**tlantic **T**reaty **O**rganization
scuba from **s**elf-**c**ontained **u**nderwater **b**reathing **a**pparatus
laser from **l**ight **a**mplification by **s**timulated **e**mission of **r**adiation

ACTIVITY

How were these acronyms formed?

sonar CWAC napalm POW

Today, people are aware of the power of acronyms, especially in newspaper headlines, and therefore tend to make titles whose initials form a pronounceable word that suggests a meaning, for example, **CARE** from **C**o-operative for **A**merican **R**emittances to **E**verywhere.

Here are some examples from technology:

FEAR — **f**ailure **e**ffect and **a**nalysis **r**eport
SMASH—**s**pecial **m**aterials **a**nd **s**pecial **h**andling
EGADS — **e**lectronic **g**round **a**utomatic **d**estruct **s**equencer (button)

When an acronym becomes part of the regular vocabulary of many people, it often loses its capitals, for example, **radar, sonar, napalm**. What difficulties might this create in the language, for example, if **FEAR** becomes **fear**?

Some recently created Canadian acronyms include:

LIP — an acronym of **L**ocal **I**nitiatives **P**rogram (introduced by the Canadian government in 1971).

Lake Koocanusa — this acronym of **Koo**tenay, **Can**ada, and **U.S.A.** was coined to name the lake formed by the Libby Dam in Montana. The lake starts in Montana but creeps across the border and up the Kootenay River. (1972)

Do you know of any other recent acronyms?

ORAL ACTIVITY

a. Create some titles so that words can be made from the initials. For example,

careful **a**ttention to **d**etail — **CAD**
careless **a**dult **d**river — **CAD**
Trans-**C**anada **R**at **E**radicator **E**xperts — **TREE**

b. Take a short word, for example, **WHIP**, and make a title with letters. For example, what might the letters stand for if these were acronyms?

CHUG MAGNA STRUT LARK

How We Make Words 6: Words Made from Proper Names

DISCUSS

What words come from these names? What is the link between the person and the word? Think of four or five other words made from names and find out what you can about the people and the words derived from their names.

Braille	Diesel	Boycott	Shrapnel
Maverick	Cardigan	Pullman	Quisling
Mesmer	McIntosh (apple)	Lynch	Chauvin

Sometimes a name evolves into a new word in the language. When Louis Pasteur invented a method of treating milk and other liquids to destroy harmful bacteria, the process was called **pasteurization**. Bikini was first of all an atoll in the Pacific, the site of atomic tests; and because the first brief swimsuits seemed to have the impact of an atomic explosion they were called **bikinis**.

ACTIVITY

What place names did these words come from? How are the places and the words associated? (Check with your dictionaries.)

| port | calico | jeans | spaniel |
| sherry | tweed | cashmere | jersey |

Literary figures sometimes become symbols for certain types of behaviour. For example, the behaviour of a romantic and impractical person is often described as **quixotic**, after **Don Quixote**, the noble but foolish hero of a famous seventeenth-century novel by Cervantes.

Don Quixote by Gustave Doré

We have adopted many words from the names of characters in literature. Here are some examples:

yahoo—'crude, brutish person': after the Yahoos, fictional people described in Jonathan Swift's *Gulliver's Travels*.

malapropism — 'the humorous misuse of a word; mistaken use of a word that resembles the appropriate one': from Mrs. Malaprop, who had a habit of doing this, a character in the play *The Rivals* by Richard Sheridan. Two examples are: "a shrewd awakening", and "the contagious countries" (rather than "contiguous").

Judas—'one who betrays a friend': from the Bible, the man who betrayed Jesus.

What kind of person is **a Scrooge? a Job? a Good Samaritan? a doubting Thomas? a Pollyanna? a Cinderella? a Daniel?**

ACTIVITY

Novelists often give their characters names that suggest their personal characteristics. Here are some characters created by Charles Dickens. Can you decide, from their names, what kind of people they were?

Mr. Murdstone	Miss Twinkleton	Mr. Pecksniff
Sleary	Mr. Crisparkle	Nathaniel Winkle
Traddles	Chuzzlewit	Uriah Heep

ACTIVITY

Many words come from names in mythology; for example, **martial** which comes from Mars, the Roman God of War. (Do you see any connection with **martial** music, and **martial** law?) Here are some other examples:

Chaos — **chaos, chaotic**	Odysseus — **odyssey**
Tantalus — **tantalize**	Pan — **panic**
Vulcan — **vulcanize**	Hercules — **herculean**
Jove — **jovial**	Amazons

What do you know of the characters from whose names these words are taken? Choose one, look up the story in dictionaries, encyclopedias, and collections of classical myths, and then tell the class what you discover about the characteristic or incident which explains the relationship between the character and the meaning of the derived word.

How We Make Words 7: Imitative Words

1.

2.

With which of the above shapes would you associate these sounds?

blick_____	bloog_____
grood_____	slitch_____
brump_____	speet_____
nikitee_____	looloo_____

Explain your choices.

What do these words seem to have in common?

slip slurp slam slush slink slouch

or these?

snide snap sneer snip snarl snuck

or these?

bump dump lump grumpy hump slump

Words such as **boom**, **cackle**, **fizz**, **cheep**, **gurgle**, **slimy**, **sludge**, and **goop** are called **imitative words** because they seem to suggest the sound or the feel of the things they describe.

Many imitative words are effective descriptions; none are exact imitations. For instance, the words used to imitate the sounds animals make differ from language to language. Make a list of English words for animal sounds, for example, **chirp**, **meow**, **moo**, **cock-a-doodle-doo**. Then look in several foreign-language dictionaries for words used in other languages, and compare these with your original list. Which words do you think come closest to being good imitations?

Unfamiliar imitative words may suggest different things to different people. What do you think these words are intended to describe?

| whiffle | squizzled | stawoo-stawoo |
| ffursh | clud | chup |

Did everyone in the class interpret them in the same way?

What letters or groups of letters tend to suggest slow movements? soft sounds? quick movements? sharp sounds? dull sounds? sizzling sounds?

ACTIVITY

Make up some nonsense words which suggest various sounds or movements. What patterns do you see?

ACTIVITY

Comic books are full of imitative words. Why do you think this is? Some words which originated in comic books, for example, **aaaaargh** and **zap**, have become common in casual speech. Look through comics for imitative words and discuss their effectiveness. If you can find some foreign comic books, look through them also, and discuss whether or not the words you find would be effective in English.

—B.C. by permission of John Hart and Field Enterprises, Inc.

ACTIVITY

In the following poem, what kind of words has the poet chosen to evoke the sound of waves on rock? What sound patterns can you find? What have poem and picture in common?

SEA CLIFF

Wave on wave
and green on rock
and white between
the splash and black
the crash and hiss
of the feathery fall,
the snap and shock
of the water wall
and the wall of rock:
after —
after the ebb-flow
wet rock,
high —
high over the slapping green,
water sliding away
and the rock abiding,
new rock riding
out of the spray.

—A. J. M. Smith

The West Wind, 1916-17, by Tom Thomson

ACTIVITY

What word can you make up to describe:

a. the sound made when someone scrapes a nail across a blackboard?

b. the feeling of a frozen metal object, for example, a can of concentrated orange juice just out of the freezer?

Try to create some other imitative words.

Repeated and rhythmic sounds are often expressed in paired words in which one vowel is changed. What sounds or ideas in the real world are suggested by these patterns? Can you add to them?

| **i** to **o** | tick tock, tick tock | sing song |
| **i** to **a** | jim jams | fiddle faddle |

What pattern do you see in the following? Can you add to the list?

superduper   teeny weeny   hillbilly
heebie-jeebies

This kind of repetition is called **reduplication**. What kinds of effects result from complete reduplication, for example, **boo-boo, a no-no, choo choo**. How do **mama** and **papa** fit into this picture?

How We Make Words 8: Borrowing

ORAL ACTIVITY

Are all the words in the following sentences of Anglo-Saxon origin? Do you think any of them are borrowed words?

I sat on a chair.
The leg of the table is broken.
We had roast beef for dinner.

We have used the words **chair**, **table**, **roast**, and **beef** for so many years that we hardly think of them as **borrowed words**, yet all of them were borrowed from French into Middle English.

Because English is a major world language, the opposite process is now taking place: many English words find their way into other languages, though their presence is not always a welcome one. The English writer William Hardcastle had this to say about borrowed words:

> The French cry into their *ouiskis* over the way their verbal inheritance is being snatched from their *bouches*. But they still don't cancel their subscriptions to newspapers which gaily report on *le steam-cracking, les picpoquets, une public relations newyorkaise*, and *le talkie-walkie*. . . .
>
> A similar groundswell has been observed in Germany. . . . [A father] was shocked to hear his daughter asking her boyfriend on the phone, "*Kannst du mich uppicken?*" . . .
>
> Today [in] West Germany . . . they fling words around like *kauboi, pinup, bluejeans* and *sexappeal* and they quite happily buy tobacco that is advertised as "superfine ready rolled". . . .
>
> Words are one of the few commodities which are not subject to tariffs and import quotas, and a free and healthy traffic is surely a good thing.
>
> —adapted from "Spit and Sawdust", © 1970 *Punch* (Rothco)

Because of the history of its speakers, English is much more hospitable to borrowing than many other languages. In our vocabulary may be found words from most of the major languages of the world. Some examples of borrowed words are:

yacht (Dutch), penicillin (Latin), algebra (Arabic), pemmican (Cree Indian), rodeo (Spanish), khaki (India), tea (Chinese), simile (Latin), and metaphor (Greek, through Latin and then French).

ORAL ACTIVITY

Why do you think we have borrowed the words in each set rather than make up or adapt our own words? Where do you think each word comes from? Check your guess with a dictionary.

(a) guava   banana   saffron   borsch
(b) kimono   culottes   mu-mu   pyjamas
(c) safari   harem   sauna   kibbutz
(d) gorilla   panda   camel   rhinoceros
(e) canoe   kayak   rickshaw   travois

English continues to borrow words, especially as we increase our knowledge of people in other countries. How many newly borrowed words can you think of that refer to food, for example, Japanese **sake** (rice wine) and Italian **pizza**?

Discuss how and why phrases in the following collage, though obviously English in origin, have been adapted to fit into the French language.

English Words Borrowed by the French

—from *Elle* magazine

DISCUSS

Read the following news item. What attitudes to borrowed words does it reveal? From what you know of how a language works, do you think people can be forced through legislation to change their language? How effective do you think the French Academy's edict will be? Will it prevent French speakers from adopting English words in the future?

'FLASHBACK' BECOMES 'RETROSPECTIF'

French bury English

PARIS (AP)—The French government began a purge today of English words from the nation's vocabulary, throwing out Anglicisms like "hit parade," "tanker" and "zoning" from official use.

A terminology commission set up by former Premier Jacques Chaban-Delmas in 1970 announced it has found 350 French words to bury the English that Frenchmen use to fill in the holes in their own language.

Thursday's Official Gazette will list the words for the edification of the nation and say that their use has become "obligatory" in government dealings. It strongly recommends the rest of the population employ them as well.

The vocabulary edict, issued with the intellectual blessing of the French Academy, seems to be part of the government's very real concern to prove that French can be adapted to expressing the needs of modern technology.

It also seems to be a kind of linguistic shoring-up for the challenge that French is expected to receive from English for dominance in the European Common Market.

The commission first attacked the areas of show business, television, transportation and space technology, and said it would get around to finance, sports, computers and tourism later.

Among the most commonly used English words or phrases to be banned from the vocabulary of the government television network are flashback, one-man show, hit parade, and features — to be replaced respectively by retrospectif, spectacle solo, palmares and varias.

In housing, zoning will become zonage, and in transportation, STOL aircraft — from the English abbreviation of short takeoff and landing — will become avion adac, which is the abbreviation of the same words in French.

Tanker is to become navire citerne. The judges kept the word pipeline intact, but insisted that it get a French pronunciation: it should sound like peepleen. Oleoduct, used by some French purists, was not mentioned.

The commission admitted failure, however, on three words that are constantly threaded through business conversation in France. They found no substitutes for hardware, software or marketing, and they will retain their place until substitutes are found.

How We Make Words 9: Affixing

English also allows the formation of new words by the process of **affixing** — adding to words, or sometimes Greek and Latin roots, units of the language which cannot stand alone called **affixes**. Affixes may be **prefixes**, those that go before the word or root, or **suffixes**, those that follow the word or root. Here are some examples:

PREFIX + WORD OR ROOT			WORD OR ROOT + SUFFIX		
un-	+ wise	= unwise	clear	+ -ly	= clearly
in- ('not')	+ decent	= indecent	joy	+ -ful	= joyful
re-	+ make	= remake	cigar	+ -ette	= cigarette
in- ('into')	+ spect (Lat. 'look')	= inspect	spect	+ -acle	= spectacle

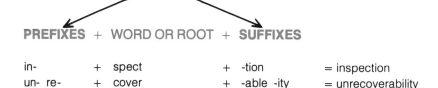

PREFIXES	+ WORD OR ROOT	+ SUFFIXES	
in-	+ spect	+ -tion	= inspection
un- re-	+ cover	+ -able -ity	= unrecoverability

Sometimes affixes are called **combining forms**. They recur in the language, carrying a fairly constant meaning. Dictionaries list affixes as elements in the vocabulary of the language.

WORD-LORE

Those proper English are losing some couth

Where did the word **couth** come from?

Prefixes

There are only about seventy-five or eighty prefixes in English. We use one prefix or a combination of two before a root or word. But these few prefixes can form many words. Some prefixes are inherited from Latin and Greek, and their meanings are often those of English prepositions and adverbs.

ACTIVITY

Make a list of about five words that begin with each of these prefixes: **sub-, re-, anti-, pre-, ab-, de-, trans-**. From the pattern within each list, work out the meaning carried by each prefix. Check your conclusions with your dictionary.

ACTIVITY

"If not actually **disgruntled**, he was far from being **gruntled**."

—P. G. Wodehouse

Make up some of your own statements along the same pattern as the above quote, using other "dis" words, for example, **disappointed**, **distraught**.

Dis, Continued

Here we go again with the "dis" word game. . . .
Census taker — discounted;
Bride — dismissed;
Tire repairman — dispatched;
Helen — disTroyed;
Pig farmer — disgruntled;
Night-club operator — disjointed.
Can you add to the list?

—Doyle Klyn, in *Weekend Magazine*

Suffixes

English uses many suffixes, and allows three or four suffixes to pile up after a word or root. But the suffixes have a fixed order.

ACTIVITY

After each word or root given in the first column, add as many suffixes as you can from the given list to make an English word. Try to rearrange the order of the suffixes. Report on what you discover. (Note that you may have to make slight spelling changes.)

WORD OR ROOT	SUFFIXES		
break	-less	-ly	-ive
civil	-ism	-ate	-ity
act	-able	-ic	-ify
vis- 'see'	-ize	-(a)tion	-ist
form	-ful	-y	-er
real	-ness	-age	

WORD WATCHING

What affixes are used here to make words?

Make your own montage of new words made with affixes.

A knowledge of the meanings of the more common Greek and Latin prefixes, suffixes, and roots in the English language is of great value. If we meet an unfamiliar word, we can often "unlock" its meaning by analysing its parts. For example, knowing that **mal** means **bad** or ill helps us to understand the meaning of such words as **malpractice**, **malnutrition**, and **malformation**. English does not mind mixing the languages it draws upon; we can find a Latin prefix joined to an Anglo-Saxon root, or a Greek suffix added to a Latin root; we are continually making new combinations.

The following words are all derived from the Latin root **scribere** 'to write'.

What is a **nondescript** person?

Can you guess what a **scriptorium** is? Check by using a dictionary. The word **manus** means 'hand'; what did **manuscript** probably mean originally?

Can you make a tree drawing similar to the one above, using the word **video**? If possible, make a tree which shows the relationship of **video** to **wit**.

It has been suggested that anyone who understands the composition of the **fourteen** words on the following page has the key to unlock the meanings of over fourteen thousand English words.

The 14 Words   Their Derivations as Keys to the Meaning of over 14 000 Words

Words	Prefix	Variant Spellings	Common Meaning	Root	Common Meaning
1. Precept	pre-		before	cap- (cep-, capt-)	take, seize
2. Detain	de-		away, from, down, off	ten- (tenu-, tent-)	hold, have
3. Intermittent	inter-		between, among	mitt- (mis-, miss-)	send
4. Offer	ob-	oc-; of-, op-	direction, opposite, against	fer-	bring
5. Insist	in-	im-, il-, ir-, em-, en-	into, upon	sist-	stand, place
6. Monograph	mono-		alone, one	graph-	writing
7. Epilogue	epi-		upon	log-	speech
8. Aspect	ad-	a-, ac-, af-, ag-, al-, an-, ap-, ar-, as-, at-	to, towards	specta-	look at
9. Uncomplicated	un-*		not	plic- (plicat-)	fold
	com-	con-, col-, cor-, co-	together, with		
10. Nonextended	non-		not	tende- (tent-, tens-)	stretch
	ex-	e-, ef-	out		
11. Reproduction	re-		back, again	duc- (duct-)	lead
	pro-		for, in front of		
12. Indisposed	in-	im-, il-, ir-	not	pon- (posit-)	put, place
	dis-	di-, dif-	apart, away		
13. Oversufficient	over-*		extra	fac- (fact-)	make, do
	sub-	suc-, suf-, sug-, sup-, sus-	under		
14. Mistranscribe	mis-		wrongly	scrib- (script-)	write
	trans-		across, beyond		

*Note that un- and over- are Germanic. The Latin equivalent of un- is in- (with its variant forms il-, ir-, im-), which is sometimes confused with (Latin) in- 'into' (see numbers 5 and 12 above).

Notice that some prefixes have variant forms, according to the letter that follows; for example,

ob- can be oc- (oc-cur), of- (of-fer), op- (op-pose)

ad- can be ac- (ac-cede), as- (as-sent), ap- (ap-position), and others

com- can be con- (con-duct), co- (co-operate), cor- (cor-relate), and others

in- (both meanings) can be im- (im-pose), il-(il-legal), ir- (ir-revocable)

ACTIVITY

Use these "keys" to unlock the meaning of the following words.

deception defer confer deduce propose intercept inference monologue desist implicate

ACTIVITY

Make ten other words by combining the roots and prefixes of the words listed in the previous Activity. Check in dictionaries to see if the words you make do exist in the English language.

Many borrowed words made up of **prefix + root** have near-synonyms of a Germanic combination **verb + particle** (**off, on, to, from, up, by,** etc.). Note the change in order. Some examples are:

Borrowed	Germanic
erupt (**ex** 'out of' + **rupt-** 'break')	break out
intervene (**inter** 'between' + **veni-** 'come')	come between
invent (**in** 'upon, on' + **veni-** 'come')	come upon

Thus speakers of English have choices, and can keep apart slight differences in meaning, using one type of word in one context, and the other for a different context: volcanoes **erupt**, but prisoners **break out** of jail; we speak of volcanic **eruptions**, but prison **breakouts**.

Sometimes the choice is a matter of style. We may have, for example:

an **introductory** question	or a **lead-in** question
oppose a suggestion	or be **set against** it
invoke the gods	or _____
precede someone	or _____
contradict someone	or _____
exceed the speed limit	or _____
emit smoke	or _____

Summary

Here is a review of the most common patterns of word-making:

1. **Compounding**—putting together two or more words to make a new word, for example, **downgrade, snowshoes**.

2. **Clipping**—making a new word by shortening an existing word, for example, **gym** from **gymnasium**, **bus** from **omnibus**.

3. **Blends**—putting together parts of two or more words to make a new word, for example, **motel, boatel**.

4. **Functional Shift**—making a new word by changing the grammatical function of an existing word (nouns into verbs, verbs into nouns, adjectives into verbs, etc.), for example, **chairs** the meeting, **tables** the motion.

5. **Acronyms**—a form of clipping in which the first letters of several words form a pronounceable word, for example, **radar** from **ra**dio **d**etecting **a**nd **r**anging.

6. **Words Made from Proper Names**—words made from the names of people, places, literary or mythological figures, for example, **mercury, ohm, bikini**.

7. **Imitative Words**—words which seem to suggest the sound or the feel of the thing they describe, for example, **burp, chug, bow-wow**.

8. **Borrowing**—words borrowed into English from other languages, for example, **yacht, beef, tycoon**.

9. **Affixing**—adding to words, or sometimes Greek or Latin roots, units of the language which cannot stand alone called **affixes**, for example, adding **un** to **wise** to make **unwise**, **ize** to **computer** to make **computerize**. (How does this pattern of word-making differ from number 1, compounding?)

WORD WATCHING

What patterns of word-making do you see here?

a step-in was a standout

do-it-yourself shelf units

THE **outperformers**

MONTREAL
...*for snowfunstylemobiling*

FUNTASTIC

Imperials are for the unmechanically minded

WARM-UP PANTS

Burrards looking east to bolster boxla lineup

NO INTEREST LAYAWAY

BUSJACKED!

The Incredible Whatsit.

SPLIT-SUEDE FUR-TRIMS

CHARGEX

ACTIVITY

Read the following list of Canadian words and identify the ways in which the words have been made. Keep in mind that one word can sometimes illustrate two or three patterns of word-making. The definitions for the following words are based on more complete definitions found in the *Dictionary of Canadianisms*.

stumpage — price paid for the right to cut trees

stubble-jumper — a prairie farmer (slang)

Vets Affairs — government department that looks after war veterans

a whoop-up—a noisy celebration or party

caribou — through French from Algonkian word meaning 'pawer, scratcher'

manning pool—central place to get work or workers

a lean-to — overnight shelter made with poles against some support

interprovincial — from province to province

ice-pool—sweepstake based on guessing the time the ice on a river or lake will break up

hydro—from Hydro Electric Commission, generalized to mean hydro-electric power

Douglas fir — a spruce tree, often over 60 m high, from David Douglas, a Scottish botanist, 1798–1834

a dozer — shortening of "bulldozer"

Canadianization — process of making something Canadian

tuque — knitted wool hat, usually tasselled at end (from Canadian French)

rink rat — a boy or man who helps with chores around a hockey rink, often in return for free skating, tickets to games, etc. (slang)

POOR MAN'S SCRABBLE

Here is a word game that any number of people can play. Try playing it in groups of six to ten.

The object of the game is to make as many words as possible. Each player takes a piece of paper and

Q	U	A	C	K
U	N	D	E	R
E		M		
S	L	I	P	X
F		T		O

draws a square of twenty-five blocks (five down and five across).

The starting player can decide which letter he wants in the middle square. Everyone must put that letter in the middle square. Each player in turn then chooses a letter which the rest of the players can put in any square they like. The game ends when all the squares are filled.

Words can go from top to bottom or from left to right, but they cannot go from bottom to top or go diagonally across the board.

Scoring

A five-letter word counts five points.

A three-letter word counts three points.

A three-letter word and a two-letter word on the same line count five points.

The highest scorer wins.

Choosing Words: "Am I Saying What I Want to Say?"

> The difference between the right word and the almost right word is the difference between lightning and the lightning bug.
>
> —Mark Twain

In speaking we have voice and gesture to help us convey our meaning. But in writing, words must speak for themselves, and if our words are not thoughtfully chosen they may not carry the message we intended.

In writing we can have second thoughts **before** what we write is given to anyone to read. We have the chance to replace the almost-right words of a first draft by more appropriate words.

Below is an excerpt from "Boys and Girls", a story by Canadian writer Alice Munro about a young girl growing up on her father's fox farm. Choose what you feel are the most appropriate words for the spaces left blank. Do they contribute to an overall "picture" or mood?

> I hated the hot dark kitchen in summer, the _____ blinds and the flypapers, the _____ old oilcloth table and _____ mirror and _____ linoleum. My mother was too _____ and _____ to talk to me, she had no heart to tell me about the Normal School Graduating Dance; sweat _____ over her face and she was always counting under her breath, _____ at jars, _____ cups of sugar. It seemed to me that work in the house was _____, _____ and peculiarly depressing.

Here is the passage as Alice Munro wrote it. Compare her choice of words with yours. What kind of picture do her words create? What do they tell you of the girl's attitude towards working with her mother? Notice that though none of the words are particularly difficult, they were all carefully chosen to suit the context exactly and to portray a particular mood or feeling.

> I hated the hot dark kitchen in summer, the <u>green</u> blinds and the flypapers, the <u>same</u> old oilcloth table and <u>wavy</u> mirror and <u>bumpy</u> linoleum. My mother was too <u>tired</u> and <u>preoccupied</u> to talk to me, she had no heart to tell me about the Normal School Graduating Dance; sweat <u>trickled</u> over her face and she was always counting under her breath, <u>pointing</u> at jars, <u>dumping</u> cups of sugar. It seemed to me that work in the house was <u>endless</u>, <u>dreary</u> and peculiarly depressing.

—from Alice Munro: *Dance of the Happy Shades*

Remember that words are never good or bad in themselves—they can be judged only in context. How adept you become at using the right language in the right place depends most of all on developing a sensitivity to the context of your writing.

ORAL ACTIVITY

As a review, discuss the following suggestions for choosing words.

1. A Good Word Suits the Occasion

Ask, "What kind of language does the occasion demand?"

2. A Good Word Is Fresh and Alive

Trite, automatic phrases usually provoke trite, automatic responses. Avoid such overworked intensifiers as **very**, **awful**, **terrific**, or **tremendous**. E. B. White calls such words the "leeches that infest the pond of prose, sucking the blood of words."

3. A Good Word Is as Simple as Possible

A show-off word is not necessarily an appropriate word. Do you think Alice Munro's line,
"I had the real watering can, my father's, though I could only carry it three-quarters full"
would have been better written this way,
"I possessed the veritable container for the purpose of irrigation, that belonging to my pater-familias, though I could only transport three-quarters of its capacity"?

4. A Good Word Is Exact

Create vivid pictures in your writing. Look at the verbs that Alice Munro uses on p. 100, for example, **pointing**, **dumping**, **trickled**. Do they carry specific images?

5. A Good Word Sounds Right in Its Context

Read aloud everything you write and remove unpleasant repetitions, clashing sounds, or monotonous rhythms.

For example,

In Tom, **suspicion** is a chronic **condition**.

As he came closer to the castle, he could catch glimpses of candlelight shining through the casements.

The wind was **blowing**, and it would probably be **snowing** before **morning**.

Rewrite these sentences to improve the sound.

6. A Good Word Is a Necessary Word

It is usually a good idea to put down as much as you can when you begin to write, and to take out as much as you can when you revise.

For example,

i. original sentence — He, in fact, worked manually, using his hands to carry out his labour.

ii. revision — He,/in fact,/ worked ~~manually using~~ ^{with} his hands ~~to carry out his labour~~.

iii. final sentence — He worked with his hands.

Summary

Incorrect words baffle and mislead. Precise words are efficient.

If language is not correct then what is said is not what is meant; if what is said is not what is meant, then what ought to be done remains undone; if this remains undone, morals and art will deteriorate, justice will go astray, the people will stand about in helpless confusion. Hence there must be precision in what is said. This matters above everything.

—Confucius (freely translated)

WORD PLAY

Here are a few examples of what can happen when writers and poets play with words — their shapes, sounds, associations, and meanings.

Words can generate words:

Puffing and globbering they drugged themselves rampling or dancing with wild abdomen, stubbing in wild postures amongst themselves.

—John Lennon: *In His Own Write*

ACTIVITY

Make up some slogans using nonsense words.

WORDS CAN MAKE PICTURES

" Mine is a long and a sad tale ! " said the Mouse turning to Alice, and sighing.

"It *is* a long tail, certainly," said Alice, looking down with wonder at the Mouse's tail ; "but why do you call it sad ? " And she kept on puzzling about it while the Mouse was speaking, so that her idea of the tale was something like this :——" Fury said to

a mouse, That
  he met in the
    house, ' Let
     us both go
      to law : *I*
       will prose-
      cute *you*.—
      Come, I'll
     take no de-
    nial : We
    must have
   the trial ;
  For really
 this morn-
ing I've
nothing
to do.'
Said the
mouse to
 the cur,
  'Such a
  trial, dear
   Sir, With
    no jury
     or judge,
      w o u l d
     be wast-
    ing our
   breath.'
  'I'll be
  judge,
 I'll be
 jury,'
said
cun-
ning
old
Fury:
'I'll
try
the
whole
cause,
and
con-
demn
you to
death.' "

—Lewis Carroll: *Alice's Adventures in Wonderland*

ACTIVITY

Make some of your own pictures with words. Making a typewritten picture is also fun.

Veni, vidi, vici.
("I came, I saw, I conquered.")
—Julius Caesar

An army marches on its stomach.
—Napoleon

Never in the field of human conflict was so much owed by
so many to so few.
—Winston Churchill (tribute to R.A.F.)

Ask not what your country can do for you—ask what you
can do for your country.
—John F. Kennedy

That's one small step for a man, one giant leap for mankind.
—Neil Armstrong

Sticks and stones may break my bones, but names will
never hurt me.
—children's rhyme

There's an iron curtain across Europe.
—Winston Churchill

He that is without sin among you, let him first cast a stone
at her.
—John 8: 7

Anyone who hates small dogs and children can't be all
bad.
—W. C. Fields

The truth shall make you free.
—John 8: 32

There's a sucker born every minute.
—P. T. Barnum

2 + 2 = 4

Chapter 4

The Shapes of Utterances

English Sentences

The making of clear and beautiful sentences in
harmony with the movement of thought is a high art.

—Stephen Leacock

The History of the Sentence—for YOU as a Sentence-Maker

When did you speak your first sentence? Do your parents or family remember when it was? what it was?

If you have a younger brother or sister or if you babysit with a young child, listen to the child's sentences. Record them if you can. How long are the sentences? Are any words omitted from the sentences?

A sentence is a mysterious thing, as is our power to make or understand one. Young children learn with amazing speed the language spoken around them. From out of the jumble of noise they hear, they somehow work out the system of the language. Are these one-word utterances "sentences"? They seem to carry full messages. For example,

"**Mummy**" may mean: "I want mummy" or "You're mummy" or "Where's mummy?"

"**Cookie**" may mean: "I want a cookie" or "This is a cookie, and I like it."

Often when children create messages in their "telegraph" form of language, adults will repeat these sentences and add to them, making them into full "adult" sentences. This may be one of the ways by which children learn to make more sophisticated sentences.

Child: Baby cookie.
Mother: Does baby want a cookie to eat?

By the time children go to school, they use all the basic sentence patterns adults use and can create new and rather long and intricate sentences. Children also understand sentences they have not heard before. Somehow children learn the grammar of the language, and show that human beings are "sentence-makers".

After we have learned to read and write with some fluency, the **written** patterns of the language have a powerful influence on our sentence structures, both oral and written. A young child might **say** this sentence:

You know, I have an uncle, and he has a dog — a big black dog — and it knows just dozens of tricks — he's really smart — and one day when we were at my uncle's place this dog heard the paper-boy, and you know what? — he ran outside and got the paper in his mouth and brought it in to my uncle, and it was all kind of wet and . . .

But he would probably not write this story in the **oral style** of strings of thoughts joined by **and**s, **but**s, **and then**s, and repetitions, but use his pencil to edit his sentences in a **written style**, with more subtle joining of ideas and more complex sentence patterns.

ACTIVITY

Try putting the child's oral sentence into edited written sentences.

What were the main changes you made?

Did everyone in the class make the **same** written sentences?

Putting your thoughts and feelings into written words is a matter of making sentences—structures that you can play with and manipulate into varied shapes and lengths to serve your purpose.

ACTIVITY

Write down **one or more sentences** that for one reason or another have stayed in your mind.

The sentences may have been a chance remark
    or something carefully constructed.
The sentences may have been about you,
    or a sport,
    or an event,
    or an idea,
    or someone you know.
Then analyse **why** this particular sentence has stayed in your mind.

What Is a Sentence?

All the following are **sentences**. Read them aloud. What is common to them all? In other words, how do you recognize them as **sentences**?

Oh, no!

Oh no?

Wait!

FOR RENT

Good!

Where?

Over there.

Yes.

Never.

Wouldn't you?

Please come here.

Tom!

Tom, will you please come here?

Tom will be here soon.

Tom will be here soon, and then you may leave.

May I leave if Tom comes?

Tom, who will be here soon, can run that machine, but I would like you to stay for an hour and help me with this one.

Mrs. Helen P. Morrison, who has been an employee of this firm for the past ten years, is a skilled and dependable worker, one whom I can recommend highly for the position of assistant manager in your company.

It is over there.

I'd never do that.

As these examples show, a sentence may be made up of one word or a large group of words, its shape and size varying with the situation. No one has been able to make a neat "capsule" definition of the English sentence. Yet everyone agrees that the sentence is a basic unit of speech.

At one time grammarians tried to define a sentence as "a group of words expressing a complete thought". But what is a "complete thought"? Could one therefore classify a book as a sentence? Sometimes a look, a nod of the head, or just a sound

expresses a "complete thought". It is probably impossible to define the idea of a "complete thought". There is little difference in the **content** of these two groups of words:

(a) the barking dogs
(b) the dogs are barking

yet everyone would agree that (a) does not seem to be a sentence and that (b) does. The **completeness** lies in the **form** of the sentence rather than in its **content**.

In **speech** the "finality" of the sentence is signalled by a change in the speaker's voice. In **writing**, this final signal is represented by a period, exclamation mark, or question mark, followed by a space.

THE FINAL PUNCTUATION MARKS OF A SENTENCE

. period
! exclamation mark
? question mark
followed by a space

ORAL ACTIVITY

Read the following sentences aloud, and see if you can "hear" the differences in the speaker's voice as signalled by the punctuation marks. What patterns of **meaning** differences are being signalled?

The boat has gone.	No.	She came alone.
The boat has gone!	No!	She came alone!
The boat has gone?	No?	She came alone?

Other punctuation marks, such as commas, semicolons, and colons, are often used in the middle of a sentence, but these marks do not signal the end of the sentence. Note the difference in the speaker's **voice** between:

How blue the water was, and how clear the sky! (one sentence)

How blue the water was! How clear the sky! (two sentences)

Because it was windy, we decided not to go out in the boat. (one sentence)
It was windy. We decided not to go out in the boat. (two sentences)

Of course, punctuation marks cannot show all the variations and subtleties of the human voice and all the facial expressions and gestures that serve as signals when people talk. Writers must therefore use with care the various sentence structures and the few punctuation marks available to them for giving the sense and rhythms intended. A "sentence sense" is largely a matter of developing a "good ear".

ACTIVITY

How good is your "sentence sense"? How well trained is your ear to hear the ends of sentences? Read this paragraph to yourself, and mark where you "hear" the end of each sentence. Then check your decisions with those of the rest of your class. Discuss any variations in the decisions.

> An animal was moving down by the snowy shore at first it looked as big as a fox but as it approached it seemed to shrink it paused by the edge of the ice-hole turned its round head and moved its trailing tail the sleek coat gleamed in the aurora until the animal slipped into the water and dived among the eddies the head appeared then vanished again further down stream where the surface was black and still a point of light spread into a widening ring in the middle of which the creature looked about with beady eyes now it began swimming against the current for a moment its back appeared among the eddies of the falls and suddenly it shot up at its starting-point on the edge of the ice
> An otter whispered Pietari but he didn't shoot

—Yrjo Kokko: *The Way of the Four Winds*

ACTIVITY

Tape-record one of your class or group discussions (for example, about a piece of literature, or a project) and transfer to paper a small part of it—preferably a part in which there are several speakers. Do the transcription without punctuation. Then punctuate it. Then play the tape and discuss where the "sentence" breaks come in speech, and how well they match the written form.

VOTE

HONEST SAM

Sentences in Conversation

When people are conversing face to face, they often use sentences such as these:

Put it there.
Where?
Beside the tool box.
Why?
Because I'll need it.
Oh, all right.
Thanks.

Nice day.
Yes, a day for gardening.
You a gardener?
Uh-huh. Built a greenhouse last spring.
Glass or plastic?
Plastic. Cheaper, even if I have to
    replace it every year. Quite a job, too.
Must be nice to have flowers all winter.

These oral sentences do not necessarily follow the full subject-predicate pattern. Some of the sentences may be imperatives, which have a grammatical pattern that omits the subject:

Put it there.   Don't do that.   Jump!

Some of the oral sentences are questions or answers to questions, in which only a piece of information needs to be expressed, because the conversation has supplied the rest:

Where? Beside the tool box. Why? Because I'll need it.

Some sentences are spoken with extra force and emotion. Like the other types, these exclamatory sentences may be shortened or full:

Wow! That's big!

Some of the oral sentences are statements, and the speakers may omit the obvious—usually the subject or a **be**—because the situation "fills" in the omitted parts:

Built a greenhouse last spring. Must be nice to have flowers all winter. Nice day.

The rapid exchange of words in most conversations allows this kind of omission. But a one-way talk or sentences on a silent page must be fully developed.

ACTIVITY

Record parts of various kinds of conversations. (You should have the speakers' permission before you record. The most natural result will come when the speakers are so well into the conversation that they do not notice when you "switch on" for recording.) Then analyse the structure of the sentences used. Is there any relationship between the fullness of the structure and the formality ("social distance") of the occasions? between the sentence structure and the topic being discussed?

Statements, Imperatives, Questions, and Exclamations

One traditional way of classifying sentences is by the type of message they contain. All of us recognize that the sentences below, though containing almost the same words, carry different messages. What are the signals that make the messages different? (Some are in the voice; some are in grammar, for example, word order.) These differences allow us to make four different categories of sentences:

(a) You took off your hat. (**Statement**—sometimes called a **declarative** sentence)

(b) Take off your hat. (**Command** or **strong request**, a form called an **imperative** sentence)

(c) You took off your hat?   (**Questions**, called **interrogative** sentences)
Did you take off your hat?

(d) How dare you leave your hat on! (Said with extra emotion and emphasis, a What a silly hat!   form called an **exclamatory** sentence)

This classification is not foolproof, as the following section shows, but can be helpful. Which types appear more often in spoken language than in written?

The Four Types of Sentences in Greater Detail

Because the statement sentence is the most complex to study and the one most often used in writing, we shall first of all look closely at the three kinds of sentence usually associated with oral language:

imperative   interrogative   exclamatory

The Imperative Sentence

Imperative sentences may vary from one to two words to a long sequence:

Eat it up!

Now!

NO SMOKING

Run for your lives!

Scalpel!

Don't!

Please do not talk while I am singing.

Don't mention that unpleasant episode during dinner.

A sentence may be a question in form, but "imperative" in tone and intention. The choice of a question form is usually made for the sake of courtesy. The intention of "command" is signalled by the voice.

Would you mind not talking while I am singing?

Will you close the window, please, John?

You'll be quiet now, won't you? (a statement with a "tag" question)

Would you care to leave now?

The question pattern gives the illusion that the other person has a choice—a matter of social convention.

A sentence can also be "imperative" in meaning but take the **form** of a statement. Put each of the following examples into the imperative form, and discuss the differences in effect.

Everyone will leave quietly by the side door.
You will stay home every school night next week.
When you finish this job at three o'clock, we will meet at the house.

What are the language clues that signal to a listener that these are "imperatives" in intent, even when statements in form?

INFORMING IDEA

Imperative sentences are classified by **form**. Other forms, such as the question or statement sentence, may convey similar "imperative" **ideas**, but are not classified as imperative **sentences**.

ACTIVITY

Try some role-playing. A father is impatient because his daughter's boyfriend is staying too late. In how many different ways can the father (or mother) ask the boy to leave? Act out the scene, and then write the script. How many of the father's sentences are imperatives? How many are questions? How many are statements? How often are "imperative" meanings conveyed without using language at all?

ACTIVITY

Listen and record the various ways in which someone tells another person that he or she disagrees with what was said. Add to your list any other possibilities you can think of. Then arrange your findings according to **form**: questions, imperatives, or statements. What are your conclusions?

ACTIVITY

Writers and speakers often use an imperative form beginning with **Notice that** . . . , **Let us**, or **Let me** in order to introduce or direct attention to a new topic or idea. Some examples are:

Let us now consider what this threat of war means to our oil supply.
Let me go back a little and . . .

Look in various essays, editorials, and other forms of thoughtful or persuasive writing for examples, and discuss their functions within each piece of writing.

ACTIVITY

Written advertisements frequently use the imperative sentence. Why? Make a collection of imperatives in advertisements, and discuss their uses.

Questions: Two Main Types

What is the difference in the **answers** expected for the following two types of questions?

A

1. Did Jim help you fix the tire?
2. Is the party at Jim's house?
3. Did you fix the boat?
4. Are you going to the party?
5. Leaving early?

B

1. Who helped you fix the tire?
2. Where is the party?
3. How did you fix the boat?
4. What are you doing tonight?
5. When will you be leaving?

The first type (A) is called a **yes-no question** because the **whole statement** is being questioned. The answer can be either **yes**, or **no**, or **maybe** (etc.), or one of these followed by the whole statement or part of the whole statement, repeated.

Yes, I'm going to the party.	Yes.
No, I'm not going to the party.	Perhaps.
Yes, I am going.	Yes, I am.
No, I'm not going.	No, I'm not.

The second type (B) is called a **wh-question**, because a **wh-** type word (**who, whose, what, where, when, why, how,** and a few others) acts as the signal for the kind of answer wanted. The person answering fills the wh- "slot" in the sentence.

Who helped you fix it? **Jim** (helped me fix it).
Where is the party? **At Jane's house.** (The party is **at Jane's house.**)
What are you doing? **Going to Jane's party. Nothing.**

These two types of questions are used most often in conversation, but they may appear in writing, for example, letters (a form of written conversation) or essays, as a device to interest and involve the reader. Some examples are:

(a) Are so-called "free" schools really free?
(b) Does TV violence affect our children?
(c) How fast are the policies of this government forcing the unions to the left?
(d) How much can one believe pre-election polls?

Usually these questions appear at the **beginning** of an extended piece of writing. (Why?)

Rhetorical Questions

Speakers and writers often use rhetorical questions. Here are some examples. How does a rhetorical question differ from an ordinary question?

Whatever shall I do with that child?

Who would have dreamed that he would be elected?

Doesn't she sing beautifully? (Try this one without the negative.)

Haven't I always kept my promises? (Try this one without the negative, too.)

Why on earth can't you be on time?

Someone using a rhetorical question does not expect an answer; the assumption is that only one answer is possible — the speaker's. Although the form is that of a question, the intent is that of a statement. Turn each of the above into the statement that is really meant. What do you discover? Why, do you think, are they called **rhetorical** questions?

Think of some situations in which rhetorical questions are used frequently. Collect examples from your reading and listening.

To Think About

Can you think of an example of someone making a **statement** in form that is really a question in intent?

Some Rhetorical Questions

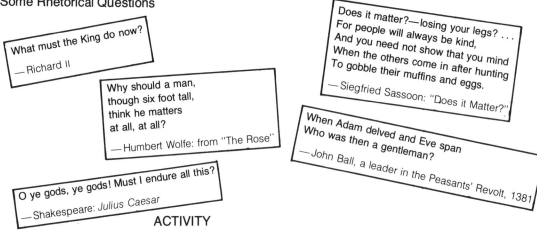

What must the King do now?

—Richard II

Why should a man,
though six foot tall,
think he matters
at all, at all?

—Humbert Wolfe: from "The Rose"

O ye gods, ye gods! Must I endure all this?

—Shakespeare: *Julius Caesar*

Does it matter?—losing your legs? . . .
For people will always be kind,
And you need not show that you mind
When the others come in after hunting
To gobble their muffins and eggs.

—Siegfried Sassoon: "Does it Matter?"

When Adam delved and Eve span
Who was then a gentleman?

—John Ball, a leader in the Peasants' Revolt, 1381

ACTIVITY

Look in essays, editorials, letters to the editor, etc. for rhetorical questions.

Questions in Advertisements

Make a collection of questions you see or hear used in advertisements.
Why did the ad writer use the question form?

Which form predominates: the **yes-no** type, the **wh-** type, the **rhetorical** type?
Do you find any interesting patterns?

There is one different type of question included in the examples below. Can you find it, and make others in a similar pattern?

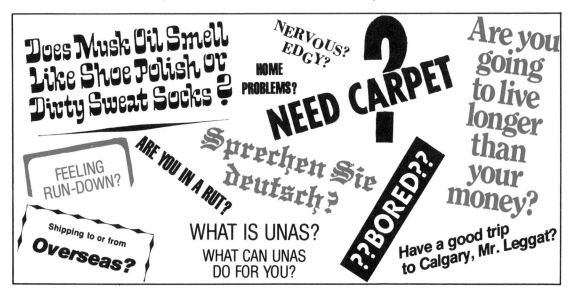

The Exclamatory Sentence

There are three main grammatical forms which signal a true exclamatory sentence. What are the differences in grammatical pattern in each of the three groups, listed below? Make other exclamatory sentences based on the same patterns.

(a) How easy it seemed then!
   How dead that tree looks!
   How quietly he works!
(b) What an idiot!
   What a boring party!
   What I suffered with that man!
(c) Good heavens!
   You miserable thief!
   You darling!
   Oh!

Some sentences are statements, imperatives, or questions in grammatical form, but spoken with voice intonation that signals extra emotion; this extra force is represented in writing by an exclamation mark. These types of sentences may be classified as "exclamatory" also, even though their grammatical form is that of another type. But they are really hybrids.

It was here only a minute ago!

Help!

Don't touch!

Don't ever say that again!

If only they would leave!

For how long must I tolerate this nonsense!

Will he be staying forever!

Exclamations occur mainly in speech. Occasionally they appear in written language other than dialogue, but the overuse of the exclamation mark lessens its effect. Usually, it is better to achieve emphasis by the right word and sentence structure.

ACTIVITY

Collect some exclamatory sentences from ads, dialogue, and other kinds of written English. Examine (a) their form, (b) their uses, and (c) their effectiveness.

You may wish to examine the examples below before doing this excercise.

Statement (or Declarative) Sentences

What does the word **statement** mean:
(a) in finance?
(b) in law?
(c) in an argument?

What meanings do these words have in common?
How do they differ in meaning?

say   declare   tell   state

A **statement** (or **declarative**) sentence is the basic form from which the other sentence types deviate. The voice signals "finality" at the end of a statement sentence by a drop in pitch followed by silence (even if only a brief silence). In writing, this signal of finality is a period.

In speech many statement sentences are "partial" because the context provides much of the information. Others are "full" statements. Most answers to questions are statements.

Here are some examples of statement sentences typical of **oral** English and of "speech on paper", as in diaries or letters:

(a) This is a poor way to start a vacation. Rain for three days.
(b) Nice day. Wish I hadn't brought my umbrella. Now I'll have to carry it around everywhere.
(c) Shopped all day. Picked up two films at half price.
(d) The silence was somehow terrifying. Not a sound. Not even a clock ticking.

Statement Sentences in Advertisements

Why are statement sentences rarely used for "lead" sentences in advertisements?

Examine the following statement sentences taken from advertisements. How accurate is the factual information they contain?

---

(1)
Your Car Could Do with a Spring Clean-up and These Famous Products Are Just What You Need.

(2)
The Department of National Health and Welfare advises that danger to health increases with amount smoked.

(3)
We care

(4)
It has a gift for celebration.

(5)
THIS YEAR'S MERCS SET NEXT YEAR'S STANDARDS

(6)
It tastes SO GOOD

(7)
Chassis tubes are a major cause of TV repairs.

(8)
They're yours for just $1.

(9)
We've got the answer

(10)
it's easy...

A Particular Kind of Statement Sentence: The Newspaper "Lead" Sentence

Newspaper items have a particular kind of structure. The opening sentence, called the "lead" or "summary lead" sentence, is usually a statement and one that gives all the main facts: what happened, who did it, when, where, how, and perhaps why. The rest of the item elaborates on each of these. The reasons for this structure are twofold: first, so that the hasty reader gets the main facts immediately and can then decide whether or not he wishes to read further; and second, to give the important facts first so that the item may be clipped off anywhere to fit into the space available.

by Jane Rosen in **New York**————— where

Thousands of angry housewives————•who

what ————**spurned their butchers here on**————— where

when————— **Tuesday** and **meat sales dropped**———— what

astonishingly by 80 per cent in

some areas as the consumer **boy-**

cott against high meat prices got———— why

under way.

ACTIVITY

Examine the first sentence of news items in several newspapers, and see how many of these questions it answers: **what happened, who, when, where, how, and why**. Then see how the following sentences elaborate upon the "lead" sentence. In how many places could the item be cut off without sacrificing important facts? If you find an item that does not follow this structure, examine it to see why.

Then either (a) write a newspaper item about something local or something imaginary or (b) rewrite one newspaper item so that it has the structure of a story told by an eyewitness to the event or by someone involved in the event. Note particularly the change in the **opening** sentence.

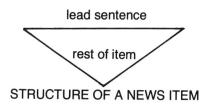

STRUCTURE OF A NEWS ITEM

SOME "LEAD" SENTENCES FROM NEWSPAPERS

Notice 1) that frequently the phrase "he said", or "Mr. S___reported", etc. is reversed in a lead sentence. (Why?) Notice 2) how follow-up sentences develop the details of the lead sentence.

Sun Staff Reporter

FORT ST. JOHN — Six persons stranded on Pink Mountain 100 miles north of here were rescued unharmed Tuesday — but had to leave their vehicles behind.

The delicate balance of the North Pacific fishing harvest was shown Monday at the opening of the 19th annual meeting of the International North Pacific Fisheries Commission.

Spokesmen for Canada, the United States and Japan — the three nations who have signed the North Pacific fishing treaty —illustrated the problems in speeches couched in diplomatic courtesies.

WASHINGTON (UPI) — Scientists reported Monday discovery in a nearby galaxy clouds of gas which suggest that the basic building blocks of life exist elsewhere in the universe as well as in our own Milky Way family of 100 billion stars.

The discovery was made by Dr. Philip Schwartx of the Naval Research Laboratory and Drs. William Wilson and Eugene Epstein of the Aerospace Corp., Los Angeles, by means of the National Radio Astronomy Observatory's 36-foot radiotelescope at Kitt Peak in Arizona.

LONDON (UPI) — Prime Minister Edward Heath confronted British trade unions today with a choice of accepting a voluntary freeze of wages and prices to halt inflation — or having one imposed by law.

By
Frank H. Nokes

Public Information Officer,
Environment Canada,
Fisheries Service

"All we've had to go on until now were field notes made by Mackenzie, Hearne, Franklin and a few others," explained federal fisheries biologist Jeff Stein when I asked him about his work on the Mackenzie River this summer.

Because of the imminent construction of a 2,500-mile gas pipeline along the Mackenzie Valley from Prudhoe Bay to Edmonton, Jeff and other federal biologists are on a massive fact-finding hunt.

They want to know the type of fish that live in the Mackenzie and its tributary streams, their age and growth rate, what they feed on, where they live, and—perhaps most important — where they spawn.

Writing Conversation: Dialogue

A conversation written down is called a **dialogue**. It requires much skill to write imaginary dialogue that sounds like real conversation. The tape-recorder has made dialogue a part of many modern reports.

ACTIVITY

Examine one of your favourite stories, novels, or magazine articles, and report on the role played by dialogue. What kinds of sentences does the writer use most effectively? What devices of punctuation are used to signal dialogue?

ACTIVITY

Examine some comic strips and cartoons and see what conventions are used to mark conversation and how it is to be read.

—© King Features Syndicate 1973

ACTIVITY

Write your own dialogue for the following two cartoons, and then compare what you have written with the dialogues written by others in your class.

—© King Features Syndicate 1973

—B.C. by permission of John Hart and Field Enterprises, Inc.

Voices on Paper

Here are some sample dialogues, all taken from Canadian stories. From each, how much information can you get about (a) the speaker or speakers, for example, age, sex, relationship, occupation, region, and (b) the situation?

1. "Have you learnt your piece for the concert?" he said.
    She nodded.
    "Mother made me a new dress," she said. "It's shot silk. It's blue and then it goes green."

2. "Just what do you think you're doing, young lady?" . . .
    "Gee, I never knew you were home yet."
    "I would have thought that on a day like this you might have shown a little respect and consideration, . . . even if you couldn't make the effort to get cleaned up enough to go to the parade."

3. "Go across the street to the Cut-Rate Store. Tell them Charlie sent you. Get them to give you sweat socks and boots. You can pay for them when you draw some money." I tried to say something but he cut me off abruptly and as I went out I could hear him mumbling, "Goddam-college-kids-no-bloody-good."

4. "I can't go, Ellen. Living off your people — charity — stop and think of it. This is where I belong. I can't do anything else."

5. "Are you deaf, Fielding?"
    "No, sir."
    "What was the last thing I said?"
    "I don't know, sir."
    "Why not, Fielding?"

ACTIVITY

Here are some oral sentences. Discuss in class or small groups

(a) the type of sentence by form,
(b) the human situation in which each of these sentences might occur.

Then choose one sentence that appeals to you, and develop around it a good dialogue — part of a play, a TV script, a cartoon, or a story.

1. "All of them in the rat-race — all of them."

2. "A sandwich maybe?"

3. "Digging ditches would be easier."

4. "Please don't tell my parents!"

5. "If you could just hear yourself!"

Summary

A sentence is a basic unit of speech. The voice signals a sense of "finality" at the end of a sentence.

One way to classify sentences is by the kind of messages they carry:

(a) statements (declarative)
(b) orders, requests (imperative)
(c) questions (interrogative)
(d) sentences expressing extra emotion (exclamatory)

The differences in the messages carried by these types are signalled by the voice and sometimes by a change in grammatical structure. To get the full message, a reader of a **written** sentence must re-create in his mind the oral utterance.

Looking at Your Own Sentences: A "Before and After" Experiment

Choose three compositions you have written recently on different topics. Then examine your own written sentences by following these questions. Compare your findings with those of others in your group or class.

1. Find the longest sentence you have used. How many words are there?

2. Find your shortest sentence. How many words are there?

3. How many questions did you use? Where do they appear in the compositions?

4. How many exclamations did you use? Where in the composition? Why did you use them?

5. Work out, roughly, the average number of words you use in a sentence.

6. Is there any relationship between your topics and the average length of your sentences?

7. How many times have you used **and** or **but**?

8. How many sentences begin with something other than the subject?

9. Find a sentence you especially like. Now rewrite it so that its structure is changed in some way. (You may wish to use parts of the sentences next to it.) Which version do you prefer out of the context of the composition? within the composition? Why?

10. Rewrite the favourite sentences chosen by two classmates from their compositions, and apply number 9 (above). What conclusions do you come to?

When you have finished this chapter, try this exercise again, and see what you have gained from doing this unit.

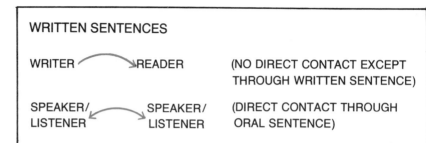

In writing, most sentences are **statements**. The exceptions are sentences in dialogue and possibly personal letters (conversations on paper) and directions for making things (usually imperatives). Because there is no direct contact between writer and reader except through the message, written sentences must be full, clear, and precise.

The Full-Statement Sentence

Defined grammatically, the full-statement sentence contains at least one main (independent) clause. Without a main clause, it is a **sentence fragment**. For example, **John has been fishing all morning** is a full-statement sentence. It contains a complete and independent clause.

But the sentences

Been fishing?
Not very.
Because John has been fishing all morning.

are not full-statement sentences. They do not contain complete and independent clauses.

Here are other examples:

Sometimes writers use sentence fragments for special effects. For example, look at the following paragraphs from Anne Hébert's description of the Quebec she knew as a child. Which sentences are full-statement sentences? Which ones are sentence fragments? How would you justify this mixture? Rewrite the paragraphs, changing each sentence fragment to a full-statement sentence, and compare the result with the original.

Burnt-over land as far as the eye can see. New growth of birch on the green moss. Long tendrils of moss, drawn from the soil, like garlands with fine sandy roots. Gathering blueberries. The barrens laden with blue fruit. The silvery mist clouding the fresh berries. That was when I was a child. Now the reign of the birches is threatened. The face of Charlebois is pitted by dead birches. Sad little white bones against the green of the forest....

Sainte-Foy. Named for a bitter victory. There where the city, the new university city, now expands. During my childhood it was a little wood. A whole summer of holidays. A brook. Green grass-snakes. Symphonies of tree-frogs. Strawberries bordering the fields. Orchards. Apples succeeding apples—the green, the white, the transparents, the Fameuses. Four houses thick-shelled with white brick. Each with its garden and its orchard. The road was called the Avenue of the Four Bourgeois. It was the country.

—"Quebec: The Proud Province" in *Century 1867—1967*

FULL-STATEMENT SENTENCE
Writing was known in Crete over 3000 years ago.
The Cretans developed a system of writing for keeping accounts.
The Greeks adopted this system.

SENTENCE FRAGMENT
Writing in Crete over 3000 years ago.
A system of writing for keeping accounts.
Adopted by the Greeks.

Here is a newspaper report about a familiar place in any city or town — the bus terminal.

Discuss the effectiveness of the sentence fragments used in this report.

Do you see any pattern in the captions of the photographs?

On the buses

By OLIVIA WARD

There's a smell about the terminal that no amount of disinfectant will erase. A backdraft of diesel fumes . . . damp, lived-in clothes . . . cigarette butts . . . stale perfume . . . hot dogs and peanuts . . . paper-cup coffee . . .

And faces. Drawn and anxious. Slack and bored. Bemused. Whistling to no one in particular through gapped teeth. Stroking a stubble of beard. Eyes darting to the clock like ping pong balls.

Taking off . . . another day in the life of a bus driver.

Pictures:

PETER HULBERT

A bus terminal lacks the slick, sterile glamour of an airport. No crisp, immaculate executives lounge on its benches scanning the financial news. No first-class passengers withdraw to the inner sanctum of VIP waiting rooms. A bus terminal has one level only — In Transit.

For some the bus trip is a ritual punishment for living in the suburbs. Others, clutching knapsacks and sleeping bags, are off to see the world. For the young, the bus station can be the launching pad of a new life; for the old, a pleasant jolt to a life running gently down. . . .

Watching . . . where does she come from? Is she worried too?

It is not only a taking-off place, but a waiting place. The short-order cafeteria buzzes with subdued talk and anticipation, magazines grow dog-eared from a hundred restless hands. Buy a package of peppermints . . . lock up your worldly goods . . . pick a pocket book . . . browse . . . wait . . .

An estimated three million people a year use the Vancouver Bus Depot. Open at 5:30 a.m., it closes at 11:45 p.m., after the last scheduled incoming trip. Lights are dimmed. Doors are locked. And the dozing wine-stained all-night people are turned out, to wander in search of another warm dry place. Another terminal.

Confusion . . . "where do I go from here?"

Exit . . . for freeway commuters, a day in the city.

Waiting . . . the newspaper helps.

ACTIVITY

Make a similar documentary article about a bus stop or some other well-known place in your own community. You could change this assignment to the exploration of a theme, for example, spring in our town, old pioneers in our community, or the gardens of our town. If possible, use a camera.

Skilled, experienced writers may use the sentence fragment to convey a sense of immediacy, for example, a series of fleeting impressions, a face-to-face conversation, or an "inner" conversation with oneself. But the full-statement sentence best deals with ideas in which sequential thought processes are involved. As a student, you should first work to master the full-statement sentence needed in formal written work. Later on, you may with full knowledge use the sentence fragment if it seems appropriate.

The mistake comes when we use a sentence fragment when a full-statement sentence is required. Here are examples of the three types of sentence fragments most commonly mistaken by students for full-statement sentences. With each sentence fragment is the corresponding full-statement sentence.

To detect the following sentence fragment errors, read aloud what is written. Your voice will indicate the error. Grammatically, the second part is not a full clause. They are modifiers of part of the main clause, and therefore dependent upon it.

Type 1

SENTENCE FRAGMENTS

These are not acceptable:

1. Some animals sleep all winter. **Such as bears**.

2. On top of the car we loaded our tent, sleeping-bags, and ground sheets. **As well as our large grub box**.

3. The lines are from a play by Shakespeare. **The greatest English dramatist**.

4. We all stood up in our seats. **To get a better view**.

FULL-STATEMENT SENTENCES

These are acceptable:

Some animals, such as bears, sleep all winter.

On top of the car we loaded our tent, sleeping-bags, and ground sheets, as well as our large grub box.

The lines are from a play by Shakespeare, the greatest English dramatist.

We all stood up in our seats to get a better view.

Type 2

SENTENCE FRAGMENTS	FULL-STATEMENT SENTENCES
These are not acceptable:	These are acceptable:
1. He had to discontinue his studies. **Because he became ill.**	He had to discontinue his studies because he became ill.
2. The sea is not silent, but full of noises. **A fact which few people know.**	The sea is not silent, but full of noises, a fact which few people know.
3. At nine o'clock we all met at the café. **Where we talked or played cards until midnight.**	At nine o'clock we all met at the café, where we talked or played cards until midnight.

Subordinate conjunctions such as **because, which, if, when,** and **that,** signal a subordinate clause, which should be attached to a main clause.

Type 3

SENTENCE FRAGMENTS	FULL-STATEMENT SENTENCES
These are not acceptable:	These are acceptable:
1. George closed the door carefully. **Forgetting, however, to turn off the lights.**	George closed the door carefully, forgetting, however, to turn off the lights.
2. The child wore a jumper dress of cotton with a white blouse. **Trimmed with braid and rickrack.**	The child wore a jumper dress of cotton, with a white blouse trimmed with braid and rickrack.
3. Our party was now reduced to twelve. **Three of our Dutch members having gone home.**	Our party was now reduced to twelve, three of our Dutch members having gone home.
	or
	Three of our Dutch members having gone home, our party was reduced to twelve.

Present participle (**-ing**) groups and past participle (**-ed**) groups are modifiers, and must be attached to a main clause.

ACTIVITY

This is an activity in eliminating the sentence fragment. If the sentences are all full-statement sentences as written, write an **S**; if there are sentence fragments, write **Fr**. Read them aloud before correcting.

1. In 1778 Captain James Cook landed on Vancouver Island. He bartered with the Indians for furs. Which he later sold in China.

2. A long bridge across the Peace River joins Dawson Creek and Fort St. John. The bridge collapsed in October 1957. Thus necessitating long detours for traffic on the Alaska Highway.

3. With twelve companions, Ulysses entered the cave of the one-eyed monster, Polyphemus. Who confined them and daily devoured two of his prisoners. Ulysses made Polyphemus drunk with wine, blinded him with a firebrand while he slept, and escaped from the cave.

4. Tennessee is bounded on the east by North Carolina. The two states being separated by the Great Smoky Range.

5. The salmon that elude the nets of the fishermen continue their journey up the brown waters of the Fraser. On and on they go, through narrow canyons and gorges, until at last they turn off into smaller streams and find their way to the gravelly spot in which they were born.

6. The ancient capital states of Nara and Kyoto recall the glories of the past. Both of them having kept much of the appearance and atmosphere of ancient Japan. In these two cities are many beautiful temples, shrines, and palaces.

7. Rescue teams today reached the wreckage of an English transport plane that crash-landed on a Swiss mountain peak in a snowstorm Tuesday. They radioed the good news that all six crew members had survived. Though two were badly injured. These two are being carried out, and should arrive at the nearest village by tonight.

8. There was nothing to do but to sit up all night fully dressed. And wrapped in blankets to keep warm. At first we talked and joked, but soon we were too cold and miserable to attempt even this.

9. Every Canadian child knows the book *Wild Animals I Have Known*. Written by Ernest Thompson Seton. This young naturalist was born in England. But was raised and educated in Ontario.

10. Every Saturday my parents drove to town and bought the weekly supplies of flour, sugar, rice, and coffee. Sometimes, as a special treat, they brought back for us a small bag of candy. This we carefully divided among us, and treasured for as long as we could make it last.

The Comma Fault

Examine the following sentences, both of which are incorrectly punctuated:

1. The teacher put the questions on the blackboard, we all began to write.

2. The vessel returned in triumph to its home port, the people flocked to the wharf to see it.

When a comma instead of a period is used to separate two sentences, the error is called a **comma fault**. The sentence in which the error occurs is called a **run-on sentence**.

If the ideas are important enough to be expressed in main clauses, the two clauses should be separated by more important marks than commas. Use either a **period**, thus making two separate sentences, as in:

Correct: The teacher put the questions on the blackboard. We all began to write.

or a **semicolon**, a mark which signals that the two clauses are related, but separate, full statements:

Correct: The teacher put the questions on the blackboard; we all began to write.

If you wish to **join** the two sentences, you may use:

subordination: **As soon as** the teacher put the questions on the blackboard, we all began to write.
When the vessel returned in triumph to its home port, the people flocked to the wharf to see it.

co-ordination: The teacher put the questions on the blackboard **and** we all began to write. The vessel returned in triumph to its home port, **and** the people flocked to the wharf to see it.

ACTIVITY

Eliminate the **comma fault** in each of the sentences below by making separate sentences or by combining the clauses with an appropriate conjunction.

1. An icy wind blew through the holes in the window, the roof leaked in several places.

2. Our school basketball team won its first six games, it lost the last four.

3. The strikers won their wage increase, jubilantly they returned to their work-benches.

4. One of the dogs suddenly growled, then both barked loudly, he froze at the foot of the ladder.

5. I have always liked small children, that is why I have decided to become a primary school teacher.

ACTIVITY

Eliminate the **comma fault** in each of the sentences below by **subordinating** some clauses. Be careful in your choice of the main clause (or clauses).

1. I asked him how much he would give me for the medal, he hesitated before replying.

2. I should like to find a copy of the most recent *Maclean's*, it has an excellent article on capital punishment.

3. Natural gas is cheap in Alberta, most homes have gas stoves and gas furnaces.

4. Both the suspects were released, they proved that they were out of town the day of the robbery.

5. Some advertisements are not honest, they grossly exaggerate, they may make false claims, therefore an intelligent reader evaluates advertising.

It is true that experienced writers occasionally use run-together sentences, and do so effectively. But these writers break the rule from knowledge, not carelessness. They understand the special effect the sentence may have within a special context. The inexperienced writer is well advised to follow the rule at first, and break it only when aware of the special effects.

ACTIVITY: A REVIEW

Write **S** if the word group is a **full-statement sentence**.

Write **Fr** if the word group is a **fragment.**

Write **Cf** if the writer has committed the **comma fault** error.

In what contexts might some of the sentence fragments be justified?

1. He left the house just before dawn.

2. Leaving the house just before dawn.

3. He left the house just before dawn, he walked briskly towards the station.

4. This country, a vast jumble of mountains, swamps, and jungle-choked valleys, with modern development only in patches along the eastern coast.

5. Parking regulations in this city are certainly out of date.

6. The ride back to town took nearly four hours, the traffic jam stretched for miles.

7. There were sudden sporadic bursts of radiation. Apparently caused by disturbances on the sun.

8. The committee has decided to meet again in a month's time. When the results of the questionnaire will be known.

9. As darkness set in, a heavy rain began to fall. I sat in misery, soaked to the skin, while mosquitoes buzzed about me constantly.

10. A dreary town, with grey frame buildings, muddy roads, no gardens, and no trees.

11. On September 1, 1905, the provinces of Alberta and Saskatchewan were created, they were each given a legislative assembly of twenty-five members.

12. Norman passed the puck quickly, it was intercepted by the defenceman.

13. A delicious aroma of bacon and eggs, coffee and toast.

14. It is hard to believe that a diamond is really only a piece of carbon. As is the graphite in a lead pencil.

Another way to practise recognizing full-statement sentences is to write your own, and then have a partner check them while you check those written by your partner.

ACTIVITY

Write a full-statement sentence for each of the following, using the ideas, not necessarily the exact words. Then check with a partner.

1. the end of a hockey game; large crowd; argument

2. a flood; emergency; truckloads of supplies

3. a high school group; visit to the provincial legislature; stirring speech

4. a party planned; icy roads; disappointment

5. a prize; hard work; a fair

6. a meeting; suggestion; anger

7. a cat; advertisement; surprise

8. a new car; delivery; guarantee; salesman

Writing Effective Sentences

The good writer wants his sentences to be more than grammatically correct. He wants them to be **clear**, **emphatic**, and **pleasing**.

Examine the style of the following paragraph:

> The oldest ballet company in Canada is the Royal Winnipeg Ballet. It began in 1938. Gweneth Lloyd came to Winnipeg in 1938. She came from England. She formed the Winnipeg Ballet Club. The company gave its first performance in 1939. The group became professional in 1949. A citizens' committee of Winnipeg backed it. It had financial troubles. It had to travel to Eastern Canada or to the United States to find large audiences. Travel to Eastern Canada was expensive. The company was unknown in the United States. The company persevered, however. The company gave a Command Performance in 1951. It was to the then Princess Elizabeth and the Duke of Edinburgh. This was a great success.

The writer of this paragraph has given much information in sentences that are grammatically correct. The paragraph, nevertheless, is not pleasing. (Why?)

The chief fault is that the various ideas are expressed as if they are all of equal importance. Many of the sentences could have been combined to emphasize main thoughts and to subordinate others.

The sentences also lack variety: they are all of the same length, and follow similar grammatical patterns (note that each sentence begins with its subject).

Below is the same material rewritten to achieve greater clarity, emphasis, and variety. Compare the two paragraphs.

> The Royal Winnipeg Ballet, first known as the Winnipeg Ballet Club, was founded in 1938 by Gweneth Lloyd. The group gave its first performance in 1939. Ten years later, with the financial help of a citizens' committee, the company was able to turn professional. But the venture was not a financial success. The company was unknown to the large audience of the United States, and travel to Eastern Canada was expensive. Nevertheless, the group persevered, and finally won acclaim and success in 1951 with a Command Performance before the then Princess Elizabeth and the Duke of Edinburgh.

Which facts has the writer emphasized, and which has he subordinated? Does the writer show more clearly the relationship between facts? Has he achieved variety in length of sentences? in kinds? Is the paragraph more pleasing to the ear? Why? Can you rewrite the last sentence to make it even better?

ACTIVITY

Rewrite the following paragraph so that it is as clear, as emphatic, and as pleasing as you can make it.

> The history of man is long. Ours is the first age with no new frontiers on land or sea. Many of our troubles stem from this fact. It is true, that, even now, there are vast areas of the Earth still unexploited and even unexplored. Dealing with them will only be a mopping-up operation. The oceans will keep us busy for centuries to come. The countdown started even for them, when the bathyscaphe *Trieste* descended into the ultimate deep. The ultimate deep is the Marianas Trench.

Sentences Should Be Clear

The first requirement of a good sentence is that there should be no question about its meaning.

A. Clarity and Unity

Decide which sentence in each pair is the clearer one.

1. a. Sir Walter Scott was incurably lame, and his *Lady of the Lake* was inspired by his enthusiasm for the wild country around Loch Katrine.
   b. Because Sir Walter Scott was incurably lame, he devoted much of his childhood to the reading of romances and history.
2. a. In his youth he studied law, and his novels are full of history, romance, scenery, and folklore.
   b. In his youth he studied law, and this knowledge is apparent in the many excellent trial scenes found in his novels.

Each of the preceding sentences illustrates an essential point about **clarity**. The first example in each pair is confusing because the writer is discussing two ideas that are not related. The sentence thus lacks **unity**. In the second sentence of each pair, although the author is also discussing two ideas, the ideas **are** related.

MAKE SURE THAT YOUR SENTENCES JOIN ONLY IDEAS WHICH ARE RELATED.

Sentences which join unrelated ideas are said to lack **unity**.

ACTIVITY

Revise any sentence that lacks unity. If a sentence is correct, write only **C**.

1. The stewardess showed us to our seats, and she was a very attractive girl, and her uniform was light blue.

2. Our school music club plans to put on Gilbert and Sullivan's *H. M. S. Pinafore* this year, and we have had excellent attendance at our weekly meetings.

3. Opening my eyes, I found that I was in a small, dimly lit room, with my hands and feet tied securely to a chair, and my mouth tightly gagged by a piece of cloth.

4. The most famous university in Paris is the Sorbonne, and my sister is working hard so she can get a scholarship to go there because she wants to be a French teacher.

5. At the foot of one of the hills, our car finally stopped, and the traffic piled up behind us, and this was one of my most embarrassing experiences.

B. Clarity and Subordination

Which sentence in each pair best emphasizes the main idea?

1. a. While I stood gazing at the blue water, I heard a shrill cry for help.

   b. I stood gazing at the blue water when I heard a shrill cry for help.

2. a. As he looked down the street, he noticed two masked men run out of the drugstore.

   b. He looked down the street, noticing two masked men running out of the drugstore.

Often in a sentence in which two ideas are related, one is obviously the main idea and the other is secondary, or **subordinate**.

MAIN IDEA

1. I heard a shrill cry for help

2. he noticed two masked men run out of the drugstore

SUBORDINATE IDEA

I stood gazing at the blue water

subordinating word: **while**

he looked down the street

subordinating word: **as**

ORAL ACTIVITY

Discuss how the following sentences on the left are improved by emphasizing the main ideas and subordinating others.

BETTER ARRANGEMENTS

1. I was alone in the cabin, and I heard a noise outside, and so I was frightened.

1. While I was alone in the cabin, I was frightened by a noise outside.
   or
   While alone in the cabin, I was frightened by a noise outside.

2. My brother came home from camp and then he found out that his dog was dead.

2. When my brother came home from camp, he found out that his dog was dead.

3. The beaver on sentinel duty caught a scent and it meant danger, and he brought his flat tail down on the surface of the water with a loud warning smack.

3. The beaver on sentinel duty, catching a scent that meant danger, brought his flat tail down upon the surface of the water with a loud warning smack.

Notice that the poorer sentences consist of vaguely related ideas strung together with **and, and so,** and **and then.** The overuse of these words indicates careless or immature writing.

Can you make other arrangements of the same idea? Some of the sentences on the right could be further improved.

In speech we often do without subordination because we are thinking in a time sequence, and can use gesture and intonation to emphasize the main ideas. But when we write, these aids are missing, and, to ensure clarity, we must use our pencil to reshape the sentences.

oral: I was getting on the bus and I noticed that my money was missing.
written: When I was getting on the bus, I noticed that my money was missing.

MAKING SENTENCES CLEAR BY SUBORDINATING THE PROPER IDEA

ACTIVITY

Improve these sentences by writing each group as one sentence. Use **subordination** and **co-ordination** correctly to relate the ideas precisely.

1. (a) I was walking along the road near our summer cottage.
   (b) I was looking for wild blackberries.
   (c) I saw something that looked like a rabbit scurry into the thicket.

2. (a) The Pacific is the largest of the oceans.
   (b) It is bigger than all the continents and islands of the world put together.

3. (a) Arthur Lismer is a Canadian painter.
   (b) He has given much of his time to teaching others.
   (c) He is known especially for organizing children's art centres.

4. (a) We gazed intently into the water under the wharf.
   (b) We could see thousands of small fish.
   (c) Some were no more than about two centimetres long.

5. (a) In the evening we found a little cave in the cliff.
   (b) It would give us some shelter from the wind and rain.
   (c) We decided to wait there until daylight.

Work in small groups (three or four people) and compare your sentences. Do you see any patterns in the structures you are using? Are you limiting yourself to one or two patterns?

C. Clarity and Pronouns

Read the following sentences and discuss the problems made by the italicized pronouns:

1. As the disease is contagious, you should not put another bird into the same cage until *it* has been thoroughly disinfected by baking or boiling. (What does *it* refer to?)
2. The best thing to do with people who write anonymous letters is to burn *them*. (What does *them* refer to?)
3. Bill wanted Tommy to go on the camping trip with him because *he* could teach *him* to swim. (Who was teaching whom?)

In these sentences the writer relies on the intelligence of the reader to decide on the reference of the italicized pronouns. The sentences are not precise. Such fuzzy writing makes hard reading. Sometimes such a sentence is more amusing than confusing. But a pronoun with alternate references can lead the reader to dangerous conclusions. If a babysitter read this note, her experience would tell her what is meant:

If the baby doesn't want cold milk, heat it.

It is unlikely that she would heat the baby instead of the milk. But look at the following sentence:

If the substance doesn't dissolve immediately in the solution, heat it.

What should be heated? the substance? the solution? Our experience does not help us. If this sentence were part of directions for an experiment, a misreading could cause a dangerous explosion.

The word or group of words to which a pronoun refers is called its **antecedent**.

```
ante- 'before'
-cedent 'going'
```

```
pro- 'for, instead of'
pro-noun
```

When a pronoun is used as a substitute word, it must have a definite antecedent. If the reference is faulty or vague, the sentence is not clear. An example:

My little brother bites his nails, and mother cannot cure him of it.

What is the antecedent of **it**? To what noun does **it** refer?

This sentence rewritten clearly would include a definite antecedent:

My little brother has **the habit** of biting his nails, and mother cannot cure him of it.

or, better, eliminate the vague **it** altogether:

My little brother bites his nails, and mother cannot cure him of this habit.

In everyday speech, we often use the pronouns **it** and **they** with rather vague antecedents and such sentences may pass unnoticed because gesture and voice intonations help to indicate meaning. In formal written language, however, we must be more precise. The problem is really one of careless sentence structure. Here are more examples:

1.   The principal listed the names of the students who are to go to the concert, but your name was not on it.

Better: The principal put on a list the names of the students who were to go to the concert, but your name was not on it.

   or: Your name was not on the principal's list of students who are to go to the concert.

2.   This year we have a new poetry book, but we do not like them very much.

Better: This year we have a new book of poems, but we do not like **them** very much.

   or: This year we have a new poetry book, but we do not like it very much.

   or: This year we have a new poetry book, but we do not like the selections very much.

3.   In British Columbia, **their** chief industry is lumbering, and **they** export much lumber to the United States.

Better: Lumbering is one of the chief industries of British Columbia, and much lumber is exported to the United States.

4.   In the movie **it** shows the ship sinking after being hit by a torpedo.

Better: The movie shows the ship sinking after being hit by the torpedo.

ACTIVITY

Rewrite the sentences so that the meaning is clear.

1. After the men got all the cattle into the corral, they were branded and earmarked.

2. My sister is terrified when it thunders, and we cannot convince her that it will not harm her.

3. Because George's father and grandfather spent their lives in the legal profession, George thinks that he will be one too.

4. After the cake has been taken out of the pan, it should be rinsed under the tap.

5. I like to listen to Spanish songs, for it is a very beautiful language.

6. Fishing in the ocean on a day like this is cold and unpleasant, but if you catch one, it is worth it.

Agreement of Pronouns

In everyday speech we often use a vague plural pronoun such as **you**, **they**, or **we** to refer to people generally, even if the antecedent is singular.

English lacks a good "cover" pronoun to express this idea. If you know any other language, investigate how that language expresses "people generally".

Informal speech

1. **Each** of you should bring **your** own sandwiches.
2. **Anyone** may take a folder if **they** wish.
3. **Every customer** may have one free package if **they** buy two.

In formal writing, however, it is more emphatic to make the pronoun agree with its antecedent. Thus, if the antecedent is a singular word such as **a man, a woman, one, anyone, everyone, everybody, nobody, no one, each, either, neither, someone,** or **somebody**, use the singular pronoun equivalent **he, she,** or **it**.

The singular pronouns such as **each, everyone,** and **not one,** do serve to stress the idea of "one and only one". To follow through with the singular is to re-emphasize this idea.

The sentences above, written formally, would be:

1. **Each** of you should bring **his** own sandwiches.
2. **Anyone** may take a folder if **she** wishes.
3. **Every customer** may have one free package if **he** buys two.

Of course, a plural antecedent requires a plural pronoun.

All the customers were writing for **their** free samples.

Ten of the Boy Scouts forgot to bring **their** sandwiches.

If a collective noun is the antecedent, use a singular pronoun if you are thinking of the group as a unit, and a plural pronoun if you are thinking of them as individual persons. The verb should be consistent.

The **City Council has** invited ten students to **its** next meeting.
The **City Council have** disagreed about giving **their** support to the local baseball team.

The **orchestra plays its** first concert of the season on May 1.
The **orchestra raise their** instruments at a signal from the conductor.

British usage tends towards the plural for a collective, for example,

The **government are** . . .
The **cabinet are** . . .
The **company have** . . .

Note:

Agreement in number between a pronoun and its reference seems to be — and usually is — a logical rule. Language, however, is not always logical. The answer to the question "Is everyone here?" would **logically** be "Yes, **he** is." This answer is obviously absurd. The movement towards the plural that we see in British usage and our oral usage is influenced by these two problems:

1. English has no singular pronoun that can refer to both sexes. To use the male pronoun, though common practice, is objected to by some; to use **him or her** is awkward (Each customer is to take **his or her** coupon to the desk.); so the plural **they (them, their)** is used to solve the problem.
2. The idea of the whole sentence is often plural. Which of these would you use? Everyone in the audience raised **his** hand? **his or her** hand? **their** hand? **their** hands?

A writer of formal English who is caught in such traps should rephrase and avoid the problem — or use the plural rather than be absurdly "correct". Would you use **him** in the following sentence?

When Prime Minister Gandhi entered the room, every photographer focused his camera, and she rewarded **them** with a smile.

ORAL ACTIVITY

Provide the preferred pronoun for formal English.

1. Long before the scheduled time, the audience had taken _____ seats.
2. Everyone in the audience felt that the speaker was talking to _____ alone.
3. Any student who does not return books on time will lose _____ library privileges.
4. If everyone took _____ responsibilities as seriously as you do, our club would be very successful in its drive for funds.
5. If all members of the club took _____ responsibilities as seriously as you do, we would be very successful in raising funds.
6. Nobody in the play knew _____ part well.
7. If anybody phones while I am out, please ask _____ to call again this evening.
8. The audience was enthusiastic in _____ reception of the singer.

MAKE SENTENCES CLEAR BY USING REFERENCE PRONOUNS PRECISELY

D. Clarity and Modifiers

Why do these "want ads" seem amusing — or muddled?

Lost: A black silk umbrella on Park Road bus by an old lady with sixteen ribs and an ivory head.

Wanted: A tutor for a Grade Ten student backward in English and Mathematics on Tuesday and Friday evenings. Phone _____.

Lost: A green boy's bathing suit at Engle Pool. Phone _____.

The ambiguity, confusion, or unintentional humour in these sentences is caused by carelessly placed modifiers.

The "tacking on" of a modifier at the end of a sentence causes one of the most frequent placement errors. Here is an example:

MISPLACED

Two fireman were sent to the hospital in an ambulance **suffering from severe burns**.

CORRECT

Two firemen **suffering from severe burns** were sent to the hospital in an ambulance.

ORAL ACTIVITY

Rephrase the following sentences which contain misplaced modifiers.

1. The farmer watched us put up our tent in his field and prepare for the night without saying a word.
2. The three boys found the tin box full of money playing near the city dump.
3. The geyser can be seen at a safe distance by all visitors spouting hot water high into the air.
4. Suddenly we came upon a tiny church wandering through the old part of town.
5. The people heard the news that the enemy had been turned back with joy.

ACTIVITY

Create some "wants ads" of your own in which misplaced modifiers make the message amusing. You could begin by looking at some real want ads in your local newspapers, and rearranging some.

Why are the following sentences confusing — or amusing?

1. While wandering among the ruins, a tiny statue in the corner met my eye.
2. At the age of six, his father died.
3. Worried about the poor weather, the picnic was postponed.

When a sentence begins with a modifier, the reader **expects** the first word or phrase that follows it to be the one modified. In the second sentence, **at the age of six** modifies **his father**, thus making the statement absurd. Such modifiers without the right word to modify are called **dangling modifiers**. Corrected, the sentences preceding would be:

1. While **wandering** among the ruins, **I** noticed a tiny statue in the corner.

2. **At the age of six**, **the boy** lost his father.
or When the boy was six, his father died.

3. **Worried** about the poor weather, **we** postponed the picnic.

Modifier		Word	Rest of sentence

Is this
the word
modified?

ACTIVITY

Here are more examples. Study them carefully.

Dangling: **Aided by his two sons**, the wheat was soon harvested.

Corrected: **Aided by his two sons, the farmer** soon harvested the wheat.

or **The farmer, aided by his two sons**, soon harvested the wheat.

Dangling: **To learn to be a good pitcher**, the ball must first be held correctly.

Corrected: **To learn to be a good pitcher, you** must first hold the ball correctly.

Now compose sentences that begin with the following modifiers. Make sure that the word you want to be modified opens the next structure.

1. In playing ice hockey, __?__

2. Without a penny in her pocket,

3. Before locking my door,

4. Running across the beach,

5. Being very tired,

6. When watching television,

7. To play tennis well,

8. After riding the merry-go-round,

ACTIVITY

Each of the following sentences has a misplaced or a dangling modifier. Rewrite the sentence so that the meaning is clear and sensible. There may be several ways to write the sentences correctly.

1. Not having done my homework, the teacher kept me in after school.

2. The teacher asked the class to be quiet at least ten times.

3. To earn money for my university fees, the local drugstore gave me an after-school job.

4. Without bothering to unpack, dinner was ordered and brought to our room.

5. When sorted by size, shape, and colour, the girls then wrap the apples in tissue paper.

6. I do not like that television program because, after becoming absorbed in the drama, a singing commercial comes on to spoil the mood.

MAKE SENTENCES CLEAR BY PLACING MODIFIERS CORRECTLY

E. Clarity and Parallel Structure

In each pair of sentences below, choose the one that seems to send its message more clearly:

1. My hobbies are collecting stamps and to play hockey.

2. My hobbies are collecting stamps and playing hockey.

1. Mary is good in sports, clever in her studies, and everyone likes her.

2. Mary is good in sports, clever in her studies, and liked by everyone.

When we list items, it is both helpful and pleasing to the reader if the items are expressed in similar grammatical form. Repetition of the same structure, which is called **parallelism**, makes a sentence easier to understand, and may also give the sentence balance and rhythm.

A sentence with parallel structures is a series of sentences made into one, with the repeated part omitted. For example:

Mary is good in sports.
Mary is clever in her studies.
Mary is liked by everyone.

Mary is good in sports,
        clever in her studies, and
        liked by everyone.

In the following examples, notice how the parallel form can sharpen comparisons and contrasts. Notice also that parallel structures can occur **within** parallel structures.

(a) **He shrugged his shoulders, shook his head, cast up his eyes, but said nothing.**

— Washington Irving

He shrugged his shoulders,
    shook his head,
    cast up his eyes,
but said nothing.

(b) The crisp feeling of the snow crust breaking under the moccasin in the winter,
the bright tangle of kinnikinnick   carpeting the forest floor in the summer,
the exploding rumble of the ice   breaking in the spring,
the pungent odor of caribou   rotting along the riverbank in the fall—
all these sensations and impressions became a part of her life.

(c) We drove across the tracks,
            up past the sailors' boarding houses,
            up   through the ancient part of the city,
                                 through an empty Place d'Armes,
            up Beaver Hall Hill through the traffic,
                            the noise,
                            the shining lights,
                            the river-like crowds of Central Montreal
                                 on a warm spring night.

— Hugh MacLennan: *The Watch that Ends the Night*

ACTIVITY

Arrange the following sentences to illustrate their parallel structure. Then discuss in groups or as a class the uses and effectiveness of the structures.

1. The horses plunged wildly and reared on their hind feet in a panic, straining against each other, pulling apart, going down underneath the pole, trying to turn and retrace their steps.

    —F. P. Grove: *Over Prairie Trails*

2. I follow the lagoon west: past the sailboats that sleep prettily at the Queen City Yacht Club; past the red-and-yellow wooden fire station; past a wild brown rabbit in a little jungle on my left; past ten adult ducks of both sexes who are noising it up on the lagoon to my right; past the old street lights that look like white cookie-jars.

    —Harry Bruce: "Flight to a Mysterious Island" in *The Short Happy Walks of Max McPherson*

3. The area is Russian or Texan in scope but the low, rocky terrain, the dearth of mighty, navigable rivers, the scattered and partial nature of the merchantable timber, the vicious winters and the brief growing season all have inhibited widespread or intensive settlement.

    — Douglas Fisher: "Ontario's Ancient North" in *Canada: A Guide to the Peaceable Kingdom*

4. The long cookhouse with the two metal pipes that served as chimneys stood silent, its sloping roof whitened by the moon, its walls dark, its windows glittering like gun metal.

    —Hugh MacLennan: *The Watch that Ends the Night*

5. In this lash and spill of water, in the slow grinding of rock and cliff, in the perpetual slide of mountain and forest, in the erosion of mountain and gumbo rangeland, in the impact of whirlpool and winter ice, the river is forever mad, ravenous and lonely.

    — Bruce Hutchison: *The Fraser*

Poetry often uses parallel structure, the effect of the language increasing as the parallelisms pile up. Here is a well-known selection from Ecclesiastes, in which parallelism is a powerful device:

For everything its season, and for every activity under heaven its time:
  a time to be born and a time to die;
  a time to plant and a time to uproot;
  a time to kill and a time to heal;
  a time to pull down and a time to build up;
  a time to weep and a time to laugh;
  a time for mourning and a time for dancing;
  a time to scatter stones and a time to gather them;
  a time to embrace and a time to refrain from embracing;
  a time to seek and a time to lose;
  a time to keep and a time to throw away;
  a time to tear and a time to mend;
  a time for silence and a time for speech;
  a time to love and a time to hate;
  a time for war and a time for peace.

—Eccl. 3:1–8.

You will find that you cannot **always** express your ideas in parallel form; the natural idiom of the language sometimes makes parallel structure awkward, in which case you would not use it. Generally, however, the repetition of a structure is smooth and effective, as the following examples illustrate.

PARALLEL

1. My ambition is
        to be a nurse at a large hospital
        or to teach in a small town.

2. I would like
        being a nurse at a large hospital
        or being a teacher in a small town.
    (or)
    I would like being
        a nurse in a large hospital
        or a teacher in a small town.

3. The librarian suggested
        that I would find the book on
        the reference shelf
      and that I could xerox the map
        I needed.
    (or)
    The librarian suggested that I could
        find the book on the reference
        shelf
      and xerox the map I needed.

NOT PARALLEL (called **LACK OF PARALLELISM**)

1. My ambition is
        to be a nurse at a large hospital
        or teaching in a small town.
    (shift from an infinitive form to an **-ing** form)

2. I would like
        being a nurse at a large hospital
        or to teach in a small town.
    (shift from an **-ing** form to an infinitive form)

3. The librarian suggested
        that I would find the book on the
        reference shelf
      and to xerox the map I needed.
    (shift from a clause to an infinitive)

ACTIVITY

Rewrite these sentences using parallelism.

1. His chief aim in life is having a good time and to do as little work as possible.

2. My counsellor advised me to study harder and that I should give up my Saturday job.

3. The police arrested him for speeding on the highway, failing to stop at a red light, and because he was weaving in and out of traffic.

4. The doctor advised Father to stop smoking, to get more rest, and that he should relax by playing golf.

ACTIVITY

Construct sentences by joining the items below and using parallel forms. Underline the parallel forms. You may wish to change slightly the wording of some sentences.

Example: (a) My uncle is generous.
  (b) He has a gentle way with children.
  (c) Everybody likes him.
My uncle is <u>generous</u>, <u>gentle with children</u>, and <u>popular with everyone</u>.

1. (a) The old woman took a key out of her purse.
   (b) She opened the door quietly.
   (c) She entered the house.

2. (a) Vincent could not remember where he had left his wallet.
   (b) He was not sure how much money was in it.

3. (a) Many of the people who settled in the Maritimes were refugees.
   (b) Some Acadians quietly returned from exile.
   (c) Some New Englanders were expelled after the American Revolution.
   (d) Some Scots were driven from their farms by the Enclosure Acts.
   (e) Some Germans sought refuge from religious persecution.

4. (a) Joan's report was on Peru.
   (b) She told about its conquest by the Spaniards.
   (c) She also described the cities of the Incas.

5. (a) Galileo made the first telescope.
   (b) With it he discovered four moons of Jupiter.
   (c) He observed spots on the sun.
   (d) He noticed the various phases of Venus.

ACTIVITY

Write four sentences of your own using parallelism. Begin by making a list, then putting the items into parallel form, then placing them all into one sentence. Use either your own topics or some of these:

1. A problem with my brother (or sister)

2. Getting ready to do homework

3. Getting up in the morning

4. How (someone) laughs

5. Suggestions for improving TV shows for small children.

INFORMING IDEA

Parallel structure is a device used to join similar ideas.

The similarity in grammatical structure helps to transmit the message clearly.

Parallel structure may also add beauty and rhythm to the sentence.

Clarity in Sentences: A Summary

The purpose of writing a sentence is usually to transmit information or to express attitudes, sometimes to ourselves but more often to others.

A confused sentence transmits a confused and confusing message.

A dishonest sentence transmits a message not tied to the truth or to clear meaning.

A written message can usually be edited by the writer, in order to ensure a clear message. Lack of clarity in sentences is usually caused by:

(a) the lack of unity — unrelated messages are put together
(b) the lack of proper subordination — the main messages are made equal to
                    lesser messages
(c) the careless use of pronouns
(d) the lack of parallelism

SOME FAMOUS SENTENCES

Why, do you think, have these sentences remained in men's minds?

For what is a man profited, if he shall gain the whole world, and lose his own soul?

—Matt. 16:26

Good fences make good neighbours.

—Robert Frost: "Mending Wall"

Something there is that doesn't love a wall.

—Frost, same poem

Don't fence me in.

—Cowboy song

Stone walls do not a prison make
Nor iron bars a cage.

—Richard Lovelace

Thirty days hath September,
April, June, and November . . .

There is always room at the top.

—Daniel Webster

Uneasy lies the head that wears a crown.

—Shakespeare: *King Henry IV Part II*

Conscription if necessary,
but not necessarily conscription.

—W. L. Mackenzie King

I can resist everything except temptation.

—Oscar Wilde

STOP!

LOOK!

LISTEN!

—(devised 1912 for U.S.
railway crossings)

$E = mc^2$

—Einstein

ACTIVITY

Language changes not only in words and their meanings, but also in sentence structure. The following sentences were written by Samuel Pepys in 1664. The sentences are from his personal diary, and therefore are closer to the oral than to the written English of that time.

Write the passage in present-day English and discuss the differences.

Up betimes and to the office; and anon it begin to be fair, after a great shower this morning; Sir.W. Batten and I by water (calling his son Castle by the way, between whom and I no notice at all of his letter the other day to me) to Deptford; and after a turn in the yard, I went with him to the Almes-house to see the new building which he with some ambition is building of there, during his being Maister of Trinity-house.

ACTIVITY

A good way to improve one's power over sentence structure is to study the structures of sentences written by others. Study the structure of each of the following sentences. Then try to write similar kinds of sentences; that is, copy the structure, not the content, of the sentences. Try them all, then choose three you like the best and explain why their structure appeals to you. Here is an example:

sentence model:
The waitress brought our coffee,
slamming the cup and saucer down so abruptly
that the coffee spilled into the saucer.

copy:
The driver arrived at the gates,
honking his horn so energetically
that the neighbours ran out into the street.

copy:
The singer approached the mike,
waving her arms so wildly
that she disconnected the electric guitar.

1. She was a big woman, sturdily built, with a firm, prominent nose, and wide-set, dark, intelligent eyes.

   —Donald Creighton: *John A. Macdonald: The Young Politician*

2. Against the green of the marsh grass the heron was a snow-white figure on slim, black stilts, tense, and motionless.

   —Rachel Carson: *Under the Sea Wind*

3. The whole history of the Canadian North can be divided into two periods — before and after the aeroplane.

   —H. L. Keenleyside (1949)

4. Later that night, alone inside the red fence waiting for Louis, Sandor sat quietly in the weeds trying to reassure himself that he had nothing to worry about.

   —John Marlyn: *Under the Ribs of Death*

5. The living room was strangely bare, its furniture worn and discolored, as though his uncle and aunt had several small children and had long ago given up the struggle with appearances.

   —Brian Moore: "Uncle T"

6. We must conquer war, or war will conquer us.

   —Ely Culbertson

Start a collection of sentences you like which you discover in your reading.

ACTIVITY

Another excellent way in which to increase your power over sentence structure is to combine short sentences in various ways, and then to decide which structure you prefer. Of course your choice within a larger unit, such as a paragraph or essay, would depend upon the surrounding sentences and the emphasis you want. But the first step is to be aware of some of the choices available to you.

Make one sentence out of the sentences in each group. Combine each group of sentences in several ways, and then star the sentence you prefer.

1. (a) Paul Kane grew up in York in the early 1800s.
   (b) He was fascinated by the Indians.
   (c) He frequently visited their encampment.
   (d) Their encampment was on the outskirts of the town.
2. (a) In 1846 Kane crossed the Rocky Mountains.
   (b) He travelled by canoe and boat and pack horse.
   (c) He painted the Indians in their primitive setting.
   (d) He painted the scenery.
3. (a) Kane brought back more than five hundred sketches.
   (b) He took great care to record accurately the details of costume.
   (c) The sketches provided him with enough material to work with for the remainder of his life.
4. (a) During his travels he kept a diary.
   (b) The diary was published in 1859.
   (c) It was entitled *Wanderings of an Artist among the Indians of North America*.
   (d) It is an interesting and important historical document.
5. (a) Antoine Lavoisier is known as the founder of modern chemistry.
   (b) This tells only a small part of his achievements.
   (c) He was a many-sided genius.
   (d) He pioneered also in physiology, scientific agriculture, economics, and public education.
6. (a) I had with me a letter of introduction to Mr. McLean.
   (b) He was the director of one of the departments of the government.
   (c) I decided to go to his office and present my letter in person.

ACTIVITY

Good sentences are based on careful observation. Here is a short paragraph based on immediate observation. Read it carefully. Then go to a favourite spot of yours, make notes on what you see, and express your observations and thoughts in a group of sentences.

> From the road, looking across the marsh, one can see a seagull a quarter of a mile away — a bright-white fleck against the sombre woods at the end of the marsh. The gull flies behind a wooded island and vanishes, but (wait) flies out the other side.

— James Stevenson: from "Environmental Impact (Illusions, Wonders & Disappearing Acts)" in the *New Yorker*

Here is the same language written in the manner of a poem. What difference does it make in effect? Try making a poem from one of your own observations.

> From the road,
> Looking across the marsh
> One can see a seagull
> a quarter of a mile away —
>
> A bright white fleck
> Against the sombre woods
> at the end of the marsh.
>
> The gull cries behind a wooded island
> and vanishes,
> but (wait) flies out the other side.

ACTIVITY : HEADLINE SENTENCES

Newspaper headlines must be short and attention-getting. They may take the form of full sentences, but usually are shortened, with unnecessary words omitted—somewhat like the sentences in telegrams.

Collect some headlines from newspapers and (a) see what proportion are full sentences, (b) what kinds of words are generally omitted from the others. To do (b), rewrite each as a full sentence. Here are a few for practice:

(1)

MYSTERY MAN BACK

(2)

Reform or die, Senate warned

(3)

MONEY MEETING

Paris talks "helpful"

(4)

Canada third in jr. skiing

(5)

Mobile home park ban set

(6)

CRACKDOWN ON UIC RIP-OFFS

(7)

ROYAL TOUR DETAILS

(8)

POT JAILS MAN, WIFE

ACTIVITY : SENTENCES IN POETRY

One revealing way to begin the close examination of a poem is to ask the questions: "How many sentences are there? How do the sentences and sentence breaks relate to the meaning of the poem?" If the poem is long, there may be patterning from sentence to sentence.

Examine this poem and, as a class or in smaller groups, discuss the above questions. Then look at three of your favourite poems in the same way.

THE GRASS

I must tell you
of the brown grass
that has twenty times
this year appeared
from under the
melting snow, reared
its version of spring
like a sea-lion coming
out of water, a-dazzle
in the sun, this
brave grass the sun
will only burn again
returning like a tiny
season.
— George Bowering

ACTIVITY

Choose five words from the list below. Think about each word awhile. Then write a sentence, using the word within an interesting sentence structure.

pine	assassination	reflection
spat	labyrinth	homestead
smoke	mortal	ideals
overthrown	entreaties	harsh

ACTIVITY

Develop one of your sentences (from the exercise above) into a more extended form, for example, a poem, a short story, a paragraph, a news item, etc.

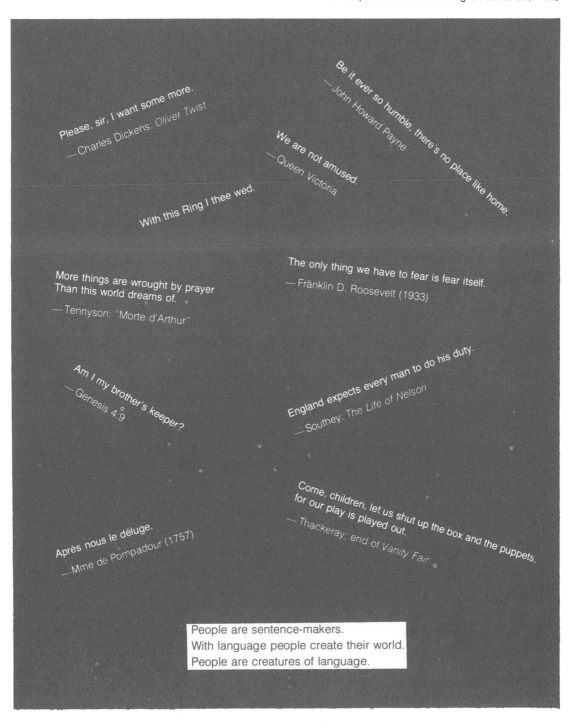

Please, sir, I want some more.
—Charles Dickens: Oliver Twist

Be it ever so humble, there's no place like home.
—John Howard Payne

We are not amused.
—Queen Victoria

With this Ring I thee wed.

More things are wrought by prayer
Than this world dreams of.
—Tennyson: "Morte d'Arthur"

The only thing we have to fear is fear itself.
—Franklin D. Roosevelt (1933)

Am I my brother's keeper?
—Genesis 4:9

England expects every man to do his duty.
—Southey: The Life of Nelson

Come, children, let us shut up the box and the puppets,
for our play is played out.
—Thackeray: end of Vanity Fair

Après nous le déluge.
—Mme de Pompadour (1757)

People are sentence-makers.
With language people create their world.
People are creatures of language.

... looking always at what is to be seen. Will you be a reader, a student merely, or a seer?

—Thoreau: *Walden*

Writing isn't simply a way we reach others. It is a dialogue with ourselves. Finding a tone to talk with begins with finding one that seems right to and for us. Talking to others begins with "talking to yourself" and with "being yourself in talking".

—Richard Hoggart: "Talking to Yourself"—The Second of the Reith Lectures, in *The Listener*

You must write and write until you begin to feel that you are saying what you want to say, in the way that you wish others to understand it.

—B. Berenson to Bertrand Russell, in *The Autobiography of Bertrand Russell*

Chapter 5

Representing Our World

Speaking and Writing, Listening and Reading

Writing: Representing Our World

Why do people write?

What situations and purposes make writing necessary?

The following conversation offers some insights.

Old John Clipper came limping along with his cane, his cap rakishly on one side of his head. "You always writin', ain't you?" he said. "Must be noice to write," he looked wistfully at my notebook. "Never could figure out how people done it." He examined a page. "All them little marks got meanin' to 'em ain't they?" he said. "Hit's a funny thing," he raised his cap and scratched his scalp, "first they's in your haid, then you puts 'em on paper, someone else sees 'em and if they can read they gits 'em in their haid. That way anybody can git same thing you got." Old John nodded, limped away slowly, then turned to call back to me, "Guess people needs be awful perticler what they writes."

—Edna Staebler: *Cape Breton Harbour*

What did Old John Clipper mean by his final remark?

How do **you** write? What are your writing habits?

It has been said that the first step in changing one's habits is to become aware that they **are** habits. Do you have any bad writing habits? What are your good ones?

Writing: A Matter of Getting Involved

How do you work up enthusiasm for writing?

How do you generate ideas?

Here is a short essay, "Tom Smith", written by a young man who thought he had nothing to say:

Sometimes I think the world is passing me by.

Who am I? Tom Smith.

Who is Tom Smith? Nobody.

I, Mr. Nobody Tom Smith, am sixteen years old; I have no special talent. I have no hobbies. I'm no good at sports. I don't like to study, so I'm no good at school, either.

My friends and I hang around the streets or the playground afternoons and evenings. Talking. Sometimes getting into trouble. Mostly doing nothing.

Other kids do things. Sometimes they have talent, sometimes just guts. But either way, they're in there pitching.

I'm always on the sidelines.

What's wrong with me? I feel I'm losing out on life. One day is like yesterday and tomorrow. Blank.

The world keeps going round and round, day turns into night and into day again, and it's all the same to me. Other people are moving, keeping up with tomorrow. I'd like to shout — STOP THE WORLD! I WANT TO GET ON!

Tom Smith thought he was uninvolved yet he managed to connect his inner thoughts (frustration at feeling left out of life) with what goes on in the outside world (the people he observes doing things). By turning his feelings of frustration into words, he has succeeded in understanding himself — and he has written well.

ACTIVITY

Have you ever thought, "What have I got to say?" Write down in your private notebook a few notes about what has happened to you this morning. Who have you talked to? Where have you been? What kind of mood were you in?

Writing may start with a curiosity about ourselves, about other people, or about any number of things we observe. Or it may start with a desire to understand or a desire to make someone else understand something. It may even be the simple passing on of information, or a desire to remember events by putting them on paper.

Most of us are involved, at least with ourselves. If you think you have nothing to write about, start with what you are presently thinking about and what you are doing.

ACTIVITY

Write short, one-sentence descriptions of:

— one sound you remember hearing this morning

— something you touched this morning

—a smell you remember from this morning
—something you looked at this morning
—something you tasted this morning

The idea here is not to remember "important" things, but to pinpoint a few of the many sensations of one morning.

What you now have on paper are a few impressions, a few details about one morning out of hundreds you have known. This is probably not sufficient material for a unified piece of writing, but it is a start. One or two notes might strike you as **related** impressions. Together they might make you think of something else. If you wrote, for example, "I woke up grumpy this morning", and later, "I heard the shrill sound of the alarm clock", you might then remember that the sound of the alarm clock makes you badtempered. Why does it make you bad-tempered? Because you have to get up and go to school? Perhaps you haven't done your homework? One thought leads to another. Ask yourself more questions and see what thoughts come to mind. What homework didn't you do and why didn't you do it? Perhaps you have trouble with that subject, or perhaps you read a good book or watched TV last night. By asking yourself questions, letting one idea lead on to the next, you have given yourself several possible subjects to write about.

Whatever you are trying to talk about, let your thoughts wander **on paper**.

> Start now, and form the habit of keeping a writer's notebook.
> Take quick notes of what you see, hear, feel.
> Write down ideas that come to you from your reading.
> Write down details of events that are or were important to you.
> Write them **down**, even if at first they seem only a jumble of notes.

Once your thoughts are on paper, they may generate other thoughts which can eventually form the basis of a composition.

ACTIVITY

Begin with a word you have some feelings about — any word. (Pick one at random out of a book or dictionary if nothing pops into your head — **luck, dancing, snakes, from, mistake, audience, illness, automobile** — any word to which you respond with some feeling.) Then let this word "generate" other words; then a sentence; then follow your sentence and develop it into a larger form (a paragraph, or two; a poem; a letter; etc.).

ACTIVITY

Write down on paper a greeting between two old friends. Let the conversation reveal something about the two people.

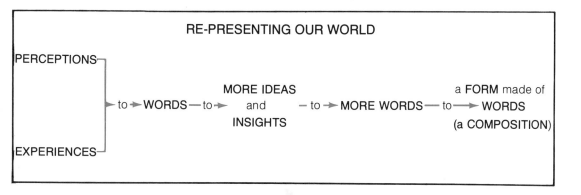

RE-PRESENTING OUR WORLD

PERCEPTIONS ⌉
                                         MORE IDEAS   a **FORM** made of
     to ► WORDS — to ►   and   – to ► MORE WORDS — to ⟶ WORDS
                             INSIGHTS   (a COMPOSITION)
EXPERIENCES ⌋

ACTIVITY

Now write down a brief description of these two people, from the view of an outsider, a watcher. You may overhear the conversation, bits of it, or none of it, as you wish. Write your description in some **form**, for example, as part of a letter to someone, as part of a story, as a poem, or as a "beginning idea" for a play.

INFORMING IDEAS

1. Writing is first a matter of getting involved—making the connection between what goes on in the outside world and what goes on inside our heads.
2. Writing begins with putting these connections, our responses to our worlds, on paper.

"Just say 'Help' . . . it doesn't have to be deathless prose!"

—GRIN AND BEAR IT by George Lichty, Courtesy of Field Newspaper Syndicate

---

Coming to Our Senses

The greatest deprivation is not to live in the physical world.

— Wallace Stevens

Look at the photograph at the top of the following page.

What do you **see** as you look?

What emotions are evoked as you look?

What do you think interested the photographer?

What senses could add to the experience of being there, yet cannot be expressed well by the photograph?

Some scientists think that we normally use only five or six per cent of our capacity to interpret the world through our senses. Some people are forced by special situations to develop one or several of the senses beyond the ordinary range. Blind persons, for example, learn to interpret different sounds with great subtlety. Most of us, however, are content to let our senses sleep.

Here are some suggested activities, and some examples of the ways in which writers use their senses to recall special moments, to evoke moods through the use of sensory detail.

To "See" → To Say → To Write

—Marian Bancroft

Our World of Sound

SUGGESTED ACTIVITIES

(a) Go outside, sit quietly, and listen for fifteen minutes. Write down the different sounds you hear. If there is a tape-recorder available, use it to pick up the sounds around you. How many sounds did the tape-recorder pick up that you didn't notice? Why did you not notice them?

Try to be aware of **particular** sounds. If your comments look like this:

traffic
wind
people talking

you are probably not listening carefully enough. If you hear traffic noises, note the kinds of traffic noises: the low hum of certain trucks, sounds that tires make. Notes like this are better because they are more specific

high-pitched giggle
whir of the bicycle pedals
shoe being scraped on pavement

Try this experiment on a dry day and again on a rainy day. Compare, for example, the sounds of cars or feet on wet pavement with the sounds of cars and feet on dry surfaces. Use the notes you have made as a basis for a short composition in which you try to present a complete picture of the sounds you heard at that particular time. What overall impression do the sounds make?

(b) Take turns leading each other blindfolded around the school corridors. Try to become aware of your other senses, for example, listen for the various rhythms and pitches of the voices around you. Can you concentrate better? Can you tell whether you are in a large or small room?

ACTIVITY

Collecting sounds with a portable tape-recorder can sharpen our listening and add to the enjoyment of remembered experience. Here are a few sounds that can bring back the memory of a trip:

(1)   the sounds of traffic on a highway
(2)   the screams of gulls
(3)   voices in the coffee shop
(4)   the sounds in quiet places —
      the lapping of water, the ticking of a clock, the sound of wind in lonely places, the tap of a branch against a window, the sounds of a distant airport, the crackle of a campfire.

These are suggestions only. Make up your own list of sounds that you remember noticing during a recent trip, or while you were walking somewhere. Become aware of the effect that conscious listening practice has on your listening powers.

De-noised

ERIC NICOL

Abroad this summer I spent several weeks in Paris and London hotels fronting on streets whose decibel output ranged well above the limit considered safe for the human ear. It was the first time I'd seen a desk clerk wearing a headset of ear protectors of the kind used by airport people who work around jets.

At the time I swore that if I got home with any vestiges of my hearing I would retreat to the primordial wilderness of one of the Gulf Islands, and just sit there till my eardrums stopped vibrating.

This I have done. Twenty-four hours, alone, on a bluff overlooking the sea. Remote from human habitation, my sole companions the creatures into whose home I had intruded on the thin excuse of owning the property.

Almost immediately the quiet of the place began gently to vacuum the pools of my inner ear, removing the auditory muck of motorbikes, trucks, buses, choppers, drunks. Within minutes I was able to distinguish the special whirr of a pair of dragonflies mating on the wing — fly the friendly skies united—and the impact of a leaf surprised by fall.

As I lay on the golden grass an ant ran up my leg carrying a load of groceries. My calf hairs gave him trouble. At the knee he wheeled around and headed downhill, clearly annoyed, and I seemed to hear him mutter:

"Wouldn't you know it? Just when you're in a hurry to get home, they hit you with a detour."

The sounds of the sea were relatively stronger. A gull breaking water to snatch a fingering. The rip of the tide. Voices (human) heard from vessels unseen, transmitted from far across a glassy strait, an obscene miracle of acoustics.

By sunset my ear was trained to the variety of subtle sound of my sourroundings. Only once was I startled, by the explosion of a quail flushed from cover. Being neither Catholic nor Protestant, she and I bore each other no malice for the detonation.

The twilight was punctuated by the small thumps of flying ants barging into things — clumsy aeronauts that they are. As I settled down for sleep in the back seat of the car, I was kept awake briefly by the sound of construction: The full moon paving a path across the strait.

The next morning was when it happened. The shocker. Just after I'd shaved in cold water and was waiting for the rising sun's rays to iron my goosepimples. I was standing on the bluff when I heard the sound, like a powerful compressor, a whoomf-whoomf, a sound that seemed to come from nowhere yet was everywhere, and coming closer.

To hear a sound you've never heard before has an electrifying effect. I promptly thought of flying saucers and of my accessibility to one that wished to be unobtrusive about picking up a sample of this planet's fauna.

Whoomf-whoomf. I looked up and saw it — the eagle. What I was hearing was an eagle — only a medium-sized eagle at that — flapping his wings overhead. Whoomf-whoomf. Fifty years of urban living, and I had only seen an eagle fly, never heard it.

My ear had learned something new. My detoxification from big-city noise was complete. Now, if I can just get my toes uncurled . . .

If you did the listening experiment you may have found it easier to hear different sounds than to find the exact words to represent them accurately. Here is how one Canadian tries to catch the "essence" of the Maritimes. What words make his description vivid?

> Vivid in my own mind are the feel of a scythe in timothy, the creak and thump of row-locks in fog, and the far-off thudding of a one-cylinder boat engine. What haunts someone else may well be the growl of a pulpmill, the whine of a lathe, Saturday night in a coal town or the ceaseless wind on Tantramar. . . .
>
> If there is one thing known in common it must be the sound of water, the many sounds of water: surf on a hundred beaches, from Bay Chaleur down the coasts of New Brunswick and The Island, round the headlands of Cape North, down the eastern and southern shores and round the coast of Fundy to Passamaquoddy and the edge of Maine. The grumbling sigh of calm bays at night, the rush of millbrooks and the soft slap on the shores of lakes. The sound of rivers that run to the beat of their names, Matapedia and Kennebecasis, Medway and Margaree . . .

—Charles Bruce: "Atlantic Cadence" in *Century 1867-1967*

How many words can you find in this passage that refer to sound?

ACTIVITY

Try writing something similar about the sounds of your own part of Canada which mean something to you.

The following poem has many references to sound. What kind of picture or mood is created? Pick out the words that refer to sound, and discuss their effectiveness. One way to do this is to replace each of these words with one of your own.

HE WAS

a brown old man with a green thumb:
I can remember the screak on stones of his hoe,
The chug, choke, and high madrigal wheeze
Of the spray-cart bumping below
The sputtery leaves of the apple trees,
But he was all but dumb

Who filled some quarter of the day with sound
All of my childhood long. For all I heard
Of all his labours, I can now recall
Never a single word
Until he went in the dead of fall
To the drowsy underground,

Having planted a young orchard with so great care
In that last year that none was lost, and May
Aroused them all, the leaves saying the land's
Praise for the livening clay,
And the found voice of his buried hands
Rose in the sparrowy air.

—Richard Wilbur

The Skills of Listening

There is something to be said for silence. Except nobody's listening. We're all tuned into the radio where "Sylvia's Mother" is playing for the fifth time in an hour. We don't really hear it. The sound is just there, filling up space, plugging the holes in our minds.

—Heather Robertson, in *Maclean's*

The quality of our language depends upon the skills we develop in speaking, listening, reading, and writing. Of these, listening and reading are receiving activities, and speaking and writing are producing activities. All four activities depend upon one another. What we listen to and what we read form the language material from which we produce speech and writing. Listening, however, is the first activity in our language development and probably takes up the most time. Why, then, are most of us poor listeners? Is it because we think of listening as a passive rather than an active process? Good listening demands highly active skills: concentration, selection, judgment, and appreciation.

A bore has been defined as "someone who talks when you want him to listen". Discuss what this excerpt reveals about talking and listening as habits —individual and cultural.

I shall never forget the horror of staying for one long week with a woman who opened her mouth as I entered her house and closed it when I departed, her vocal cords amputated only by the slam of a door. Every single thought — the state of her silver, the flies on her geraniums — sparked off in the remotest nodule of her brain, and travelled instantly to her larynx, from thence, magnified unto the hundredth part, to boom into my shrinking ears. I longed, then, for silence as an addict for a fix and learned what an instrument of torture the human voice can be.

Just after this noiseful visit ended I went on a journey to Kuwait and for the first time came up against the social silence of the Arab. Invited to visit the home of a Kuwaiti minister, I was ushered into a large sitting-room and placed in a seat against one wall. The minister sat in a seat against the opposite wall. We sat. I did my best to fill the crushing silence with nervous chat—a lovely picture, an enviable table, what was the oil output per annum? Politely he answered and when he had answered, fell silent. Slowly I realized that silence between two people, even between such strangers as we were, was considered entirely natural—it simply did not occur to my host that conversation could be for conversation's sake.

Later, the minister's wife and two teen-aged sons came to sit with us. We smiled, we shook hands, we nodded companionably, we sat there for an hour or more saying nothing. A strange experience for a Westerner bent on verbal exchange — odd and nice and restful.

And yet in the last analysis, in spite of the soft sweet lure of quiet and meditation, I am again convinced that talk is more important, more golden than silence, with all its disadvantages.

— Jill Tweedie: "What's Wrong With the Too-Silent Majority?" in *The Guardian*, Manchester

Are You Listening?

Many of us, when accused of "not listening", tend to blame the uncomfortable surroundings, physical fatigue, or boredom with the material presented. But most of us miss a great deal even when the situation for listening is almost perfect. Often our response after listening to a good speech or a panel discussion, or after participating in a lively conversation is merely: "I enjoyed that" or "That was interesting." Good listening depends, even in ideal situations, upon highly developed listening habits.

The intelligent listener has the ability:

(1) to ask pertinent questions
(2) to summarize the content of a speech, or discussion
(3) to make notes—recording significant points
(4) to distinguish between fact and opinion
(5) to understand the context in which words are used
(6) to detect propaganda devices (name calling, glittering generalities, for example)
(7) to challenge the speaker's ideas
(8) to stimulate discussion

What does the following poem reveal about the part listening plays in relationships between people?

TWO FRIENDS

I have something to tell you.
I'm listening.
I'm dying.
I'm sorry to hear.
I'm growing old.
It's terrible.
It is, I thought you should know.
Of course and I'm sorry. Keep in touch.
I will and you too.
And let me know what's new.
Certainly, though it can't be much.
And stay well.
And you too.
And go slow.
And you too.

— David Ignatow

ACTIVITY

I suspect that human ears are about as dull by comparison to porpoise ears as our sense of smell would be in comparison to that of a bloodhound.

— Roger Payne: "Whales and their Songs" in *The Listener*

What can you find out about the hearing apparatus of the porpoise? of other animals? What are the potentials and limitations of the human ear? Do some reading. Then write a hundred to a hundred and fifty words about some aspect of "hearing" that interests you. Use the quotation above as an opening sentence, if it fits the material you decide upon.

The Senses of Smell and Taste

What is your favourite smell? your favourite taste? What smell or taste has a special meaning for you? (Why?)

The senses help us to recall memories in vivid images. To tell someone else about "what happened" we try to re-present these images.

> Perhaps smell is . . . for many of us the sharpest of the senses of childhood.
>
> — Richard Hoggart: *Speaking to Each Other About Literature*

Do you remember when you were a child and it rained after a dry spell and there was a very particular, intensive earthy smell in the air? Do you remember how people smelled when they hugged you? Do you recall the brilliant colors of leaves, flowers, grass, and even brick surfaces and lighted signs that you experienced as a child? Furthermore, do you recall that when father and mother stepped into the room you *knew* how they felt about themselves, about life, and about you — at that moment.

— Herbert A. Otto: "New Light on the Human Potential" in *Saturday Review*

REMEMBERED ODOURS

Yes, and the smell of hot daisy-fields in the morning; of melted puddling-iron in a foundry; the winter smell of horse-warm stables and smoking dung; of old oak and walnut; and the butcher's smell of meat, of strong slaughtered lamb . . . ; and of brown sugar melted with slivered bitter chocolate; and of crushed mint leaves, and of a wet lilac bush; of magnolia beneath the heavy moon, of dogwood and laurel; of an old caked pipe and Bourbon rye, aged in kegs of charred oak; the sharp smell of tobacco; of carbolic and nitric acids; the coarse true smell of a dog; of old imprisoned books, and the cool fern-smell near springs; of vanilla in cake-dough; and of cloven ponderous cheeses.

— Thomas Wolfe: *Look Homeward, Angel*

ACTIVITY

Write a short piece about your own "remembering", but concentrate upon the sense of touch.

The Art of Seeing: To Know the Look of Things

The artist, whether working with words or with paint, clay, a camera, or another medium, is a "see-er", someone who sees familiar things in a new way.

In presenting a series of photographs, Malvina Bolus, editor of *The Beaver*, makes this comment — one that applies equally to a "maker" in words and a maker on film:

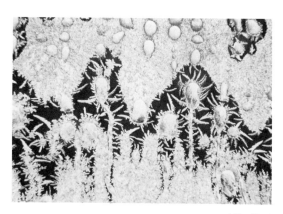

—Lillian Allen

THE ART OF SEEING

In all nature there is ever changing and ever wonderful design, the patterns created by growing things, by wind and weather — the whorl of a shell, the tracery of a snowflake, the rhythm of a feather, the rippling shadow of reeds in water.

Such creations are there for all to see, but only a few are sufficiently perceptive. One of those few is Lillian Allen, until recently professor of housing and design in the Home Economics faculty at the University of Manitoba. The designs of nature she translates and adapts for the decorative alleviation of man's stark reality, and the beauty she sees she imprints forever on a speck of film in a man-made camera. In this way she brings to others both pleasure and new vision.

> . . . things we have passed
> Perhaps a hundred times nor cared to see;
> And so they are better, painted — better to us,
> Which is the same thing. Art was given for that.
>
> —Robert Browning: "Fra Lippo Lippi"

ACTIVITY

In this excerpt from *Wolf Willow*, Wallace Stegner is recalling his boyhood experiences in a Saskatchewan town. List the words and phrases in these paragraphs that reflect the various senses. Then discuss their effectiveness in making the reader "be" in the author's world.

Upstream from the draw that held the dump, the irrigation flume crossed the river. It always seemed to me giddily high when I hung my chin over its plank edge and looked down, but it probably walked no more than twenty feet above the water on its spidery legs. Ordinarily in summer it carried six or eight inches of smooth water, and under the glassy surface of the little boxed stream the planks were coated with deep sun-warmed moss as slick as frogs' eggs. A boy could sit in the flume with the water walling up against his back, and grab a cross-brace above him, and pull, shooting himself sledlike ahead until he could reach the next cross-brace for another pull, and so on across the river in four scoots.

After ten minutes in the flume he would come out wearing a dozen or more limber black leeches, and could sit in the green shade where darning needles flashed blue, and dragonflies hummed and stopped in the air, and skaters dimpled slack and eddy with their delicate transitory footprints, and there pull the leeches off one by one while their sucking ends clung and clung, until at last, stretched far out, they let go with a tiny wet *puk* and snapped together like rubber bands. The smell of the flume and the low bars of that part of the river was the smell of wolf willow.

—Wallace Stegner: *Wolf Willow*

> If . . . you go in for too much taking the Big Picture you miss something very valuable in the smaller picture. . . . [You must] "know" where you are, and this means, among other things, your street, your apartment block, your window box, the faces of friends around you.
>
> —James Reaney: "James Reaney's Canada" in *Maclean's*

ACTIVITY

Now try writing a short piece from your own memory. Start by forming small groups and exchanging memories. Listening to someone else's memories may awaken your own. Keep rough notes.

ACTIVITY

Advertisements catch the reader's attention by making strong appeals to his senses of touch, taste, smell, etc. Such appeals may be within an illustration, or within the language, or both. Sometimes one sense is used to describe another sense, for example, a **velvet** taste, a **smooth** cigarette.

Make a montage of phrases, cut from advertisements, which are effective in appealing to the various senses of the reader.

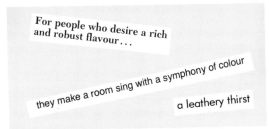

For people who desire a rich and robust flavour...

they make a room sing with a symphony of colour

a leathery thirst

What words would you use to respond verbally to this visual stimulus?

FOR ORAL DISCUSSION

Each of the two following selections emphasizes kinds of observations which are important in writing. How are these two views alike, and how do they differ?

(1)   Isaac Babel, in a short story significantly named "Awakening", recalls his first attempts at writing. He tells how an old man called Nikitich gave him his first lesson:

"I was sure you did a bit of scribbling," said Nikitich. "You've the look. You're looking in *that* direction all the time; no eyes for anywhere else."

He read my writings, shrugged a shoulder, passed a hand through his stiff gray curls, paced up and down the attic.

"One must suppose," he said slowly, pausing after each word, "one must suppose that there's a spark of the divine fire in you."

We went out into the street. The old man halted, struck the pavement with his stick, and fastened his gaze upon me.

"Now what is it you lack? Youth's no matter—it'll pass with the years." . . .

He pointed with his stick at a tree with a reddish trunk and a low crown.

"What's that tree?"

I didn't know.

"What's growing on that bush?"

I didn't know this either. . . .

"What bird is that singing?"

I knew none of the answers. . . .

"And you dare to write!" . . .

(2)   ## TO LOOK AT ANY THING

To look at any thing,
If you would know that thing,
You must look at it long:
To look at this green and say
"I have seen spring in these
Woods," will not do — you must
Be the thing you see:
You must be the dark snakes of
Stems and ferny plumes of leaves,
You must enter in
To the small silences between
The leaves,
You must take your time
And touch the very peace
They issue from.

— John Moffitt

What do you think the poet means in the line, "You must **be** the thing you see"?

Knowing the name of a thing is recognizing that it

is distinct from other things. To **be** the thing is to know **why** it is distinct; to understand the qualities which make one thing different from all others is an act of the imagination.

ACTIVITY

Look again at the photograph on page 149. Imagine yourself to **be** one of the people inside the picture, or one person looking at the scene, or one **thing** within the picture. Start by listing in phrases what you see, feel, and smell, etc., and then develop some of your phrases into sentences. Let the material then develop into some form—a story, a description (for example, to a blind person), or a short play.

Widening the Connections: Exploring Your World AND Yourself

To "see" is not merely to observe a physical world. A human being is more than a camera. To "see" means to **respond** to that world with feelings and emotions, and to make new "connections". In writing, we make discoveries about ourselves. By putting our experiences into words, we discover who we are in relation to others.

> Writing is an activity of self-exploration and discovery.

Different Ways of Responding to and "Re-presenting" Our Experiences

In the next few pages are illustrations of some different ways in which people have responded to the experience of "winter". Each of the responses involves two views: the outside world that is observed, and the inner world of feelings and "ideas". Each of the responses has taken a shape— a poem, a piece of prose, and a photograph. What other kinds of responses are possible?

What are the physical and emotional points of view in the following word-pictures of winter?

After the red leaf and the gold have gone,
Brought down by the wind, then by hammering rain
Bruised and discolored, when October's flame
Goes blue to guttering in the cusp, this land
Sinks deeper into silence, darker into shade.
There is a knowledge in the look of things,
The old hills hunch before the north wind blows.

—from Howard Nemerov: "A Spell before Winter"

The day grays, its light withdrawing from the winter sky till just the prairie's edge is luminous. At one side of the night a farm dog barks; another answers him. A coyote lifts his howl, his throat-line long to the dog-nose pointing out the moon. A train whoops to the night, the sound dissolving slowly.

High above the prairie, platter-flat, the wind wings on, bereft and wild its lonely song. It ridges drifts and licks their ripples off; it smoothens crests, piles snow against the fences. The tinting green of Northern Lights slowly shades and fades against the prairie nights, dying here, imperceptibly reborn over there. Light glows each evening where the town lies; a hiving sound is there with now and then some sound distinct and separate in the night, a shout, a woman's laugh. Clear — truant sounds.

—W. O. Mitchell: *Who Has Seen the Wind*

What sounds are heard and described? How do they contribute to the general mood? Underline all the verbs, and discuss their effectiveness. Is the phrase, "truant sounds" a good ending? Why?

Look at the black and white photograph of "Winter" (Lake Ontario). In what ways does it differ from the photograph taken by Lillian Allen (p.153)?

Suppose the photographer of this black and white picture had wanted to enlarge one section of her photograph and shape it into a different pictorial composition. How might this change in focus

—Marian Bancroft

change the feeling one experiences when looking at the photograph?

ACTIVITY

"Be" one of the children in this photograph, and describe in words this scene from that child's view. You may "be" there, or look back upon it. You may change the season if you wish. If you do, how might it change the emotional point of view?

ACTIVITY

Have a group of students present the music of Antonio Vivaldi's "Winter" from his *Four Seasons*. Jot down words and phrases that occur to you while listening.

ACTIVITY

Jot down a list of words and phrases that form **your** response to one of the other seasons. Try to think in images, and to use your various senses. Group those that are related to one **point of view**, that is, a way of "seeing" physically as well as responding emotionally. Then re-present that view in any medium you wish — with words, paint, film, music, etc.

What do you see in this photograph?

This is how one person explored with his camera something very ordinary — part of a door.

" . . . things we have passed
Perhaps a hundred times nor cared to see;"

Here is how a poet responded to the idea of "doorknob":

KNOB

Conceptually a blob,
the knob
is the smallest object which,
hitched
to a larger,
acts as a verger.

It enables
us to gain access to drawers in end tables;
it shepherds
us into cupboards.

Prouder than buttons yet humbler than handles
knobs avoid scandals
and keep themselves stiff.
When one (as on a bedpost) turns decorative, it is as if
Everyman were to
Become a chorine in a Broadway revue.

—John Updike

ACTIVITY

Explore — with a camera, paints, words, or any other medium — any commonplace object within your everyday experience. Present your material so that your viewer, hearer, or reader will see it "with new eyes". If you use a camera or drawing, write captions or write quotations from poetry which seem to reflect the feelings within your picture.

Point of View and the Reader

Here is a poem that presents a "view" of modern North American life. To read this poem with any understanding, you must first know the physical point of view—who is viewing the scene, and where that viewer is. Discuss the poem in groups, and decide upon the physical (or "outer") point of view. Then discuss the "inner" view of the poet.

SOUTHBOUND ON THE FREEWAY

A tourist came in from Orbitville,
parked in the air, and said:

The creatures of this star
are made of metal and glass.

Through the transparent parts
you can see their guts.

Their feet are round and roll
on diagrams — or long

measuring tapes — dark
with white lines.

They have four eyes.
The two in the back are red.

Sometimes you can see a 5-eyed
one, with a red eye turning

on the top of his head.
He must be special —

the others respect him,
and go slow,

when he passes, winding
among them from behind.

They all hiss as they glide,
like inches, down the marked

tapes. Those soft shapes,
shadowy inside

the hard bodies — are they
their guts or their brains?

— May Swenson

> My task . . . is, by the power of the written word, to make you hear, to make you feel — it is, before all, to make you *see*.
>
> — Joseph Conrad, from his Preface to *The Nigger of the "Narcissus"*

> The writer sees ⟶ responds ⟶ writes.
> The reader, in turn, will "see" and respond to what has been written.

Sometimes the response to a work produced in one medium can be reinterpreted to produce a work in another medium. These young people, for instance, are responding to a poem by using movement, rhythm, and music.

WHAT DO YOU "SEE"?

Wheatfield with Crows, July 1890, by Vincent Van Gogh

Look closely at this painting by Vincent Van Gogh and think of a painting as a kind of pictorial writing. In that sense, what "message" do you get from this painting? Ask yourself the following questions, and then respond to this painting with a short paragraph.

1. What words would you use to describe the blue of the sky?
2. What words would you use to describe the "sea of grain" that meets the blue sky?
3. Are the crows flying towards or away from the viewer?
4. The grassy road in the middle of the painting seems to come to "a dead end". Why?
5. What does the dirt path in the foreground suggest to you?
6. The sky seems to be rolling in some direction. How do you respond to that part of the painting? How do the colours affect the direction of the various movements within the painting?
7. What words suggest the emotion conveyed to you by the whole composition? peaceful? threatening? turbulent? enclosing?

Summary

When a painter, photographer, or writer wishes to represent a scene or a person, he decides two things:
1. the physical point of view — the outer world
2. the emotional point of view — the inner world
   Every painting, picture, photograph, piece of sculpture, or piece of writing is an **exploration** of a subject. Each detail strengthens the general feeling or idea the artist wishes to communicate — though, of course, all attempts to "re-present" an experience are incomplete and imperfect. (No painting ever says everything about a face; no painting of a face **is** a face.)

Some Hints to Help You Become a Better Writer

To compose is more than just writing one sentence after another, although it may **begin** that way. A composition is a contraption made of words, in which the parts — words, sentences, ideas — work together. Composing means choosing, moving things around, until the final effect is like a machine that runs smoothly.

The ways in which writers compose may vary. But all effective writing, when analysed, reveals its shape and, from the beginning, the direction in which the thought is to be developed.

An example:

Suppose you decide to write a paragraph on "Study Habits". If your opening sentence is:

My study habits reflect my inability to concentrate.

you have given your reader several clues to your line of approach.

The word **my** tells your reader that you are writing from a personal point of view.

The phrase **inability to concentrate** suggests the attitude you have to the subject and the thought you will expand.

You have set limits upon what you will say from then on. The whole paragraph must be about your own study habits and how they reflect your inability to concentrate. You might then begin to plan—to jot down ideas to support the main thought — something like this:

"My Study Habits"
Main idea: Inability to concentrate
Sub-ideas:
(a) staring at the pages and hoping for interruptions such as a telephone call from a friend, or family visitors
(b) deciding to stretch out on the couch and think
(c) feeling hungry — a trip to the kitchen to restore my strength

(d) deciding to call a friend in order to find out what's going on in the real world
(e) returning to my book with the sports section of the evening paper (must keep up with the news)
(f) going to bed — after all, the real work can be done tomorrow

The whole composition is thus an **expansion** or development of an idea by means of detail.

Getting Started

Good writing needs hard work **before** the real writing begins. Inspiration sometimes provides an idea for a piece of writing, but there are certain things to be done, and usually in a certain order. Here is an effective pattern of preparation:

---

1. **Find a subject** — something related to your own thoughts and experiences.
2. **Limit your subject.** It is better to expand one narrow topic than to range vaguely over a whole field; for example, not "Hockey", but "The Effect of the Forward Pass".
3. **Determine your purpose.** Sometimes it helps to set your purpose on paper; for example, "My purpose is to convince my classmates that all high school students should wear a school uniform."
4. **Gather your materials.** Begin by putting down the details you know about the subject. Then add new material from reading and discussion.
5. **Select the details** that develop your main idea.
6. **Arrange these details** in some order.

Now you are ready to begin writing your first draft.

What follows is an expansion of this pattern of composing.

GETTING STARTED: FINDING A SUBJECT

Reflect upon your experiences and interests. What places have you seen? What interesting people do you know? What family situations, humorous or sad, can you describe? What makes you happy or sad? What are your hopes, your fears, your ambitions? These questions make you think about the world **you** know, and thus provide the best source for topics.

LIMITING THE TOPIC

A limited or narrowed topic is a part of a wide subject. Narrowing a topic is like "zeroing in" with a camera from the "big picture" to one interesting part of the scene.

The "Big Picture":

—Marian Bancroft

Narrowed topics:

—Marian Bancroft

—Marian Bancroft

Another example:

wide topic — Transportation
limited topic — Air Transport
more limited yet — Jet Transport
more limited yet — Jet Transport and Weather Forecasting.
           or — The Length of Runways for Jet Passenger Planes
           or — The Concorde and Noise Levels

If you consider these carefully, you will see that you must know **enough** about a limited topic to develop it. Almost anyone can write a paragraph on "Air Transport", but a limited topic demands much more specific knowledge.

The narrow topic will, however, make a **better** paragraph, because you must expand it by using details.

> Failure to narrow the topic is the most common feature of poor writing.

ACTIVITY

Defend your choice of **one** of the following topics for a paragraph by listing at least **six** suitable details. State whether your knowledge comes from direct experience or from reading, conversation, radio, or television.

Tracking a Cougar or Criminal or Lost Article, etc.
Changing a Tire or Diapers or Hair Colour, etc.
Managing Teachers or Younger Brothers, etc.

ACTIVITY

For each of **three** of the following general subjects suggest **two** specific topics that would be suitable for a short composition. (In other words, **limit** the topics.)

1. An Ideal School
2. Hitchhiking
3. David Thompson
4. Eskimo Art
5. Wilderness Parks

Here is a piece on the broad topic "Winter". Discuss how the writer limits the topic in the first sentence to "the **still** reality of winter" and then expands the topic by giving detailed images.

We sleep, and at length awake to the still reality of a winter morning. The snow lies warm as cotton or down upon the window sill; the broadened sash and frosted panes admit a dim and private light, which enhances the snug cheer within. The stillness of the morning is impressive. The floor creaks under our feet as we move toward the window to look abroad through some clear space over the fields. We see the roofs stand under their snow burden. From the eaves and fences hang stalactites of snow, and in the yard stand stalagmites covering some concealed core. The trees and shrubs rear white arms to the sky on every side; and where were walls and fences, we see fantastic forms stretching in frolic gambols across the dusky landscape, as if Nature had strewn her fresh designs over the fields by night as models for man's art.

— Henry David Thoreau: *A Winter Walk*

ACTIVITY (FOR GROUP DISCUSSIONS AND WRITING)

After reading the following classifications of "inner" experience and discussing them in groups, choose one that interests you. List concrete incidents that would make it "visible". Then write a short composition.

1. Experiences with Emotions (Discuss **one**): Fear, Guilt, Confidence, Hopes and Ambitions, Disappointment, Shyness
2. Experiences with Language (Discuss **one**): The First Book I Remember Reading, Books I Used to Like, Books I Read Now, The Sections of the Newspaper I Like to Read

DETERMINE YOUR PURPOSE: DECIDE ON THE CENTRAL OR CORE IDEA

Once you have chosen your topic and have limited it, you must find a central idea for it. Sometimes you may need to do quite a bit of writing and working with words before you hit on the purpose and the idea you want to develop.

Determining a Purpose: An artist decides to depict a greenhouse

—Sinclair Healy

—Sinclair Healy

—Sinclair Healy

The artist has a subject — a greenhouse.
His sketches are like the writer's "lists" of ideas
and phrases. Then he finds his "topic" —the one he
will develop into a pictorial composition.

The final selection — the artist's "composition"

—painting by Sinclair Healy photographed by Marian Bancroft

When you write, the central idea may take any of a number of forms, for example,

it can express a preference: **I like oranges better than pears**.

it can express an opinion: **Mandarin oranges are juicier than any other oranges**.

it can state a fact: **Most of the oranges we get in Canada are imported from California, Florida, or Israel.**

The **topic sentence**, containing the central idea, is usually the first sentence in the paragraph. Sometimes it is at the end. Occasionally, it is omitted, but when it is, the idea is implied.

In the following paragraph the core idea is stated in the first sentence. Find in this first sentence the "key" words that tell the reader the purpose of the whole piece. The ideas expressed by these key words are then expanded in the rest of the paragraph.

Albert Einstein was, in my opinion, the most authentic great man that I have ever known. I have known eminent men of various kinds: statesmen from Gladstone to Lenin and Sir Winston Churchill, poets from Browning and Tennyson and Mallarmé to T. S. Eliot, and most of the philosophers of the past sixty years. But none of these men made upon me the impression of massiveness and insight that was made by Einstein.

—Bertrand Russell, in *The Vancouver Sun*

In the last sentence the author has narrowed his topic even further. The words **massiveness** and **insight** are the key words and the writer's "promise" for what will follow.

ORAL ACTIVITY

Look at the following paragraph. What words in the opening sentence are the key words? How does the remainder of the paragraph develop these?

We forgot our own danger for a few minutes as we watched the fleeing wilderness people in their pitiful pilgrimage towards the swamp. Everything that could walk, or crawl, or fly was there — friend and foe oblivious of each other in the titanic struggle for self-preservation. Thousands of terror-filled creatures there were that never reached the safety of the swamp. Behind us, through stifling smoke, we saw dozens of birds — fluttering like falling leaves, trying to dodge the fire and the wind. Lost, they fell in the flames.

—John R. Barrett: "Red Invader"

The first two sentences of the next paragraph imply a question: "What makes an airplane fly?" Does the paragraph answer the question? What evidence, if any, does the paragraph give to support this answer?

What makes an airplane fly is not its engine nor its propeller. Nor is it, as many people think, some mysterious knack of the pilot, nor some ingenious gadget inside. What makes an airplane fly is simply its shape. This may sound absurd, but gliders do fly without engines, and model airplanes do fly without pilots. As for the insides of an airplane, they are disappointing, for they are mostly hollow. No, what keeps an airplane up is its shape—the impact of the air on its shape. Whittle that shape out of wood, or cast it out of iron, or fashion it, for that matter, out of chocolate and throw the thing into the air. It will behave like an airplane. It will *be* an airplane.

—W. Langewiesche: *Why an Airplane Flies*

ACTIVITY

Divide into groups and discuss ideas that could develop from the following topics. Then each group write an appropriate opening sentence for three of the topics.

1. Final Bell — Friday Afternoon
2. Our Family at Breakfast
3. Fishing for Compliments
4. At the Drive-In
5. Racing
6. Never Again!

Developing a Paragraph

DEVELOPING A CENTRAL IDEA: FULFILLING A PROMISE

Good paragraph development means including enough concrete detail, examples, or explanations of fact to support the point the writer wishes to make. Some ideas may require only three sentences for adequate development; others may require more. The topic sentence of the paragraph makes some kind of promise to the reader. It says in effect:

"This is what I saw happen." (**narration** or **reporting**)

or "This is a place you should see." (**description**)

or "Here is the way to do it." (**exposition**)

or "Here are my views on the problem." (**argument**)

A paragraph that does not give enough details to interest the reader is "undernourished" and needs more substance.

Here is an example of an underdeveloped paragraph. It contains the basic facts, but does not amplify these by detail.

The six months' journey from England to Vancouver Island must have been very wearisome. Often the ship hit storms or long stretches of calm. Sometimes epidemics broke out, and many passengers died. Usually there was a shortage of food or fresh water. How eagerly the immigrants must have looked forward to the end of the voyage!

Here is the same paragraph fully developed. What details have been added to each of the basic facts given in the first paragraph?

Immigrants travelling from England to Vancouver Island in the Hudson's Bay Company supply ships found the long voyage of six months almost interminable. On the journey almost every kind of weather was encountered: gales and high seas in the Bay of Biscay; trade winds and calms in the tropics; snow, hail, thunder and lightning in the vicinity of Cape Horn; in the Pacific, sometimes heavy seas and storms, but often, from the Mexican coast northward, monotonously good weather and gentle winds. Some passengers never arrived at their destination: a voyage was seldom completed without an outbreak of smallpox or a death from scarlet fever or from measles, and the rigours of the trip were too great for the strength of very young children or of aged men. The supplies of fresh food and water taken on at Cape Verde were exhausted long before a ship reached Vancouver Island, and for months the passengers lived on cheese and biscuits full of weevils. As the weeks lengthened, everyone, growing tired of the dreadful emptiness of the landscape, longed to reach shore. On the last stage of the voyage, the craving for the privacy of a house and for the satisfaction of a filling meal of fresh meat, fresh vegetables and fresh butter became almost unbearable.

— Margaret Ormsby: *British Columbia: A History*

PATTERNS OF DEVELOPMENT IN COMPOSING

Here are some frequently used methods of developing a paragraph topic:

1. giving details or illustrations or examples
2. pointing out similarities and differences
3. defining
4. giving reasons

Frequently, writers use a combination of several methods. **Have something to say, and include enough details to complete the main idea, and the method will take care of itself.**

Here are some examples of methods of development. Studying these may help you.

1. Giving Particulars, Details, or Examples

I was running for my life! Leaping from ice-block to ice-block and frantically jumping crevasse after cre-

vasse, I sought to escape from the monstrous pile of ice that was crashing down behind me. But dodge as I could it was getting closer and closer. . . . Suddenly a gigantic crevasse loomed in front of me — I was trapped! In desperation I looked around at the grinding ice surging toward me.

— Sir Edmund Hillary: *High Adventure*

The above paragraph is a piece of **narration**. The details make the writer's experience become "alive" for the reader. What details and particulars does the writer use to expand the key idea **running for my life**?

Discuss how the following piece is developed by the accumulation of details.

We watched things: we watched people build houses, we watched men fix cars, we watched each other patch bicycle tires with rubber bands. We watched men dig ditches, climb television poles — I can hear the sound now of climbing irons on a pole, this was a race of heroes! —we watched trains at the station, shoe-shine men at the station, Italian men playing *boccie*,[1] our fathers playing cards, our mothers making jam, our sisters skipping rope, curling their hair. For at least a month I watched my sisters making beads: they cut paper into long triangular strips, put glue on them, wrapped them around hatpins, and then I think they varnished them. I don't recall that they ever wore them, but I'm here to tell you they made them. They also did something called tie-dyeing: it was a rage, and it produced handkerchiefs of unbelievable ugliness.

We strung beads on strings: we strung spools on string; we tied each other up with string, and belts and clothesline.

We sat in boxes; we sat under porches; we sat on roofs; we sat on limbs of trees.

We stood on boards over excavations; we stood on tops of piles of leaves; we stood under rain dripping from the eaves; we stood up to our ears in snow.

We looked at things like knives and *immies*[2] and pig nuts and grasshoppers and clouds and dogs and people.

We skipped and hopped and jumped. Not going anywhere —just skipping and hopping and jumping and galloping.

We sang and whistled and hummed and screamed.

What I mean, Jack, we did a lot of nothing.

— reprinted from "Where Did You Go?" "Out." "What Did You Do?" "Nothing." by Robert Paul Smith

[1]*boccie*, bowling   [2]*immies*, marbles

ACTIVITY

Write your own piece using the same method of development by detail. Possibilities are:

"A Lazy Day at Home" (or at School, at Summer Camp, on the Job)
"I Like to Keep Busy"
"Sick in Bed"

2. Making Comparisons or Contrasts

Most of us think we can separate clearly the two activities we call "work" and "play". Follow closely the writer's arguments and examples to see how he uses comparisons and contrasts to develop his ideas of work and play.

The function of the machine is to save work. In a fully mechanised world all the dull drudgery will be done by machinery, leaving us free for more interesting pursuits. So expressed, this sounds splendid. It makes one sick to see half a dozen men sweating their guts out to dig a trench for a water-pipe, when some easily devised machine would scoop the earth out in a couple of minutes. Why not let the machine do the work and the men go and do something else. But presently the question arises, what else are they to do? Supposedly they are set free from "work" in order that they may do something which is not "work". But what is work and what is not work? Is it work to dig, to carpenter, to plant trees, to fell trees, to ride, to fish, to hunt, to feed chickens, to play the piano, to take photographs, to build a house, to cook, to sew, to trim hats, to mend motor bicycles? All of these things are work to somebody, and all of them are play to somebody. There are in fact very few activities which cannot be classed either as work or play according as you choose to regard them. The labourer set free from digging may want to spend his leisure, or part of it, in playing the piano, while the professional pianist may be only too glad to get out and dig at the potato patch. Hence the antithesis between work, as something intolerably tedious, and not-work, as something desirable, is false. The truth is that when a human being is not eating, drinking, sleeping, making love, talking, playing games or merely lounging about — and these things will not fill up a lifetime — he needs work and usually looks for it, though he may not call it work.

—George Orwell: *The Road to Wigan Pier*

ACTIVITY

Develop one of the following sentences into a short composition by the method of **contrast**.

1. The winters on the coast are not at all like those inland.

2. Television and radio are both entertaining, but for different reasons.

3. Living by a lake is pleasant, but there is nothing like the smell of salt water.

3. Defining

When developing a paragraph by definition, the writer usually tries to answer the question, "What is the exact and precise nature of this thing?" To supply a satisfactory definition, he may use all the other devices — examples, descriptive details, contrast, and so on. Literally, to **define** means 'to set limits to'.

The term "old-timer" may seem vague to the uninitiated; but in most communities where it is in current use its meaning is in fact precise. The old-timer is the man who has been on the scene from the beginning, or very nearly the beginning, of the life of the community. A man may live to be a hundred or more in Toronto or Montreal but this means nothing, for the life of the city reaches much further back than a century; but if he lives to be a hundred in Estevan or Maple Creek or Whiskey Gap he can count on being stuffed and put in a museum.

—Edward McCourt: *Saskatchewan*

ACTIVITY

Try to make a satisfactory definition for two of these; do not use a dictionary until you have finished.

a sonnet   a keepsake   country music   pollution
a student   a pupil   a word   proton

ACTIVITY

Discuss the importance of defining one's terms in argument. For instance, many people talk about "democracy" or "freedom". Do they all define the word in the same way? Can they agree on a common definition?

Scientific definitions are, in a sense, universally accepted, and universally changed when a new discovery arises. To change definitions of words dealing with human relationships is much more difficult. (Why?)

4. Giving Reasons

In the following paragraph the writer gives us his opinion in the topic sentence. To convince us, he must give us specific reasons for thinking as he does.

> Of all America's great rivers the Fraser is probably the most unfriendly to mammalian life. The fish it tolerates and breeds in countless swarm. The vegetable growth it burrows out and sweeps away wherever its tides can reach. The animal touches these waters at its peril. Among the animals, the river has seen man for a fragment of time hardly worth recording in the ages of its experience and it holds him in contempt. It crushes his vessels. It tugs and chews forever at his bridges. It heaves its avalanches against his fragile railways. It gnaws his little plots of habitable land, overwhelms his dikes, silts up his harbours, and awaits the day of his going.

—Bruce Hutchison: *The Fraser*

Notice:

1. the strong attitude expressed in the general topic sentence: **most unfriendly**.
2. a series of specific examples of the river's **unfriendliness** to mammalian life.
3. the use of vigorous, descriptive verbs, rather than adjectives — verbs such as **burrows**, **sweeps, crushes, tugs, chews, heaves, gnaws**, and **overwhelms** — to describe the fury and unfriendliness of the river.
4. the striking concluding sentence with the suggestion that man is just an incident in the life of the river.

FOR DISCUSSION

Usually the topic sentence suggests to the reader the method or methods the writer will use to develop his idea. For instance, what method or methods of development are suggested by each of the following topic sentences?

1. Fifty years ago air travel for the ordinary person was almost unheard of.
2. Central heating means heating a house from one appliance.
3. The city of Vienna has been the home of many eminent composers of music.
4. We are now beginning to realize the high price of living in an automobile civilization.
5. A snake's hearing is very different from ours.
6. Teachers are human.
7. You may wonder why I no longer skate.
8. Who are the Amerindians?

Read the following paragraph and study the analysis that follows it.

> As for me, I was a crybaby. My circulation was poor and my hands always got blue and white in the cold. I always had a runny nose. I was skinny and small, so that my mother anxiously doctored me with Scott's Emulsion, sulphur and molasses, calomel, and other doses. To compound my frail health, I was always getting hurt. Once I lost both big-toe nails in the same week, and from characteristically incompatible causes. The first one turned black and came off because I had accidentally shot myself through the big toe with a .22 short; the second because, sickly thing that I was, I had dropped a ten-pound bottle of Scott's Emulsion on it.

—Wallace Stegner: *Wolf Willow*

Topic sentence: As for me, I was a crybaby.
Central idea: weakness and frail health
Supporting ideas: poor circulation — hands cold — runny nose — frail — skinny and small — victim of mother's doctoring — accident-prone — lost toe nails twice

Writing Skills To Notice

1. The writer had previously been talking about the heroes honoured and admired by the ten-year-old boys of a prairie town — "good shots, good riders, . . . stoical endurers of pain". What phrase in the topic sentence shows that this paragraph is in contrast with what went before it?

2. Notice how the author expands a general statement through giving particular details. For example,

   general statement: My circulation was poor

   detail: hands got blue and white in the cold

   With what details does he develop the general statement, "I was always getting hurt"?

3. How does the reference to the ten-pound bottle of Scott's Emulsion in the final sentence suggest the writer's attitude to himself?

ACTIVITY

Write a short piece in which you develop a picture of yourself as a ten-year-old from your point of view at your present age.

Sometimes, making an outline of a composition **after** it has been written helps a writer to discover whether or not the paragraph has been properly or fully developed, and provides the writer with the clues necessary for revision. Try doing this with your piece about yourself as a ten-year-old.

These questions may help you to make sure that you have used an effective method of paragraph development:

1. Does my paragraph have something to say? (**substance**)

2. Does my opening show the reader the direction in which I am going to go? (**topic sentence** or **topic guide**)

3. Does my paragraph have **sufficient detail** to support my main idea? (a well-nourished piece of writing)

4. Does my paragraph stick to the topic? (**unity**)

Examine the following paragraph:

TROUBLE-MAKER

He is the silent one. He never speaks up on issues. He never sounds off in the letter column of his local newspaper. He never writes to his member of Parliament. He is as quiet as a clam. And in his wish to offend nobody, he offends Democracy. How could Democracy succeed if all of us, like this one, withheld our opinions, our ideas, our criticisms? Voting on election day is only part of a citizen's duty. Active, day-by-day participation in government, in society, is a responsibility for each and every one of us. The silent trouble-maker fails to understand this. In his worship of "law and order", he never dares to question an oppressive law, never distinguishes "order" from stagnation. He is the apostle of social decay, not Democracy.

—adapted from "Nationwide Insurance" in the *Atlantic Monthly*

Does this paragraph meet the standards of effective development mentioned above?

Why is the opening sentence good? What does it do?

What key word is repeated in the paragraph?

Does the paragraph give a sense of completeness?

The paragraph has faults that you would do well to avoid: for example, the expression "sounds off", though effective, is almost slang. Phrases such as "quiet as a clam" and "each and every one of us" are clichés, tired and outworn expressions. No piece of writing is ever perfect. But, considered as a whole, this paragraph says what it wants to say, and says it clearly and emphatically.

ACTIVITY

1. Under the general topic "Speak Up!" list at least five issues about which you think you should

"speak up". These issues may be international, national, or personal; but make sure they are real and important to **you**.

2. Choose one of the issues, limit it, and then write a short composition on the model of "Trouble-Maker".

   If you choose a wide topic such as "School Citizenship", limit it to a specific issue, such as:

   Locker Litter
   The Homework Scrounger
   The Sidewalk Hog

Unity

A writer without a focus often wanders around a subject and introduces unrelated items. In other words, a paragraph has **unity** when it focuses on and develops **one** idea, **one** impression, or **one** event.

ORAL ACTIVITY

Discuss the lack of unity in the following paragraph, using the check list of questions on page 172 as a guide.

> The prairie-dog is a plump, tawny rodent, weighing about one kilogram and measuring thirty-five to forty-two centimetres from nose to tail-tip. It belongs to the squirrel family and is related to the marmots. I have often seen as many as thirty or forty prairie-dogs on the edge of a dried-out slough. Of the five species of prairie-dog, it is the black-tailed species that builds its towns in the Great Plains. Its front feet are equipped with long digging claws. The badger also has long claws for digging. The ears of the black-tailed species are small, and its eyes—which are especially adapted to the detection of aerial predators—are so high on its head that they are about the first things to appear as the animal emerges from its burrow.

ACTIVITY

Develop one of the following topics into a unified piece of writing.

1. A Day in the Country

2. Curtain-time

3. An Embarrassing Moment

4. Popping Corn

5. Entering the Harbour (the City, etc.)

Coherence

A close reasoner and a good writer in general may be known by his pertinent use of connectives.

—Samuel Coleridge

If the sentences within a piece of writing read like separate statements, the reader is forced to deal with the ideas in pieces, sentence by sentence. If, however, the ideas flow easily into one another, the paragraph has **coherence**. Coherence means literally "holding together".

The following paragraph lacks coherence. (Why?)

> I did not do well in examinations. I did not do well on my entrance examination to Harrow. The Headmaster was Mr. Welldon. Mr. Welldon took a broad-minded view of my Latin prose. Mr. Welldon showed discernment in judging my general ability. Mr. Welldon's discernment was remarkable. I was found unable to answer a single question on the Latin paper. I wrote my name at the top of the page. I wrote down the number of the question. It was number 1. I put a bracket around the number. I could not think of anything connected with the question that was either relevant or true. There arrived from nowhere in particular a blot and several smudges. I gazed for two whole hours at the blot and smudges. The merciful ushers collected my piece of foolscap with all the others. The ushers carried my paper up to the Headmaster's table.

Now read the paragraph as originally written by Sir Winston Churchill in his book *My Early Life*. Comment on the devices (indicated by italics) used by Churchill to achieve coherence.

I did not do well in examinations. *This* was especially true of my entrance examination to Harrow. The Headmaster, *Mr. Welldon*, *however*, took a broad-minded view of my Latin prose: *he* showed discernment in judging my general ability. *This* was the more remarkable, *because* I was found unable to answer a single question on the Latin paper. I wrote my name at the top of the page. I wrote down the number of the *question*: 1. After much reflection I put a bracket around *it* thus: (1). *But thereafter* I could not think of anything connected with *it* that was either relevant or true. Incidentally there arrived from nowhere in particular a blot and several smudges. I gazed for two whole hours at *this sad spectacle: and then* merciful ushers collected my piece of foolscap with all the others *and* carried *it* up to the Headmaster's table.

This refers to the previous statement. Note that such a use of *this* is often considered a weakness in writing, because it can be imprecise. What other device could avoid this possibility of vagueness?

The Headmaster's name is not important, so is subordinated. The *however* signals a reversal in some way of the previous ideas.

He, a pronoun (pro- -noun), serves to refer to someone already named.

This is like the first *this* in function.

Now analyse the remaining devices of coherence within the paragraph. Then write your own version of the paragraph.

The preceding example illustrates two important points about coherence within a paragraph.

1. There must be good **sentence sequence**. The ideas in the paragraph must be linked to help the reader move easily from one sentence to the next.

2. There must be **variety in sentence structure**. Variety prevents monotony, and a nice mixture of short and long sentences provides a pleasing rhythm, a feeling of naturalness.

Guideposts and Bridges

WAYS OF LINKING SENTENCES

Here are some linking expressions that are useful for connecting ideas:

FOR TIME ORDER	FOR PLACE ORDER	TO ADD IDEAS	TO SHOW CAUSE AND EFFECT	TO CONTRAST IDEAS
after	inside	moreover	so	yet
then	outside	besides	hence	however
at last	nearby	also	consequently	but
finally	near at hand	too	thus	nevertheless
when	above	furthermore	as a result	still
soon	within	in addition	accordingly	on the other hand
before long	straight ahead		for this reason	
meanwhile	turning the corner		therefore	**TO REPEAT IDEAS**
next	around the bend			pronouns
a little later	as we came closer			nouns
	behind me			possessives

Examples

(a) **SHOWING PLACE ORDER:**

As we approached the gates, we could see the students hurrying across the campus. **Once inside**, we mingled with the crowds **in front of the library**. Suddenly we caught sight of Tom **not ten feet away**.

Do the expressions in bold type tell the reader where the speaker is?

(b) **TO REPEAT IDEAS:**

Margaret gave John a book for **his** birthday. **He** liked **the gift** very much.

How do **he**, **his**, and **the gift** repeat ideas? Broken glass and smashed furniture were everywhere. **The mess** showed how furious the fight had been.

How does **the mess** repeat an idea?

(c) **TO CONTRAST IDEAS:**

For months we planned for this day. **But** at the last minute the whole affair was postponed a week. Better a week late, **however**, than not at all.

Omit the two connectives. What does each connective signal to the reader?

True coherence lies in the **logical development of thought**. Connecting words are useful, but are not substitutes for natural continuity. For instance, look at the following series of sentences:

What a wet day it was! I wished I had not gone out. I was soaked to the skin.

It would be foolish to add connectives and write the sentences like this:

What a wet day it was! Because of this, I wished I had not gone out. Furthermore, I was soaked to the skin.

ORAL ACTIVITY

Pick out the connectives in the following paragraph, and discuss how each helps the reader to follow the description.

The slope into Alberta was much more gentle and regular than that by which we had climbed from British Columbia. First there was a rocky region of slate-grey mountain lakes, with occasional quarries and small mines, then the landscape changed to little craggy ranges of hills where mining villages alternated with cattle ranges and small mixed farms. Right from the beginning, on this drier side of the mountain, the forests were more meagre than on the coastal face, and they quickly became more scattered until we ran into a rolling prairie, rather like the Wiltshire Downs, where the only trees were the willows and aspens in the gullies and in the valleys which the few rivers had cut into the deep prairie soil. Here the rain of the west gave way to snow, the sky was shut in with leaden clouds, and the thin fall of flakes increased in volume as we travelled eastward. The ground, however, was still too warm for the snow to lie, except in occasional pockets on some colder slope.

—George Woodcock: *Ravens and Prophets*

Ideas must also cohere when you move from one paragraph to another. The first sentence of the new paragraph is the connecting one. It looks **back** to what was said, and looks **forward** to the idea about to be developed.

ORAL ACTIVITY

Discuss how the opening sentence of each new paragraph in the following newspaper editorial makes the transition from the previous paragraph coherent for the reader.

Tribute on a Tombstone

A countryman was looking about an old rural cemetery, seeking traces of his pioneer ancestors buried there more than a century ago. He came upon sad evidence of the hard life of the early settlers in Ontario. There were tombstones, for instance, which recorded the deaths of young children, perhaps from diphtheria or some such plague of those times.

One headstone, however, cheered the observer immensely. It bore an epitaph offered by a husband to his deceased wife. The roughly carved letters read: "She made home pleasant." What a wealth of wonderful meaning those four words contained!

They suggested this pioneer wife and mother maintained a clean, neat log cabin and that she tended her family well, in sickness and in health. But above all they implied she was a woman of pleasant disposition, cheerful, optimistic and kindly.

This was no shrewish wife, making the lives of those around her miserable with her petty nagging. Nor was she one to complain ceaselessly about her harsh lot amid all the deprivations of pioneer life. She made her home pleasant because she herself was pleasant.

This simple epitaph on the old tombstone has a lesson for all those still alive. We can create pleasure for others just by being pleasant ourselves. A happy disposition can provide happiness which mere money cannot buy. Fortunate are those who have such a temperament and doubly fortunate are those who have such a person in the home.

ACTIVITY

Work in small groups. One person will supply the others with the first paragraph of an article he likes— not a narrative, and not from a newspaper (unless it is an editorial). Each person in the group will write the opening sentence of the next paragraph. Then the group will compare and discuss their choices, looking especially at the "clues" in the first paragraph that led them to write their sentences.

A REVIEW

Here is an excerpt from Laurie Lee's account of his childhood in England. Look back through this chapter about writing, and then discuss in groups some of the features of good writing you see in this piece.

Afterwards you may wish to write about some memory of your own — of a certain day, or episode, or — as here — of a certain room.

Indoors, our mother was cooking pancakes, her face aglow from the fire. There was a smell of sharp lemon and salty batter, and a burning hiss of oil. The kitchen was dark and convulsive with shadows, no lights had yet been lit. Flames leapt, subsided, corners woke and died, fires burned in a thousand brasses.

"Poke round for the matches, dear boy," said Mother. "Damn me if I know where they got to."

We lit the candles and set them about, each in its proper order: two on the mantelpiece, one on the piano, and one on a plate in the window. Each candle suspended a ball of light, a luminous fragile glow, which swelled and contracted to the spluttering wick or leaned to the moving air. Their flames pushed weakly against the red of the fire, too tenuous to make much headway, revealing our faces more by casts of darkness than by any clear light they threw.

Next we filled and lit the tall iron lamp and placed it on the table. When the wick had warmed and was drawing properly, we turned it up full strength. The flame in the funnel then sprang alive and rose like a pointed flower, began to sing and shudder and grow more radiant, throwing pools of light on the ceiling. Even so, the kitchen remained mostly in shadow, its walls a voluptuous gloom.

The time had come for my violin practice. I began twanging the strings with relish. Mother was still frying and rolling up pancakes; my brothers lowered their heads and sighed. I propped my music on the mantelpiece and sliced through a Russian Dance while sweet smells of resin mixed with lemon and fat as the dust flew in clouds from my bow. Now and then I got a note just right, and then Mother would throw me a glance. A glance of piercing, anxious encouragement as she sidestepped my swinging arm. Plump in her slippers, one hand to her cheek, her pan beating time in the other, her hair falling down about her ears, mouth working to help out the tune — old and tired though she was, her eyes were a girl's, and it was for looks such as these that I played.

"Splendid!" she cried. "Top-hole! Clap-clap! Now give us another, me lad."

So I slashed away at "William Tell", and when I did that, plates jumped; and Mother skipped gaily around the hearth-rug, and even Tony rocked a bit in his chair.

Meanwhile Jack had cleared some boots from the table and started his inscrutable homework. Tony, in his corner, began to talk to the cat and play with some fragments of cloth. So with the curtains drawn close and the pancakes coming, we settled down to the evening. When the kettle boiled and the toast was made, we gathered and had our tea. We grabbed and dodged and passed and snatched, and packed our mouths like pelicans.

Mother ate always standing up, tearing crusts of the loaf with her fingers, a hand-to-mouth feeding that expressed her vigilance, like that of a wireless-operator at sea. For most of Mother's attention was fixed on the grate, whose fire must never go out. When it threatened to do so she became seized with hysteria, wailing and wringing her hands, pouring on oil and chopping up chairs in a frenzy to keep it alive. In fact it seldom went out completely, though it was very often ill. But Mother nursed it with skill, banking it up every night and blowing hard on the bars every morning. The state of our fire became as important to us as it must have been to a primitive tribe. When it sulked and sank we were filled with dismay; when it blazed all was well with the world; but if — God save us — it went out altogether, then we were clutched by primeval chills. Then it seemed that the very sun had died, that winter had come for ever, that the wolves of the wilderness were gathering near, and that there was no more hope to look for. . . .

But tonight the firelight snapped and crackled, and Mother was in full control. She ruled the range and all its equipment with a tireless, nervous touch. Eating with one hand, she threw on wood with the other, raked the ashes and heated the oven, put on a kettle, stirred the pot, and spread out some more shirts on the guard. As soon as we boys had finished our tea, we pushed all the crockery aside, piled it up roughly at the far end of the table, and settled down under the lamp. Its light was warm and live around us, a kind of puddle of fire of its own. I set up my book and began to draw. Jack worked at his notes and figures. Tony was playing with some cotton reels, pushing them slowly round the table.

—Laurie Lee: *Cider with Rosie*

Revising a Composition: Learning by Re-Doing

How Natural Is Natural?

When George Shuba, famous for being the second ball player ever to pinch-hit a home run in

the World Series, was once complimented on his "natural" hitting ability, his response was the following:

"In the winters ... for fifteen years after loading potatoes or anything else, even when I was in the majors, I'd swing at the clump six hundred times. Every night, and after sixty I'd make an X. Ten Xs and I had my six hundred swings. Then I could go to bed.

"You call that natural? I swung a 44-ounce bat 600 times a night, 4200 times a week, 47 200 swings every winter. Wrists. The fast ball's by you. You gotta wrist it out. Forty-seven thousand two hundred times."

—Roger Kahn: *The Boys of Summer*

Good writing, when finished and presented to readers, seems natural — as if it had flowed effortlessly from the pen of the author. But behind most good writing lies the hard work of revision — that is, cutting, adding, rewording, reorganizing, and checking. The heat of composing results in the first draft; revision makes the finished product. Revision, which means literally 'looking again', demands a clear, critical mind, one that keeps the **reader** in view.

The writer, Alan Sillitoe, explains the importance of revision in his own work:

When I'm writing by hand, my first draft, I always feel marvellous, I'm writing, I'm doing something, that's the best time! The sweat comes when I'm revising. When I've got my first typed copy I go through and through it and it's torment. I don't want to make too heavy weather of it because what does anybody care, but it's blackened with corrections until I can't read it, with additions and subtractions. So I type it again. Clean, marvellous, I think it's a final draft. Then I start reading it, and in about two months' time it's black. Type it again. I think, final, terrific, send this off. I start reading it and I think, oh, this doesn't go here at all, and I start shuffling it in its new arrangement, and so on.

—Alan Burns: "The Loneliness of the Writer" in the *New Statesman*

A Guide for Revision

1. Write your first draft well ahead of the revision. The more time between the two, the more objective your criticism will be.
2. Use double spacing and ample margins in the first draft, so that your revisions can be made on it.
3. Read your first draft aloud. Pretend that you are a reader who knows nothing about the subject, is hard to interest, and wants precise information or arguments.

   In order to be a competent critic of your own work, you must play two roles—that of the reader who asks questions and criticizes, and that of the writer who answers and defends.
4. Read your work several times, each time looking critically at specific points. You cannot deal adequately with paragraph structure, sentence structure, diction, and mechanics all at once. Take each in turn.

Check List for Self-Criticism

PARAGRAPH STRUCTURE

1. Does my opening sentence give the reader a clue as to what I intend to say?
2. Does everything that follows fulfil this promise?
3. Do the ideas advance step by step towards a conclusion?
4. Are the ideas linked from sentence to sentence and from paragraph to paragraph, so that my reader can follow easily the expansion of my main thought?
5. Does the paragraph contain enough details to give a sense of full development and completeness?

SENTENCE STRUCTURE

1. Are all the statement sentences grammatically complete and separate?
2. Are modifiers placed so that my reader cannot mistake my meaning?
3. Are subordinate thoughts made subordinate, and important thoughts emphasized?
4. Is there variety in both sentence length and sentence structure? (Are other orders or combinations possible?)

DICTION

1. Are the words direct, concrete, and unpretentious?
2. Do the verbs carry the burden of my ideas?
3. Can I defend the use of every word in this composition?

MECHANICS

Check these:
1. paragraph indentation

2. end-of-sentence punctuation
3. spelling, including capitalization and possessives
4. correct reference and case of pronouns

THEN: Read aloud for necessary punctuation signals to the reader. Some errors are more easily heard than seen.

FINALLY: Rewrite neatly (or type) for submission.

True Ease in Writing comes from Art, not Chance,
As those move easiest who have learn'd to dance.

—Alexander Pope: "An Essay on Criticism"

Kinds of Paragraph

Although paragraphs are generally classified as **narrative**, **descriptive**, or **expository**, most paragraphs have within them elements of two or even three of these types. Longer compositions are usually a mixture of the three types: it is difficult, for example, to tell a story without describing a character or a setting; and an exposition usually contains some narration and description. What is important is to know your main purpose. Is it to relate an incident, tell a story, describe a person or scene, or to explain something?

Narrative Paragraphs

A narrative paragraph is the simplest to organize, because the development is usually in the order of time.

A good narrative paragraph:

1. begins where the action is relevant to the central idea of the paragraph. Avoid a long preamble.

For example, if you wish to relate a boating incident, omit all such details as getting out the boat and the storm coming up, and start with the accident itself.

Which would be the better opening for such a paragraph?

(a) One day my brother and I decided to go fishing. We went down to the lake and rented a rowboat for an hour. After we . . .

(b) We had been warned not to overload the boat, but had paid no attention.

2. is interesting because it includes significant details, rather than a series of general statements.

Use good, active, descriptive verbs:
The day was rather windy, and the waves were high.
Better: A gusty east wind whipped the waves around us into two-metre peaks.

3. moves towards a climax and then ends.

Here are some examples to study and discuss.

The lorry had been ordered to arrive at the rest-house at seven-thirty for loading, and by eight-thirty we thought we should be well on the road. It was very apparent that we were new to Africa. At ten o'clock we were pacing round and round our mountain of luggage on the veranda, cursing and fuming impotently, scanning the road for the truant lorry. At eleven o'clock a cloud of dust appeared on the horizon and in its midst, like a beetle in a whirlwind, was the lorry. It screeched to a halt below, and the driver dismounted. I noticed an assortment of odd passengers sitting in the back, about twelve of them, chatting happily to each other with their goats, chickens, bags of yams, calabashes of palm wine, and other necessities of travel spread out around them in the lorry. I stormed down to interview the driver, and it was then I learned that it is better not to inquire why a lorry is late in the Cameroons: I was treated to at least six different and contradictory reasons, none of which satisfied anyone except the driver. Wisely leaving the subject, I turned my attention to the crowd in the back of the vehicle. It transpired that this was the driver's wife, this was the driver's wife's cousin, this was the father of the motor-boy, and this was the motor-boy's mother-in-law, and so on. After a prolonged altercation which for shrillness and incomprehensibility could not have been rivalled by any race on earth, they were removed, together with their household goods and livestock. The driver then had to turn the lorry for loading, and my faith in his abilities was rudely shattered when he backed twice into the hibiscus hedge and once into the rest-house wall. Our baggage was then loaded with a speed and lack of care that was frightening, and, as I watched, I wondered how much of our equipment would be left intact on arrival at Manfe. I need not have worried. It turned out later that only the most indispensable and irreplaceable things got broken.

—Gerald Durrell: *The Overloaded Ark*

ORAL ACTIVITY

1. Why does Durrell begin two sentences in the same way: "At ten o'clock . . ." and then, "At eleven o'clock . . ."?

2. What details does he give rather than the following general statements?
   (a) The passengers had brought their belongings with them.
   (b) The driver had brought his relatives with him.
   (c) I doubted that he could drive well.
   (d) The lorry had still not arrived at ten o'clock.

3. Is the phrase "like a beetle in a whirlwind" a good one? Why?

4. Pick out effective verbs the writer uses.

5. Could this paragraph be turned easily into a scene of a play or a movie? Explain.

6. What does the final sentence do for the paragraph?

7. Does this narrative paragraph contain description?

8. What means does the writer use to achieve natural continuity, that is, coherence?

Here is part of a novel about early Canadian pioneers, which contains a narrative about a fire. What devices does the author use to make you as reader "see" this fire—"outwardly" and "inwardly"?

They ran for the houses then and snatched up buckets and formed lines, men, women, and the older children, passing water from the sea, in the atmosphere of hell itself, in a tremendous hiss and crackle that drowned all their voices together, in a choking darkness where none could see more than ten feet and dead leaves whirled, burning like comets. And the little ones and the sick and old stood in the chill sea water at the foot of the slope, whimpering with fright and pain. Mercifully, the final struggle was short. The dribbles of water flung over those crisp wooden roofs and walls were pathetically useless. The westernmost street burst into flame all at once, and as the flames came on, those struggling people were forced back, down the slope, down the beach, and into the water.

Yes, after all their hope and labour and their long enduring they found themselves driven into the sea from which they had landed several months before. And as the fire died at last for lack of fresh fuel and the smoke thinned, they saw the blackened hillside and the rows of naked chimneys standing like tombstones over the ashes of their homes and hopes. Sumter Larrabee, badly burned about the hands, stood there with the rest, the tide lapping about his boots. To his dying day he never forgot that moment, the silence, the smoulder, the gaunt tottering chimneys, and never spoke of it but in a hushed voice.

—Thomas Raddall: *A Harp in the Willows*

ORAL ACTIVITY

1. What vivid details are found in the two paragraphs?

2. What is the effect of the repetition of phrases in the last sentence of the first paragraph?

3. What details make vivid both the scene and the mood of the second paragraph?

4. How does the writer achieve a sense of finality?

With language we can stretch or shorten time. In the following poem, for example, two seconds are stretched out to a kind of "psychological time".

Notice the part played by close observation and the use of detail.

Try writing a piece of your own in which time is stretched or shortened.

FOUL SHOT

With two 60's stuck on the scoreboard
And two seconds hanging on the clock,
The solemn boy in the center of eyes,
Squeezed by silence,
Seeks out the line with his feet,
Soothes his hands along his uniform,
Gently drums the ball against the floor,
Then measures the waiting net,
Raises the ball on his right hand,
Balances it with his left,
Calms it with fingertips,
Breathes,
Crouches,
Waits,
And then through a stretching of stillness,
Nudges it upward.

The ball
Slides up and out,
Lands,
Leans,
Wobbles,
Wavers,
Hesitates,
Exasperates,
Plays it coy
Until every face begs with unsounding screams —
And then
                And then
                        And then,

Right before ROAR-UP,
Dives down and through.

— Edwin A. Hoey

ACTIVITY

Write a short narrative of one or two paragraphs about some event that you experienced or witnessed.

A suggestion:

Think of a **place**, and try to recall an incident that happened there (for example, an episode on a bus, train, or airplane, at school, in a department store, or on the street).

Before turning in your work, make sure that you have fulfilled the requirements of a good narrative paragraph.

Descriptive Paragraphs

Nearly everyone, at some time, must describe someone or something. Notice the close observation in the following descriptive paragraph. Remember that you cannot describe what you have not observed.

Frank O'Connor is of medium height and build; he has heavy silver hair, brushed back; dark, heavy eyebrows; and a mustache. His voice is bass-baritone in pitch and very resonant — what has been described as juke-box bass. His accent is Irish, but with no suggestion of the "flannel-mouth", his intonation musical. He enjoys talk and needed no urging regarding the subject of the interview. His clothes tend toward the tweedy and casual: desert boots, corduroy jacket, rough tweed topcoat; and a bit of California touch evident in a heavy silver ornament hung on a cord around his neck in place of a tie.

— *Writers at Work: The "Paris Review" Interviews*

A factual description, such as the above, has the accuracy of a photograph.

In the following descriptions, how much is fact, and how much is a revelation of the writer's attitude to his subject?

He [Crane] was tall, but exceedingly lank, with narrow shoulders, long arms and legs, hands that dangled a mile out of his sleeves, feet that might have served for shovels, and his whole frame most loosely hung together. His head was small, and flat at top, with huge ears, large green glassy eyes, and a long snipe nose, so that it looked like a weathercock perched upon his spindle neck, to tell which way the wind blew. To see him striding along the profile of a hill on a windy day, with his clothes bagging and fluttering about him, one might have mistaken him for the genius of famine descending upon the earth, or some scarecrow eloped from a cornfield.

— Washington Irving: *The Legend of Sleepy Hollow*

— © Walt Disney Productions: *The Adventures of Ichabod and Mr. Toad*

This is a description of a region in Saskatchewan.

Desolate? Forbidding? There was never a country that in its good moments was more beautiful. Even in drouth or dust storm or blizzard it is the reverse of monotonous, once you have submitted to it with all the senses. You don't get out of the wind, but learn to lean and squint against it. You don't escape sky and sun, but wear them in your eyeballs and on your back. You become acutely aware of yourself. The world is very large, the sky even larger, and you are very small. But also the world is flat, empty, nearly abstract, and in its flatness you are a challenging upright thing, as sudden as an exclamation mark, as enigmatic as a question mark.

— Wallace Stegner: *Wolf Willow*

If you used a photograph or painting to express this feeling, what would it look like? See if you can find photographs that "express" a region or place— or, if you wish, a feeling.

In the following poem, Walt Whitman uses particular, concrete pictures to describe an inner feeling or mood.

What mood do these words suggest: **veiled, living columns of the temple, holy Sabbath, incense, songs of birds in deep recesses, aloft, silence?**

Practise reading this poem aloud so that the sounds and rhythms match the mood.

WOOD ODORS

Morning after a night-rain
The fresh-cool summer-scent
Odors of pine and oak
The shade

Wandering the negligent paths
— the soothing silence,
The stillness and the veiled
The myriad living columns of the temple
The holy Sabbath morning

Incense and songs of birds
in deep recesses
But most the delicate
smells fitting the soul
The sky aloft, seen through
the tree-tops
All the young growth &
green maturity of May
White laurel-blossoms within reach
wood-pinks below — overhead stately tulip-
trees with yellow cup-shaped
flowers,

The meow
meo-o-ow of the cat-bird
cluck of robin, gurgle
of thrush delicious

Over and under these, in the
silence, delicate wood-odors
Birds flitting through the trees
Tangles of old grape-vines

—Walt Whitman

Perhaps you would like to try to write in prose or poetry a concrete description of a mood (for example, sadness, grief, joy, gaiety, anticipation, or peace).

OVERWORKED PHRASES

In description, words should re-create images of sight, sound, odour, and touch. The writer who observes accurately is more likely to use fresh and original language, not someone else's tired phrases.

Description is marred by outworn and overworked phrases such as:

babbling brook	sparkling or twinkling eyes
twinkling stars	strong silent men
purple peaks	magnetic personality
snow-capped peaks	pearly teeth
twittering birds	pretty as a picture
crack of dawn	brown as a berry
wee small hours	blushing bride
devouring seas	the bitter end
patter of rain	with bated breath
sun sinking to rest	in breathless silence
carpet of grass	thrill of a lifetime
clear as crystal	white as a sheet
cold as ice	wend my way

"Words in a pair?
Writer, beware!"

Poetry provides fresh language — a fresh stream running into the mainstream of the language. Reading poetry keeps us aware of the possibilities that lie within the language.

ACTIVITY

After reading the following excerpt from Rupert Brooke's poem "The Great Lover", make a list of things you like or dislike.

You may wish to make a more limited list, such as:

Sounds I Like
Smells I Like
Sounds I Hear on a Sunday Morning
Things I Like to Touch
Sounds I Hear When I Go Camping
Things I Remember at Camp, etc.

These have I loved:
    White plates and cups, clean-gleaming,
Ringed with blue lines; and feathery, faery dust;
Wet roofs, beneath the lamp-light; the strong crust
Of friendly bread; and many-tasting food;
Rainbows; and the blue bitter smoke of wood;
And radiant raindrops couching in cool flowers;
And flowers themselves, that sway through sunny hours,
Dreaming of moths that drink them under the moon;
Then, the cool kindliness of sheets, that soon
Smooth away trouble; and the rough male kiss
Of blankets; grainy wood; live hair that is
Shining and free; blue-massing clouds; the keen
Unpassioned beauty of a great machine;
The benison of hot water; furs to touch;
The good smell of old clothes; and other such —
The comfortable smell of friendly fingers,
Hair's fragrance, and the musty reek that lingers
About dead leaves and last year's ferns. . . .

ACTIVITY

Choose one topic from the suggestions given below, and write a short descriptive composition.

1. a person (for example, a baby, a friend, a relative, a well-known person, a person who impressed you)

2. a crowd (for example, shopping, in a bus, at an accident, at a party, at the rink)

3. a costume (for example, of the past, for a party, at a masquerade)

4. a memory

Expository Paragraphs

Exposition is the kind of writing we use most often —to explain, to give information, or to answer questions on examinations. In argument, a special kind of exposition, we try to convince others of our opinions and views. Good exposition demands careful preparation and careful planning, and thorough knowledge, because if we do not know, we cannot explain.

GIVING DIRECTIONS

We are often asked to give directions; we must tell someone how to make something, or how something works, or explain how an experiment is conducted, how a game is played, or how a machine operates. To explain well, we must:

1. have accurate knowledge of the process—all the reader needs to know.
2. know what is important and what is not.
3. analyse the process into steps and arrange these steps in order.

How well have these standards been applied in the following expository paragraphs?

Dumas's skin-diving technique consisted of floating face under water and breathing through a schnorkel tube. When he spotted some attraction below, he would execute a maneuver called the *coup de reins*, literally 'stroke of the loins', the technique the whale uses to sound. For a floating man, it consists of bending from the waist and pointing the head and torso down. Then the legs are thrown up in the air with a powerful snap and the diver plummets straight down. Lightning dives require well-trained, wide-open Eustachian tubes to deal with the rapidly mounting pressure.

—Capt. J.-Y. Cousteau: *The Silent World*

"Cutting out", it was fittingly called, and this performance was, and still is, the highest art of the cowboy. Cutting out required a specially trained pony, one that could "turn on a dime", and a rider who had a sharp eye, good muscular reflexes, and who was an artist at handling a lariat. After selecting an animal to be separated from the herd, the rider and his horse would begin an adroit game of twisting and turning, or sudden stops and changes of pace. Range cattle were adept at dodging, and if a cowboy's pony was not a "pegger" the chased animal would soon lose itself in the herd. Some horses never learned the art of cutting out; others seemed to sense instinctively what was demanded of them. For the latter the work was pure sport and show. Working with the best type of cutting pony, a cowboy could drop his reins over the saddle horn and by pressure of a knee indicate the cow he wanted, leaving the rest of the action to his mount. If calves were being cut out, the objective was usually the mother cow. The calf would follow her out of the herd into the open where it could be roped with ease.

—Dee Brown and Martin F. Schmitt: "A Roundup" from *Trail Driving Days*

What do you learn from the opening sentence? What does the reader expect because of the statement, "the highest art of the cowboy"? What does the word "fittingly" suggest about the author's attitude?

Why does the writer put "turn on a dime" within quotation marks? What technical words of "cow-punching" are within quotation marks? Why?

EXERCISES ON GIVING AND FOLLOWING DIRECTIONS[1]

Here are directions for the diagram below:

"Draw a straight horizontal line. Then place on it, 1.25 cm apart, three equilateral triangles of different sizes with the largest on the left and the smallest in the middle. Now draw above the line a semicircle that bisects the bases of the two outside triangles. Put an x in the part of the triangle that is also within the semicircle. Print 'Keep off the grass' in the part of the semicircle outside all the triangles."

---

[1]Suggested by an article by Eric W. Johnson in the *English Journal*, Feb. 1958, where the article is expanded in detail.

ACTIVITY

Give precise directions for a diagram of your own design. Write them so clearly that a person cannot go wrong.

Read the directions to your class, and have the class draw the diagram as a test of the precision and clarity of your exposition. Two or three volunteers may put their diagrams on the blackboard. Did they follow your directions, or were your directions imprecise?

ACTIVITY

Write precise directions for doing one of the following:

1. making a bed

2. packing a suitcase

3. setting your hair

4. the care and cleaning of a record

5. placing a long-distance call person-to-person, or by direct dialling

6. looking after house plants

Have these read aloud to the class for criticism.

ARGUMENT

"Facts Are Sacred; Opinions Are Free"

Argument is a form of exposition that aims to present evidence or give reasons in support of an opinion. Argument attempts to convince and move others to action. Because democracy is based upon free expression of opinion, we should become skilled in presenting our arguments and in assessing the arguments of others.

When preparing to write, take time to state your opinion in one sentence. Such a statement will give direction to your argument, for example,

University education should be free.

All examinations should be abolished.

There is too much emphasis in Canada on professional sports.

Then list the factual evidence to support this opinion. Few problems are one-sided. Your argument is strengthened if you consider the evidence of opposing points of view. You are entitled to your opinion if you can defend it honestly.

The editorial pages and "Letters to the Editor" sections of newspapers and magazines are important forums for the exchange of opinion.

The following argument is in the form of a letter to the editor, in answer to statements made in an article in *Maclean's* magazine. (Note that only a portion of the letter is quoted here.)

What qualifications has the writer to speak on the subject?

Does giving his qualifications help his argument?

What facts and arguments does he put forward?

As an academic chemist with no particular designs on the health of my fellow citizens, I find it hard to understand the reasons for the emotional, even slightly hysterical reaction to the word "chemical", especially chemical added to foods, as exemplified in your article on food pollution (Sept. 10). There seems to be an assumption that any substance found in nature is good and anything produced by man is probably bad. Yet the people who feel this way probably ride on synthetic rubber tires, use synthetic gasoline, oil, and anti-freeze, drink out of synthetic plastic glasses, wash them with synthetic detergents, and in a thousand other ways accept contact with the chemist's creations. How does the chemist who prepared salt, white sugar, vinegar, and other traditional chemical additives to food become a monster when he develops synthetic sodium glutamate (to enhance meat flavors), synthetic sweeteners (as a boon to diabetics), or synthetic vanillin (a cheap purified version of the substance that gives vanilla its flavor)? Is this the same prejudice that allows oranges and butter to be colored, but not margarine? Do they object to iodized salt, chlorinated water, pasteurized milk, and synthetic vitamins added to butter and flour?

—P. M. Laughton, Chairman, Department of Chemistry, Carleton University, Ottawa

The following editorial from *Maclean's* argues in a different manner, more lightly. (This is only the beginning of the article.)

If I wake up on Boxing Day with my usual bout of Christmas liverishness I shall have to exercise all my reserves of self control to refrain from picking up the nearest gift hockey stick and taking off after certain men in white coats. I am speaking of those agricultural Frankensteins who during the past fifteen years have transformed our traditional Christmas fare — turkey, chicken, goose, and duck—into table birds that have the appearance, texture and taste of a toasted watermelon.

What has happened to those noble tom turkeys of my youth, the long, lean, big cousins of the pheasant that used to run up to forty pounds in weight and came to my family's table redolent of the wild autumn berries on which they'd fed in ditch, hedgerow and copse? Where have they gone, those crackling cockerels, capons and big fat hens that filled our Christmas season with the appetizing aroma of poultry raised on a natural diet of corn and grit? When shall we taste again those geese and duck that had enriched their flesh on the succulent life that swims in pond and stream?

ACTIVITY

Look in newspapers and magazines for short editorials or letters on a controversial subject in which you are interested. Then write an editorial or letter supporting or opposing the arguments.

Where possible, use facts to support your arguments.

ACTIVITY

Write a short argument about some subject in which you are interested. Treat it lightly, as:

The "Manly" Art of Wrestling

or seriously, as:

Everyone in Canada Should Be Bilingual

Some topics on which you may have an opinion are:

The Curriculum	Violence in Sports
Women's "Lib"	Television (Heroes, Use of
Land Use	Prime Time, Presentation of
	News, etc.)

ACTIVITY

Advertisements are arguments. They set out reasons to convince you to buy products.

Examine carefully some advertisements taken from magazines or newspapers. Choose advertisements for products you have used. What arguments are presented? What facts are presented? Are the arguments valid? Write a paragraph analysing the arguments presented.

The "How to" type of exposition is often used by skilled writers for humour or satire. In the following paragraph, for example, James Thurber uses the "how to" or "recipe" style to show the "ingredients" of a soap opera.

A soap opera is a kind of sandwich, whose recipe is simple enough, although it took years to compound. Between thick slices of advertising, spread twelve minutes of dialogue, add predicament, villainy, and female suffering in equal measure, throw in a dash of nobility, sprinkle with tears, season with organ music, cover with a rich announcer sauce, and serve five times a week. A soap opera may also contain a teaser ("Be sure to tune in next Monday for a special announcement"), a give-away ("Send in a box top and twenty-five cents for a gorgeous lovebird brooch"), a contest offer ("Complete this sentence and win a Bendix washer"), or a cowcatcher or hitchhike; that is, a brief commercial for another of the sponsor's products, such as a Kolynos plug on an Anacin program. It is the hope of every advertiser to habituate the housewife to an engrossing narrative whose optimum length is forever and at the same time to saturate all levels of her consciousness with the miracle of a given product, so that she will be aware of it all the days of her life and mutter its name in her sleep.

—James Thurber: *O Pioneers!*

You may wish to try this kind of "tongue-in-cheek" exposition. Here are a few suggestions for topics:

How to Catch a . . .

How to Make a . . .

How to Be Unpopular

How to Tell Fish Stories

How to Be a World Traveller Without Going Anywhere

How to Prepare for an Examination

How to Sell . . .

How to Get Homework Done

You may also try to turn one of your serious expository paragraphs into a humorous one — or turn your "tongue-in-cheek" exposition into a serious one.

In words, in whispering, stumbling words, in the litter and ceaseless drift of words, is my . . . searching for my own identiy . . . [and] the articulation that will go on, at the heart of all experience, till at last all burdens are laid down and I need no more words, not even amen and goodnight.

—Walter Nash: *Our Experience of Language*

... she'll vish there wos more, and that's the great art o' letter writin'.

—Dickens: *Pickwick Papers*

Ottawa June 20, 1884

My dear Professor

Pardon me for stealing your Hat. I owe you a new one. Get one from Clark Wright or anywhere else & charge it to me.

Will you kindly send me the Bismuth prescription.

My address is St. Patrick P.Q. We hope to get off tomorrow. Love to Louisa,

yours etc.

John A. Macdonald

(letter from Sir John A. Macdonald to his brother-in-law, the Reverend Doctor James Williamson)

—*Affectionately Yours—The Letters of Sir John A. Macdonald and His Family*, ed. by J. K. Johnson.

Chapter 6

"Yours sincerely"

Writing Letters

Postcard addressed to:
  Miss H. D. Wilson,
  St. Andrews,
  N.B.,
  Canada.
dated 1880.

"Talking on Paper": Informal Letters

Speak with the pen!—that is what the best letter-writers do, whether they are literary artists, such as Lamb and ... Keats, ... or the unknown pen-gossips.

—E. V. Lucas: *Fireside and Sunshine*

Since the beginning of writing, the letter has provided one of the widest opportunities for self-expression. Friendships, dreams, and ambitions, troubles, adventures, and conspiracies have all found their way into the letter. Its range is wide, from the chit-chat of friends, to the innermost reflections of St. Paul writing to the Corinthians.

"Why Don't You Write?"

—© 1972 United Feature Syndicate, Inc.

"Write when written to" is the first rule of letter-writing. If you are not methodical by nature, follow Lewis Carroll's advice:

If the letter is to be an answer to another, begin by getting out that other letter and reading it through, in order to refresh your memory as to what it is you have to answer, and as to your correspondent's present address.... Next, *address and stamp the envelope*. "What! Before writing the *letter*?" Most certainly.

A letter reveals the personality of the writer. Make sure that its appearance, tone, language, and content represent you at your best, with no pretensions and no posing.

ACTIVITY

How often do you write letters? To whom do you write? How many of your letters are requests? thank-you letters? newsy letters? What kind of letters do you like to get? Why? Discuss in groups and then report to the class.

The Form of the Letter

The conventions we follow when we write a letter will depend most of all on our relationship with the person to whom we are writing. If we are writing to a very close friend, the form of our letter may be quite casual. But when we are writing more formal letters, such as thank-you notes, or letters to adults we don't know well, the form becomes more important. Keep in mind the receiver of the letter. What will he or she best respond to?

There are five parts to a formal letter: **heading, salutation, body, complimentary close,** and **signature.** In most cases the heading should be conventional. Accurate dates and return addresses are especially important. (Why?) The salutation, complimentary close, and signature express the relationship that exists between writer and the reader.

Look at the skeleton letters on pages 191–4. Why do you think most of us agree to follow these conventions of form? Why do we address envelopes the way we do? Can you think of a better way to set up a letter? an envelope? What recent changes in addressing letters have you noticed?

Arrangements

Two forms of arranging the five parts of a letter are used:

1. **the indented form** — most frequently used when we write in longhand.
2. **the block form** — used in most typewritten letters. (Why?)

Choose the one you like.

Open and Closed Punctuation

We also have a choice of two kinds of punctuation in the headings.

1. The **closed** form has a comma at the end of the first three lines and a period at the end of the last line:

Indented

> 2511 Wallace Crescent,
> Vancouver, B.C.,
> V6R 3V3,
> February 10, 1976.

Block

> 2511 Wallace Crescent,
> Vancouver, B.C.,
> V6R 3V3,
> February 10, 1976.

2. The **open** form has no punctuation at the ends of the lines in the heading, but within each line there is conventional punctuation.

Indented

> 2511 Wallace Crescent
> Vancouver, B.C.
> V6R 3V3
> February 10, 1976

Block

> 2511 Wallace Crescent
> Vancouver, B.C.
> V6R 3V3
> February 10, 1976

Block Form—Open Punctuation

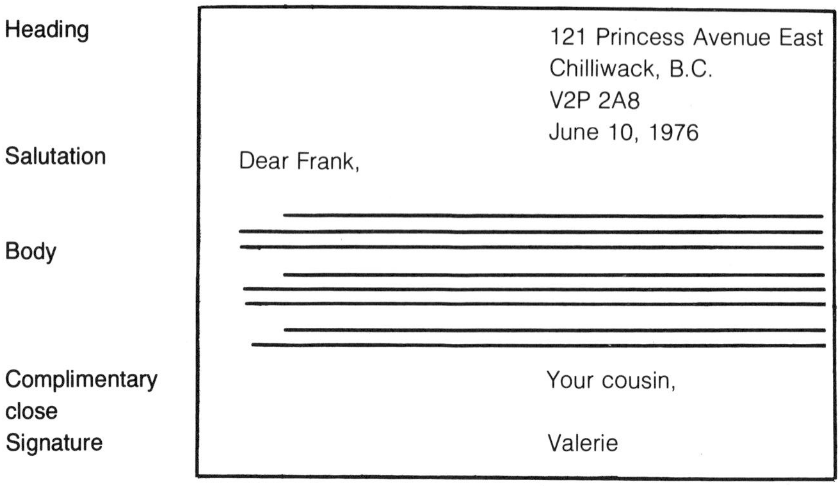

Heading

121 Princess Avenue East
Chilliwack, B.C.
V2P 2A8
June 10, 1976

Salutation

Dear Frank,

Body

_____

Complimentary
close

Your cousin,

Signature

Valerie

Indented Form—Closed Punctuation

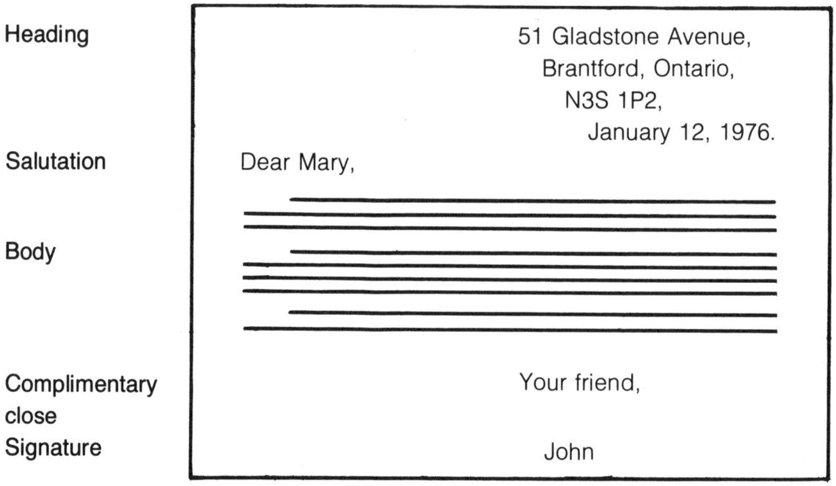

Heading

51 Gladstone Avenue,
Brantford, Ontario,
N3S 1P2,
January 12, 1976.

Salutation

Dear Mary,

Body

_____

Complimentary
close

Your friend,

Signature

John

ACTIVITY

Write out, punctuate, capitalize, and arrange the following items correctly:

Headings:

100 south drive toronto ontario M4W 1R6 january 15 1976

suite 5 lakeview apartments 95 wendover drive hamilton ontario L9C 2S8 february 20 1976

Salutations:

dear cousin frank   dear jane

dear mr cannon   my dear miss thomas

Closings:

yours very sincerely mary   yours tom

your affectionate son richard

your loving niece judy philips

What does **postal code** mean? How is the Canadian postal code system organized? Why is it used?

ADDRESS LABELS

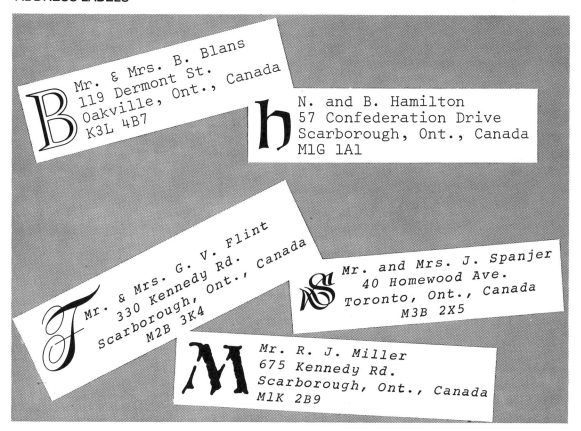

Design your own!

The Envelope

The standard format of the envelope helps to get your letter — whether personal or business — to its destination as quickly as possible. The block form with open punctuation is now the more common choice, but you may use the indented form or closed punctuation. Here are two examples.

(a) Block form, and open punctuation:

Return address (Why necessary?)	R. E. Smythe 2511 Wallace Crescent Vancouver, B.C. V6R 3V3
Mailing address	The Macmillan Company of Canada Limited 70 Bond Street Toronto, Ontario
Postal code	M5B 1X3

(b) Indented form, and closed punctuation:

Return address	R. E. Smythe,
	  2511 Wallace Crescent,
	    Vancouver, B.C.,
	      V6R 3V3

Mailing address	Mr. Arthur Lambert,
	  58 Ormiston Road,
	    Winnipeg, Manitoba,

Postal code	R2J 2Z2

ACTIVITY

Get this "letter perfect"!

1. Copy the following letter in correct form (including paragraphing) on a page of personal stationery, to show that you know how to arrange a friendly letter on paper. Use your best handwriting.

2. Place the letter in its envelope and address it properly. Do not seal the envelope.

trout creek motel bonner's ferry idaho 03429 july 20 1976 dear sydney we arrived late this evening after an exciting trip from banff it is too late to try out the trout stream at our door but not too late to tell you about some of our adventures in the canadian rockies much has happened since i last wrote to you from calgary tom and i thought nothing could be more exciting than the stampede i don't know how many rolls of film we used to catch the chuckwagon races bronco busting and calf roping to say nothing of the colourful costumes of indians we persuaded father to give us an advance on our allowance after we arrived in banff we didn't want to miss the bears in the park or the scenery around lake louise and needed more film once out of the park we settled back just to enjoy the scenery when we got near the border between british columbia and idaho we stopped to eat dad said we could have anything we wanted because we would not get another chance until morning tom and i had jumbo hamburgers and chips and washed it down with pop after we left the cafe we stopped at a service station for gas while dad was busy we went inside and bought a dozen oranges at the customs the officer asked us if we'd bought anything when i mentioned the oranges he looked disgusted and asked me to hand them over he took them and tossed them in a garbage can conveniently placed for those stupid enough to forget regulations boy i wish i had one of them now but i'll have to settle for water tonight tomorrow we plan to do a bit of fishing if we get up early enough after that it's home to vancouver thanks for giving us such an interesting time on your father's farm tom and i enjoyed our weekend with your uncle near winnipeg your sincere friend gordon p.s. by the way our new address will be 2511 wallace crescent vancouver b.c. V6R 3V3

THE APPEARANCE OF A LETTER

The appearance of a letter will vary according to the relationship between the writer and the reader. But whatever the shape or size of the paper you use or the colour of the ink, the important thing is to make your letter legible. Who wants to receive a letter that can't be read?

Before the invention of the telephone the letter was **the** medium for communication for people separated by distance. The following paragraph illustrates the importance of the conventions of letter-writing for the pioneers of nineteenth-century Canada:

Letter writing was of course an art, and the fashionable Spencerian script needed much practice. Both books of exercises to upgrade the penmanship and books on how to write letters were very popular among the less educated and were available in French and English. Men always used white paper but ladies might use delicately tinted papers. Scented notes were in and out of fashion from time to time. Letter-writing books contain examples to cover every contingency from asking for a loan to writing a love letter. One of the most charming is "Chesterfield's art of letter-writing simplified. Being a guide to friendly, affectionate, polite and business correspondence, containing a large collection of the most valuable information relative to the art of letter-writing, with clear and complete instructions how to begin and end correspondence, rules for punctuation and spelling, etc." It was published at thirty-five cents in 1857, sent anywhere in the United States and the Canadas. One copy owned by a man, inscribed "Lytton, British Columbia, 1871" has been found. The concern for proper form reached far into the wilderness.

—Una Abrahamson: *God Bless Our Home: Domestic Life in Nineteenth Century Canada*

Where does the word **stamp** come from? What does it tell you about the earliest kinds of postage stamps?

Have a stamp-collector give a talk about how stamps are designed.

THE PENNY POST: 1839—40

The same decades that saw the rapid growth of the railway system and the electric telegraph, saw the triumph of the penny post, established by the unselfish and tireless efforts of Rowland Hill, supported by the popular demand, against the indifference of statesmen and the angry obstruction of the unreformed civil service. Prior to this great change, the poor who moved in search of work either inside the island or by emigration overseas, could seldom exchange news with the parents and friends they had left behind, owing to the heavy charge made for the receipt of letters. Rowland Hill's plan for a postal delivery prepaid by a cheap adhesive stamp, enabled the poor, for the first time in the history of man, to communicate with the loved ones from whom they were separated. And since the business world found cheap postage a boon, and since it proved a great financial success after it had been forced upon the obdurate Post

Office, the new method was soon imitated in every civilized country in the world. In this great reform the State had necessarily to be made the instrument, but the thought and the leadership had come from an individual, backed by public opinion.

—G. M. Trevelyan: *English Social History*

Notes of Invitation.

Mr. Walter Hood presents his regards to Miss Jennie Mason, and requests the pleasure of escorting her to the Grand Opera, to-morrow evening.

246 Monroe Ave., April 10.

—ACCEPTANCE.—

Miss Jennie Mason presents her compliments to Mr. Hood, and accepts with pleasure his kind invitation to accompany him to the Opera.

April 11th

—Una Abrahamson: *God Bless Our Home: Domestic Life in Nineteenth Century Canada*

QUESTIONS FOR DISCUSSION

1. What does the letter do that the telephone doesn't?
2. Is the telephone (like the letter before penny postage) a convenient system of communication only for those who can afford it?
3. Why do you think Canadians use the telephone more than the people of any other country?
4. Why do businesses still prefer a letter rather than a telephone call for certain kinds of procedures?

Two commemorative Canadian stamps issued in 1968-69.

—NASA

TELSTAR—The experimental communication satellite built by American Telephone and Telegraph and launched by NASA. This photograph is a composite showing the actual spacecraft in a space environment. The star background was taken by Mt. Palomar Observatory from which NASA made the composite.

FOR DISCUSSION

1. How do you think the form of letters may change in the future?
2. What is **Canunet**?
3. How important is the **look** of a letter: the mistakes, the handwriting, the spacing — all the personal signals that accompany the words?

The Body of the Letter

The important part of a letter—the real "letter"—is the body, that is, what you write between "Dear—" and "Yours sincerely".

Here, for instance, is a letter that initiated the atomic age and started a chain of events that has changed all our lives. Notice that important news can be expressed with restraint and simplicity.

August 2, 1939.

The President,
White House,
Washington.

The results of the research recently pursued by E. Fermi and L. Szilard, submitted to me in manuscript, have revealed that we may in the immediate future expect to find the element uranium capable of being transformed into a new and considerable source of energy. This new phenomenon may also lead to the construction of excessively powerful bombs. A single bomb of this type, transported by ship and allowed to explode in a port, could destroy the whole port and the surrounding territory.

A. Einstein

A. Einstein

"He builds a nice fire but he has nothing to say!"
—GRIN AND BEAR IT by George Lichty, Courtesy of Field Newspaper Syndicate

Who Is Your Reader?

When we write informal, personal letters we have an advantage: receptive readers. Good letters establish and strengthen a relationship. They demonstrate an awareness of the reader and capture just the right tone. Good letters are also informative and legible, and invite a response.

correspondence:
cor — 'with, together'
re — 'back, in return'
spondere — 'to promise'

ORAL ACTIVITY

Do you keep letters? If so, why? What makes a letter worth keeping? What makes a letter worth answering?

ACTIVITY

Writing a letter, like writing in a diary, is "talking on paper". You may have been using a diary to develop this habit of "talking on paper" without worrying about the formal conventions of writing. If you have, choose some notes from your diary that interest you (a description of a place you have been to, a day you enjoyed, or someone you met) and incorporate your notes into a letter to a friend. What difference does your audience make to the way you shape the material? What do you leave out? What do you add?

HINTS ABOUT THE CONTENT OF INFORMAL LETTERS ✓

1. Before writing, re-read the letter you are answering. (Why?)
2. Avoid long apologies for not having written sooner.
3. Be natural. Avoid meaningless superlatives such as "darling", "lovely", and "wonderful" — leave the gushing to the oil-wells.
4. Keep your reader in mind. Do not become so engrossed in your own interests that you forget the interests of the person to whom you are writing.

ACTIVITY

Imagine someone coming to your town as an exchange student. Write a letter to this student giving information about activities in your town, suggesting what to bring, and asking your friend what he or she would like to know that you haven't mentioned.

Now write the reverse letter, as though you were the exchange student asking questions about your visit. You might imagine that you are going somewhere in Quebec, in which case you could try writing the letter in French.

ACTIVITY

Write two different letters about one event that took place in your home town (a) to someone who knows your home town, and (b) to someone who doesn't. In other words, use the same material but treat it differently.

ACTIVITY

Imagine that a classmate has been in the hospital two weeks. List topics that you think would interest her or him.

Occasions for Social Notes

Although most of the friendly letters we write are just "visits on paper", some situations require special kinds of letters. Among the most frequent are the thank-you note, the "bread-and-butter" note, the informal invitation and reply, the note of congratulation, and the expression of sympathy. Because these social notes are sometimes difficult to write, many people rely on cards printed to suit almost any occasion. Such cards are rarely as effective as a personal note in one's own handwriting.

Thank-you Notes

Be prompt to acknowledge a gift or a kindness. The best thank-you letter is the one that is **sincere** and **immediate**.

Something like the following letter is usually adequate.

March 5, 1976.

Dear Aunt Susan,

Thank you for your gift of Edward McCourt's **Saskatchewan**. Reading it helped me to remember the many towns we saw on our trip last summer.

Please give my best to Uncle John. Tell him I'm still working on my boat, but hope to have it ready for our holidays at Lake of the Woods.

Thanks again for the book. Dad is reading it now and there's a strange, far-away look in his eyes.

Your nephew,
Tom

The "Bread-and-butter" Note

When you have stayed overnight or have spent a weekend in someone else's home, good manners demand that you acknowledge this hospitality in a letter to the hostess. Your note should be specific, expressing how much you enjoyed and appreciated your visit — and it **must be prompt**.

Even though you may have been the guest of the son or daughter, the first letter you write is to the mother of your friend. Make her feel that all her efforts for you were worth while.

Here is a sample:

Wednesday

Dear Mrs. Booth,

Thank you for giving me such a good time at your house over the long weekend. I don't know when I have had so much fun. The party on Saturday must have taken much of your time and I want to say a special thank-you for the trouble you took to arrange it.

Please remember me to Mr. Booth. He probably experienced the noisiest weekend of his life. I'm still enjoying the stories he told about his camping trip last summer.

Sincerely yours,
Mary Thomson

Informal Invitations

Most informal invitations can be made over the telephone, but an invitation to a special party is more appropriate if written. A class invitation to parents, such as the following, is an example.

Room 110
Sir Winston Churchill High School
December 15, 1975

Dear Mr. and Mrs. Thomas,

Our class is giving a tea for parents. It will be in the Home Economics room from three-thirty to five on Thursday afternoon, December 18. We would be pleased to have you come.

Sincerely yours,
Jean Davidson
Class Secretary

All written invitations must be answered promptly, and should show that you have not misunderstood the place and time of the occasion.

12 Elm Park Road
Winnipeg, Manitoba
R2M 0V9
December 16, 1975

Dear Jean,

Thank you for your invitation to your class tea from three-thirty to five o'clock on Thursday afternoon, December 18. My husband and I are delighted to accept.

Sincerely yours,
Margaret Thomas

---

12 Elm Park Road
Winnipeg, Manitoba
R2M 0V9
December 16, 1975

Dear Jean,

Thank you for your invitation to your class tea from three-thirty to five o'clock on Thursday afternoon, December 18. Unfortunately, Mr. Thomas and I are unable to attend. I hope we will have another opportunity to meet your class.

Sincerely yours,
Margaret Thomas

The Letter of Congratulation

The letter of congratulation should be a spontaneous expression of encouragement and good feeling. Your own sincerity will tell you what to write.

The Letter of Sympathy

At no time is a letter appreciated more than in time of distress. Gentleness and sincerity expressed in a note can be truly comforting. But it is probably the most difficult of all letters to write and so personal that a textbook should not suggest a model. If your sympathy is genuine, you will take the time to find the words to express it. A note, which has cost you time and effort, is much better than a printed card.

ACTIVITY

Write an appropriate note for three of the following situations:

1. Your aunt and your uncle will soon celebrate their twenty-fifth wedding anniversary.

2. Ask your grandparents to send you a history of your family. Tell them you are writing a report entitled *Family Tree*.
3. You have just returned from a weekend holiday in a lakeshore cottage. Write your bread-and-butter letter.
4. Your grandmother has sent you a pair of woollen socks that she knitted herself. They are rather gaudy and much too small. Write an appropriate thank-you letter. (This one is difficult.)
5. Write a letter to your parents telling them what you have learned in the past month.

Postcards

ACTIVITY

Make up some humorous postcards of your own along the line of the examples shown, using real, historical, or fictitious characters that interest you.

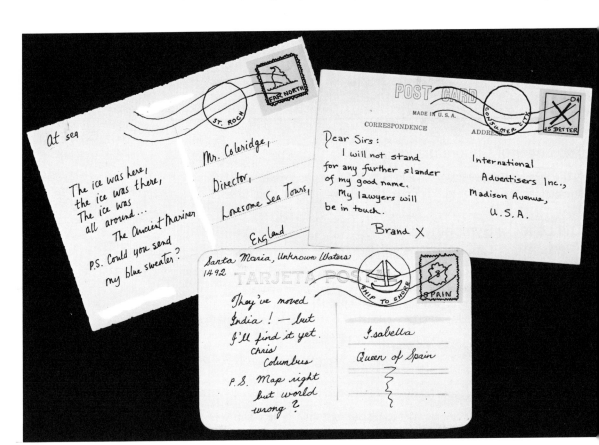

ACTIVITY

Imagine that you are on a holiday and writing postcards to three people who know each other and are likely to share their news from you. Rather than sending the same message to each, try writing each postcard so that it contains a special message for each person.

Some Letters to Read

The great mathematician and philosopher Alfred North Whitehead once observed that history should be written more from letters because good letter writers "put in what we want to know, how people felt about things, how they died, what they ate and more, what they worried about, and all those immediacies which make the life of an epoch live again."

On the following pages are some letters written at different times in history, in a variety of situations. Read them and then discuss whether these letters from the past possess Whitehead's characteristics of the good letter.

LETTER 1

Here is an interesting letter written home by a young man at Christmas-time. Despite faulty punctuation and spelling, this is a good letter. Why?

Can you find in his style of writing and choice of language any evidence of his knowing the Bible?

December 1876

Dear Old Zell

I dare say you will be surprised to hear again so soon from your "nere do weal" but I must write to wish you all a very merry Christmas & a happy New Year & many of them dear old girl. I hope you will think of me when you drink Absent friends. Of course we are preparing to keep Xmas as best we can, as decorating our rooms with flags, evergreens, appropriate mottoes & last but by no means least our arms & accoutrements, saddlery & all burnished till they flash & sparkle in the bright firelight like the cut glass pendants of a chandeleir, altogether it looks very pretty & reminds one of the Christmas feasts in olden times when the walls were garnished with the arms of the baron & his retainers, with here & there a stag head Stag heads are so plentiful here that no one thinks of sticking one on the wall as a curiousity; Our feast consists of venison, buffalo tongues & beef which our old coun-

trymen say is equal to the "roast beef of old England" so much for a foundation, prairie chicken, mountain grous, jack rabbit & antelope choops   as ballast all kinds puddings, pies, tarts, &c almonds, raisons, walnuts, hazelnuts, Brazil nuts, all kinds of sweetmeats, of course the largest plum duff ever recorded & would you believe it whiskey ad lib   yes such is the degeneracy of the age that we the Mounted temperance association, we who are paid to slay kill & utterly destroy all whiskey traders are all flaming drunk under the Commissioners very nose but he having no nose smells not. Col McLeod has been ordered to Ottawa & we expect that his reign will be a short & merry one & we are all ready to cry "La roi est mort, vive la roi".

The Winter so far has been milder than any I remember in Canada with scarcely any snow. first we have a little snow, then a little frost & then a Chinook wind which you must feel to understand   for instance two of us were doing sentry looking out for whiskey traders on top of a high bare hill one very cold day, we took it in turns to go down for a warm every hour well I was down in the hollow running quarter heats against time when I lifted up mine eyes & lo my chum was lying comfortably in the snow taking a smoke, of course I went up to enquire whence this thusness & discovered that a wind as warm as we get in July was blowing right through the Coutanie pass, on a cold day you feel a puff of hot air all of a sudden & the snow if there is any disappears at the rate of an inch an hour till eather snow or wind call time. whence it comes or wither it goes we know not but we accept it as it is & are thankful. Our horses are herded on the open prairie & are doing well they are to be kept out all winter

Good bye dear old girl
Believe me ever
Your loving brother
F C with fond love to
you T C & the Atoms

The writer of this letter, which is now in the Manitoba Provincial Archives, was twenty-three-year-old Frances Fraser Galt "Frank" Carruthers from Toronto. He had enlisted in the North West Mounted Police the previous year and was stationed at Fort Macleod (in present Alberta) when he wrote to his older sister Georgiana, affectionately known as Zell. The T C mentioned at the end was Thomas Clarkson, his brother-in-law.

LETTER 2

For many parents the most special letters from their children are those their children first wrote.

Does your family have a letter you wrote when you were very young?

Here is Winston Churchill's first letter to his mother.

My dear Mamma I hope you are quite well I thank you very very much for the beautiful presents those Soldiers and Flags and Castle they are so nice it was so kind of you and dear Papa I send you my love and a great many kisses Your loving Winston.

LETTER 3

The copy of a letter written by Sir Walter Raleigh to his wife (on the night before he expected to be put to death (1603)). Note: spelling and punctuation have been modernized.

You shall now receive, dear wife, my last words in these my last lines. My love I send you, that you may keep it when I am dead; and my counsel, that you may remember it when I am no more. I would not, by my will, present you with sorrows, dear Besse. Let them go to the grave with me, and be buried in the dust. And, seeing it is not the will of God that ever I shall see you any more in this life, bear it patiently and with a heart like thy self.

First, I send you all the thanks which my heart can conceive, or my words can express, for your many travails and cares taken for me, which — though they have not taken effect as you wished—yet my debt to you is not the less; but pay it I never shall in this world.

Secondly, I beseech you, for the love you bare me living, do not hide yourself many days after my death, but by your travails seek to help your miserable fortunes, and the right of your poor child. Your mourning cannot avail me; I am but dust.

You shall understand that my land was conveyed *bona fide* to my child. The writings were drawn at midsummer twelvemonths. My honest cousin Brett can testify so much, and Dalberie, too, can remember somewhat therein. And I trust my blood will quench the malice that have thus cruelly murdered me; and that they will not seek also to kill thee and thine with extreme poverty.

To what friend to direct thee I know not, for all mine have left me in the true time of trial; and I plainly perceive that my death was determined from the first day. Most sorry I am (God knows) that, being thus surprised with death, I can leave you in no better estate. God is my witness I meant you all my office of wines, or all that I could have purchased by selling it; half my stuff, and all my jewels; but some on't for the boy. But God hath prevented all my resolutions; even that great God that ruleth all in all. If you can live free from want, care for no more; the rest is but vanity.

Love God, and begin betimes to repose yourself on Him; therein shall you find true and lasting riches, and endless comfort. For the rest, when you have travailed and wearied all your thoughts over all sorts of worldly cogitations, you shall sit down by Sorrow in the end. Teach your son also to love and fear God, while he is yet young, that the fear of God may grow up with him. And the same God will be a husband unto you, and a father unto him; a husband and a father which can not be taken from you.

Bayly oweth me two hundred pounds, and Adrian Gilbert six hundred pounds. In Jersey I have also much money owing me. Besides, the arrearages of the wines will pay my debts. And, howsoever you do, for my soul's sake, pay all poor men.

When I am gone, no doubt you shall be sought by many, for the world thinks that I was very rich; but take heed of the pretences of men and of their affections; for they last not but in honest and worthy men. And no greater misery can befall you in this life than to become a prey, and afterwards to be despised. I speak not this (God knows) to dissuade you from marriage — for it will be best for you, both in respect of the world and of God. As for me, I am no more yours, nor you mine. Death hath cut us asunder; and God hath divided me from the world, and you from me.

Remember your poor child for his father's sake, who chose you and loved you in his happiest times. Get those letters (if it be possible) which I writ to the Lords, wherein I sued for my life. God is my witness, it was for you and yours that I desired life. But it is true that I disdain myself for begging it. For know it (dear wife) that your son is the son of a true man, and one who, in his own respect, despiseth Death, and all his misshapen and ugly shapes.

I cannot write much. God he knows how hardly I steal this time, while others sleep; and it is also high time that I should separate my thoughts from the world. Beg my dead body, which living was denied thee; and either lay it at Sherborne, if the land continue, or in Exeter church, by my father and mother. I can say no more. Time and Death call me away.

The everlasting, powerful, infinite and omnipotent God, that almighty God who is goodness itself, the true life and true light, keep thee and thine; and have mercy on me, and teach me to forgive my persecutors and accusers; and send us to meet in His glorious kingdom. My dear wife, farewell. Bless my poor boy; pray for me; and let my good God hold you both in His arms.

Written with the dying hand of sometime thy husband, but now (alas!) overthrown.

Wa. Raleigh

Yours that was; but now not my own,

W. R.

ACTIVITY

Imagine yourself as some well-known historical or fictional character or as someone participating in an historical event. Write a letter to one of your present friends or to your real family describing what is happening to you. Think about the style of the letter as well. What kind of letters were written at the time you imagine yourself writing? (An interesting book to read as a model is *The Ides of March* by Thornton Wilder, a fictitious set of letters between Julius Caesar and certain people involved in his life.)

LETTER 4

Here is an example of a letter written out of necessity. Does the bricklayer tell his employer what he needs to know? Do you like the letter? Why?

From a Bricklayer to the Firm for Whom He Works

Dear Sir,

By the time I arrived at the house where you sent me to make repairs, the storm had torn a good fifty bricks from the roof. So I set up on the roof of the building a beam and a pulley and I hoisted up a couple of baskets of bricks. When I had finished repairing the building there were a lot of bricks left over since I had brought up more than I needed and also because there were some bad, reject bricks that I still had left to bring down. I hoisted the basket back up again and hitched up the line at the bottom. Then I climbed back up again and filled up the basket with the extra bricks.

Then I went down to the bottom and untied the line. Unfortunately, the basket of bricks was much heavier than I was and before I knew what was happening, the basket started to plunge down, lifting me suddenly off the ground. I decided to keep my grip and hang on, realizing that to let go would end in disaster —but half way up I ran into the basket coming down and received a severe blow on the shoulder. I then continued to the top, banging my head against the beam and getting my fingers jammed in the pulley.

When the basket hit the ground it burst its bottom, allowing all the bricks to spill out. Since I was now heavier than the basket I started back down again at high speed. Half way down, I met the basket coming up, and received several severe injuries on my shins. When I hit the ground, I landed on the bricks, getting several more painful cuts and bruises from the sharp edges.

At this moment I must have lost my presence of mind, because I let go of the line. The basket came down again, giving me another heavy blow on the head, and putting me in the hospital.

I respectfully request sick leave.

ACTIVITY

Do you know of any stories or novels where a letter or letters play an important part? Find two or three examples and discuss the kinds of letters and their importance in the plot. What do they reveal about the characters who wrote them?

ACTIVITY

Look at letters used in advertisements. What are the advertisers trying to do?

ACTIVITY

As a class or in groups, examine carefully the Letters to the Editor in a recent newspaper of your area. How good are the letters for their purpose? Could you write some of them in a more effective way? Write a letter, individually or as a group, to your local newspaper about some issue you feel strongly about, or in answer to one of those you have examined.

LETTER 5

Here is a small piece of a letter written in 1911 by Louis Hémon to his mother. Why have the Canadian Public Archives treasured such a letter?

1230 Rue St Hubert
Montréal
Canada
28 Oct. 1911

Ma chère maman,

Tu trouveras ci-dessus ma nouvelle adresse. Je suis à Montréal depuis le commencement de la semaine, mais viens seulement de retenir une chambre.

Ma lettre de Québec vous aura appris que j'ai fait un excellent voyage. Depuis le temps a été assez beau et encore clément, sauf un peu de neige hier. Mais c'etait une pauvre petite neige genre européen qui fondait à mesure; la vraie ne viendra guère qu'en Novembre. Aujourd'hui le soleil brille. Le climat et le régime me vont à merveille. Le pays me plait et je crois que ça marchera bien.

Je commence à parler canadien comme un indigène. Je prends les "chars" (tramways électriques) je parle tout naturellement de la "chambre de bains" et de la "chambre à dîner" sur le même "plancher" (étage) etc. C'est une langue bien curieuse.

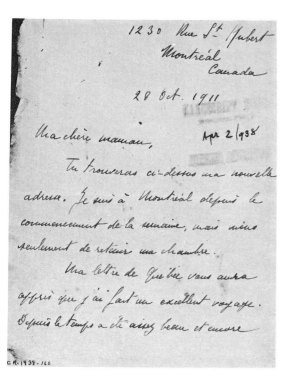

—Public Archives of Canada; Louis Hémon Papers (M.G. 30, D 47)

LETTER 6

Not all letters in a country's archives are from famous people. Sometimes a letter from an ordinary citizen seems to reflect a time in history. Here is the beginning of such a letter, one sent by a woman in Saskatchewan during the Great Depression of the 1930s to the Prime Minister of Canada. In even this section of the letter, something of the woman's character shines through her words. Discuss what kind of person you think she was, and what caused her to write this letter.

R. B. Bennett Papers (M.G. 26, K, Volume 644)

ACTIVITY

In the *Dictionary of Canadianisms*, look up these phrases which became part of Canadian vocabulary during those years: **Dust Bowl**, **Dirty Thirties**, **Hungry Thirties**, **Bennett buggy**, **Bennett Barnyard**, **Anderson chariot**, and **pogey** (or **pogy**).

NELSON'S LAST LETTER

The following letter has been preserved in the British Museum, London.

—reproduced by permission of the British Library Board —Egerton MS. 1614, f. 125

Victory Oct: 19th: 1805
Noon Cadiz ESE 16 Leagues

My Dearest beloved Emma the dear friend of my bosom the signal has been made that the Enemys combined fleet are coming out of Port. We have very little Wind so that I have no hopes of seeing them before tomorrow May the God of Battles crown my endeavours with success at all events I will take care that my home shall ever be most dear to you and Horatia both of whom I love as much as my own life, and as my last writing before the battle will be to you so I hope in God that I shall live to finish my letter after the

Written to Lady Hamilton on board the *Victory*. The letter, dated October 19, 1805, is followed (overleaf) by a postscript dated the twentieth, the eve of Trafalgar, and concluding with the words, "May God Almighty give us success over these fellows and enable us to get a Peace." Below is a note in Lady Hamilton's hand: "This letter was found open on His Desk & brought to Lady Hamilton by Capn. Hardy. Oh miserable wretched Emma oh glorious & happy Nelson."

ACTIVITY

As a class project, make a collection of historical letters. Write to local and provincial museums and to local historical societies, and see what you can find. Do not neglect the older people in your own district. Some students may wish to make a collection of family letters, or of their own letters which mark important events in their own lives.

—"Staatliche Kunstsammlungen Dresden — Gemaldegalerie Alte Meister"

Vermeer of Delft — **Girl Reading a Letter by an Open Window**

Only by the form, the pattern,
Can words or music reach
The stillness.

—T. S. Eliot: "Burnt Norton"

The System of English
English Grammar

Part One

What Is Grammar?

Examine the following pairs of sentences. How do you know that the two sentences, though much alike, give different messages?

(a) Tom chased the dog.
 The dog chased Tom.
(b) Tom chased the dog.
 Tom chases the dog.
(c) Tom chased the dog.
 Tom chased the dogs.
(d) Tom hit the dog.
 Tom, hit the dog.
(e) Tom was wrong.
 Was Tom wrong?
(f) Tom is here.
 Tom's is here.

We react to the differences in these sentences because we know the **system** of the English language. Grammar is simply the study of a language system, of how people arrange and change the words of a language into patterns in order to communicate.

Many people think of a language as just a set of words, each word tied to a meaning. But when we learn a new language, we find that sending messages in that language involves more than knowing vocabulary. We must also discover how the people of that language:

1. put their words together in various patterns (see sentences (a), (d), and (e) above), and
2. change the forms of the words to make differences in meaning (see sentences (b), (c), and (f) above).

Because we already know how to **use** the English grammar system, learning about English grammar for us is simply learning to notice and describe the patterns we already know, and to name the various parts and patterns of the system.

A knowledge of the **vocabulary** of grammar enables us to speak accurately about language. A

good mechanic, in order to discuss mechanical problems, must know the names of the parts of an engine as well as how they fit together. In the same way, people using language and such "tools" as dictionaries and handbooks need to know certain terms to understand and talk about the system.

> Grammar is not something strange and artificial. Its study consists mainly of observing what we already know about the language. The most convincing reason for this study is expressed in these words:
>
> **Language is man's earliest and greatest invention; to study its complex structure and varied history is to realize one important dimension of our humanity.**
>
> — W. Nelson Francis

What Grammar Is Not

He ain't ready yet.
He don't care about going to school.
Him and me are friends.

We often hear people say that sentences such as those above are not "good grammar". It would be more accurate to say that the speakers of such sentences are not employing "good usage" or "standard English". Grammarians once thought that language was built on logical and unchangeable "rules", and that a study of grammar meant a study of how a language **should** work. Modern grammarians know that all living languages change and that no language is completely logical. The word **ain't**, and the expression **he don't**, for example, were acceptable in England up to the 1890s; they are still "English", even though they are not acceptable now as standard English.

Learning grammar is learning how language **is** used, not how it **should** be used. Studying grammar reveals the patterns of the English language. But problems involving the distinction between standard and non-standard expressions are mainly problems of **usage**, not of grammar.

> **Grammar** — is a description of the system of a language.
>
> **Usage** — refers to "language etiquette" — statements about the degree of acceptance of certain items in the language.

Every Language Has Its Own System

Every language has its own system — its own sound system, its own vocabulary, its own way of marking notions such as "plural", "past time", and "action", and its own way of putting the pieces together to make a sentence.

It is probably true that all languages have some characteristics in common. All languages, for example, seem to have something corresponding to our "verbs" and "nouns", and some ways to ask questions and make negatives. But how these notions are expressed in actual speech varies from language to language. Here are some examples of how language systems vary. What differences do you see?

English: The house is red.

Latin: Domus rubra est.
or Rubra domus est.
or Domus est rubra.

German: Das Haus ist rot.

French: La maison est rouge.

The same idea expressed in Eskimo would be something like:

The house, looking-like-flowing-blood-it-is. [1]

Can you change the word order in the English sentence without changing the meaning? Compare with the Latin sentences.

Does Latin seem to need a word like **the**?

---

[1] Edmund Carpenter, F. Varley, and R. Flaherty: *Eskimo*

If we changed **house** to **sky** in the English sentence, would anything else have to change? The sentences in the other languages, however, become:

Latin: Caelum rubrum est.
or Rubrum caelum est.
or Caelum est rubrum.

German: **Der** Himmel ist rot.

French: **Le** ciel est rouge.

Note that in English **the** serves all nouns; but the French grammar system uses **le** with some nouns, **la** with others, and **les** for all plurals; and the German grammar system uses variations of three forms, **der**, **die**, and **das**, according to both number and case — quite bewildering to anyone who doesn't know the system.

Each language also has its own rules as to what structures make a sentence. Therefore the definition of "sentence" is not the same for all languages. In Chinese, for example, if the pattern is this:

PLACE ADVERBIAL NOUN ADJECTIVE
outside the city trees tall

it is a sentence. But if the order of the noun and adjective is changed to this:

PLACE ADVERBIAL ADJECTIVE NOUN
outside the city tall trees

it is **not** a sentence. Neither of these patterns would make an English sentence, for English full-statement sentences require not only a verb, for example:

Outside the city **are** tall trees.
Outside the city **grow** tall trees.

but also that the verb "agrees" with the number of the noun, for example,

Outside the city **are** tall trees. (**grow** trees)
Outside the city **is** a tree. (**grows** a tree)

Chinese people learning English find this "agreement" odd, because the notion of "number" is already marked in the noun (tree: tree**s**). But the grammar of any language is completely arbitrary — it is what it is.

If you know or are learning another language, what parts of its grammar system do you find "odd"?

Some of the "rules" of our own grammar are intricate. We don't notice them because we learned them as children—how, we do not know. But when a non-English speaker makes an error, then we begin to realize how much we, as native speakers, "know" when we talk. Our language seems ordinary until we examine it.

What part of the English grammar system is not understood by the Spanish speakers who wrote these signs for English tourists:

LETTERS BOX	PARCELS POST
SHOES REPAIR	PEANUTS VENDOR

The use of the plural (letters, shoes, peanuts, etc.) is logical and sensible, but the English grammar system does not allow the -s, and the signs are not "English".

PRESCRIPTIONS...
COSMETICS...

"Of course I wrote 'two teethbrush' on the list. The plural of 'tooth' is 'teeth,' isn't it?"

—reproduced with permission—The Register and Tribune Syndicate

---

INFORMING IDEA

Every language has its own system — its grammar. The grammar of a language is arbitrary, not "logical".

Basic Principles of the English Grammar System

1. Word Order

Why do the following word groups give different messages?

(a) The car hit the tree
   The tree hit the car

(b) a flower garden
   a garden flower

(c) Only Tom has a dime
   Tom has only a dime

(d) The teacher is here
   Is the teacher here

(e) How big is he
   How big he is

(f) to escape a fire
   to a fire-escape

The most important principle in the English language system is **word order**. A child as young as four has learned this feature of English grammar. He can demonstrate that he knows, for instance, that **Train push duck.** is not the same as **Duck push train.** Until we examine our language, we often do not realize how fixed English word order is. In what order are these five words: **big, three, the, hunting,** and **black** placed before the word **dogs**?

———, ———, ———, ———, ——— dogs

Where could you add **very** to this group?

In the above, the word order is fixed. We automatically put each word into its proper position. Which word in this next sentence is **not** fixed—that is, can change its position without changing the basic meaning of the sentence?

I shall soon finish my homework.

If we are not aware of the importance of word order in English, we can write sentences that are ambiguous (carrying more than one meaning) because the words, when grouped in different ways, give different meanings.

Can you change the word order in these two sentences so as to remove the possible ambiguity?

1. I paid for my plane ticket for my trip yesterday.
2. The teacher checked the girl who was talking crossly.

As you study English grammar, watch particularly for **word order**, and the possible changes in meaning brought about by changes in order.

ORAL ACTIVITY

Change the following statements to questions by changing word order.

(a) He is here.
(b) The prisoner has escaped.
(c) There is a guard at the gate.
(d) They are not leaving.
(e) They aren't leaving.
(f) Jack will arrive before lunch.

ORAL ACTIVITY

What is the difference between:
    He is looking good.
and: He is good looking.

Can you make similar pairs?

2. Patterns

Which words will fit into the spaces shown below, to make patterns that are "English"?

(a) She is a very _____ girl.
    (beautiful, beauty, beautify, beautifully, French, France, dazzling, dazzle, intelligence, intelligent)

(b) Don't _____.
    (go, gone, went, going, departure)
(c) The baby began _____.
    (to cry, cry, crying, cried, has cried)

The grammar of the language dictates that certain kinds of words, but not others, may go together in patterns. Conscious knowledge of the patterns allowed by the system of English gives us greater power to choose and manipulate the patterns.

When studying grammar, look for patterns.

ORAL ACTIVITY

Which one of each group is an exception to the pattern of the others? How do you know?

1. (a) to run
   (b) to steal
   (c) to you
   (d) to keep

2. (a) jumping off
   (b) looking in
   (c) holding on
   (d) telling me

3. (a) a little house
   (b) a little slow
   (c) a little baby
   (d) a little stick

4. (a) to be here
   (b) to be taken
   (c) to be helped
   (d) to be driven

5. (a) They have it.
   (b) He has finished.
   (c) You have gone.
   (d) They have started.

6. (a) Stop that noise.
   (b) Drive much faster.
   (c) Pass the cream.
   (d) Hold this parcel.

ORAL ACTIVITY

Change **sloog** and its variations into English words that fit the pattern.

- (a) I will **sloog** him at once.
- (b) A huge **sloog** was in the box.
- (c) A very **sloogy** cat watched the bird.
- (d) We wrapped it in a small piece of **sloog**.
- (e) I wanted to **sloog**, but was afraid to.
- (f) He drove fast but **sloogily**.
- (g) It was a **sloogish** day.

3. Additions to Word Forms: Inflections and Derivational Suffixes

There are two kinds of suffix used in English to change meaning: **inflectional suffixes** (or **inflections**) and **derivational suffixes**.

(a) INFLECTIONS (INFLECTIONAL SUFFIXES)

In 1957–58 a psychologist, Dr. Jean Berko, tried a language experiment with children four to seven years of age which revealed that children of this age know some of the major rules of the English grammar system. As you read what the children were asked (orally, of course), think of these questions:

What general rules of the English grammar system have the children learned?

Why did Dr. Berko use nonsense-words to test the children's knowledge of English grammar?

1. Inflection of nouns for plural:

The children knew a major rule of English grammar: that to make a word like **wug**, or any noun, mean "more than one" (**plural**) we add an **s** sound or variant of it to the singular form. This change in a form of a word to make plurals is called **inflection for number**.

THIS IS A WUG.

NOW THERE IS ANOTHER ONE.

THERE ARE TWO OF THEM.

THERE ARE TWO _____.

—from: *Word* 14. 150-77. 1958.

Dr. Berko repeated the experiment with such nonsense words as **lun**, **gutch**, and **niz**. What do you think the children said? Why did Dr. Berko use these particular forms?

2. Inflection of nouns for possessives:

If the children were asked the following pattern, what would they probably say?

This wug has a hat.   This bik has a hat.
It is the _____ hat.   It is the _____ hat.

This ending is called the **possessive** inflection. In speech the possessive forms are pronounced the same as the plural, but in writing they are marked also by an apostrophe:

wug's hat   bik's hat   wugs' hats (plural)

3. Inflections of verbs:

If we change **wug** to fit into these patterns, what happens?

I wug every day.

Yesterday I _____.

I wug, and my dog _____ too.

I am _____ right now.

I have _____ every day for a week.

The word **wug** used in this way (a class called verbs) has at least three possible inflectional suffixes:**-s** (for singular number, with a noun)

      -ed (for **past tense**, or after **have** or **had**)

      -ing (often after the verb **be**)

All these suffixes which occur with a class of words are called **inflections**. All new nouns and verbs coming into the language take the regular inflections of their class:

Nouns: **-s** for plural; **-'s** for "possessive"
Verbs: **-s**; **-ed**; **-ing**

Each inflection carries a meaning, for example, "plural", "possessive", "past", etc.

Two other classes of words sometimes have inflections:

4. Adjectives:

Today is wuggy, but yesterday was _____, and tomorrow will be the _____ of all.

5. Adverbs:

He walks bikly, but Joe walks _____, and Amos walks the _____ of all.

These forms **-er**, **-est** are inflections that signal **degree**. Other examples are: nice, nic**er**, nic**est**; fast, fast**er**, fast**est**; and friendly, friendli**er**, friendli**est**. Longer adjectives and adverbs do not inflect, but use **more** and **most** to express the same idea:

beautiful
more beautiful
(the) most beautiful

intelligently
more intelligently
(the) most intelligently

Note:

There are a few irregular inflections such as goose, **geese**; child, **children**; write, **wrote**, **written**; good, **better**, **best**. These are "leftovers" from former times. Most irregular forms are found in commonly used words and give little trouble. New words coming into the language are always inflected regularly. Examples are:

snowmobile (noun) — two snowmobile**s**; the snowmobile**'s** engine
snowmobile (verb) — they snowmobile; he snowmobile**s**; she snowmobil**ed**; he is snowmobil**ing**

Not her best
good enough

Creamier, tangy-er, softer-to-taste Cottage Cheese now in new fresh-looking containers!

ACTIVITY

Some of the following words can be inflected. Which ones cannot? Write all the forms of those that can be inflected.

poor	blacken
few	by
quick	law
quickly	small
window	ask
because	know
black	of
pretty	

ACTIVITY

Try Jean Berko's experiment with some children three to eight. Report on your findings.

(b) DERIVATIONAL SUFFIXES

A second kind of suffix may act as a grammatical device in English.

How would we change the **form** of the words in bold type to fit into the spaces and be "English"?

The flowers **attract** attention.
The flowers are very _____.
She arranged the flowers _____.
The flowers were the main _____.

The **origin** of the story is Hungarian.
The story _____ in Hungary.
The _____ story came from Hungary.
The story came _____ from Hungary.

These suffixes (-ive, -ly, -tion, -ate, -al) and others like them are a grammatical device that helps to mark some words as nouns, verbs, adjectives, and adverbs. For example, a word ending in -tion (attraction, prevention, attention, etc.) is probably a noun;

and a word ending in -ize (dramatize, legalize, modernize, etc.) is likely to be a verb. Because this kind of suffix allows one word to be derived from another (**original** and **originate** from **origin**, for example), it is called a **derivational suffix**—an excellent device for extending the use of a word in the language. Derivational suffixes differ from inflectional suffixes in several important ways:

1. There are many derivational suffixes. Here is a list of words illustrating only a few of them:

   bushy selfish harmonize alertness musical painter remarkable versify electrician electricity hourly historic selective selection

   There are very few inflectional suffixes.

2. A derivational suffix often allows a word to move from one class to another, for example, **please** (verb) to **pleasure** (noun) to **pleasurable** (adjective) to **pleasurably** (adverb). An inflectional suffix operates with one class (for example, plural inflection -s or -es for nouns; -d or -ed for pasts of verbs).

3. A derivational suffix does not apply automatically to a full class. For example:

   attract can become **attraction**
   and **produce** can become **production**
   but **manufacture** does not become **manufaction**
   and **influence** does not become **influention**

   Nor can thousands of other verbs use the suffix -tion or -ation to form a noun; try **drink**, **supply**, **care**, **nourish**, and **read**, for example. In contrast, an inflectional suffix applies to almost any member of a class; nearly all verbs use the inflection -d or -ed to make a past form, for instance.

4. A word can have up to three or four derivational suffixes; for example, to **ideal** we can add **-ize**, and then **-ation**; to **press** we can add **-ure**, then **-ize**, then **-ation**. But a word can have only one inflectional suffix (except noun plural and possessive, as in **boys'**, which is marked in spelling only). Once an inflectional suffix is added to a word, no other suffix can be added.

SUFFIXES

Derivational	Inflectional
a large number of them	very few
can change a word from one part of speech to another, for example, music (noun) to musical (adj.)	runs through one class, for example, plural inflection for nouns (cat — cats), past inflection for verbs (scratch — scratched)
is arbitrary — does not apply automatically, for example, wide — width, but not narrow — narrowth	applies automatically to nearly all members of a class (for example, Nouns: book — books; Verbs: look — looks, looked, looking; Adjectives: big — bigger, biggest; Adverbs: soon — sooner, soonest — but most adverbs and many adjectives use **more** and **most** for comparison, rather than the inflections)
a word can use many, for example, **intend** + **-tion** + **-al** + **-ly** (intentionally)	closes off a word; we cannot add to prettiest, fills, or intends

---

ACTIVITY

Make words using the following derivational suffixes. Can you use more than one suffix in a word?

-ance or -ence	-ism	-ish	-al
-(i)ous	-age	-ic	-ist	-er
-ment	-(i)fy	-ward(s)	-ive

Watching for clues in **word forms** is an important part of learning about the system of the language.

Grammar is the study of the system of a language. Every language has its own system.

Some basic devices characteristic of English grammar:

1. a more or less fixed word order
2. patterns of words that we recognize
3. changes in word form:

   (a) inflectional suffixes—English has very few (a small set) of the final suffix of a word — for example, amusements

   (b) derivational suffixes — amuse**ment**, arrival

The Parts of Speech

Into how many classes could we put these words?

lion	of	bar	rattlesnake
the	quarterly	pull	honesty
rubber	rubbery	taking	noble
Arthur	use	by	between
ice-cream	Canadian	soon	not
when	honestly	see	chosen
pretty	which	eye	walks
into	very		

One of the first tasks of someone trying to describe a language is to classify the elements of the language.

Traditionally, the classes into which we put words are called the **parts of speech**. The parts of speech are categories set up by grammarians according to some system. But language, which is made by people and always changing, is not entirely regular. It has wayward exceptions. Although most English words are easy to classify, a few are difficult, and some do not fit a general pattern.

Examples: Only I understood. (What is **only**?)
You had better go. (What is **better**?)

As the scholar Edward Sapir says, "All grammars leak." In fact, there is as yet no perfect system for classifying all English words — and grammarians sometimes differ. Nevertheless, most words fit into some pattern.

As speakers of English, we recognize the various classifications even if we cannot fully define them. We "know", for example, that **dogs** is a noun in this sentence:
The **dogs** are fighting again.

but a verb in this sentence:

My little brother **dogs** my footsteps all day long.

We understand these sentences because we "know" the function of **dog** in each sentence. If we didn't, we wouldn't understand the sentence — or speak English at all. Even a young speaker knows the difference between a noun and a verb, although unable to **name** the classes "noun", "verb".

Rather than classify words by definitions, we will in this section try to see **how** we recognize the class into which a word fits — to discover the clues in the English system that give us this unconscious knowledge. We will look especially at: **word order**, **patterns** of words in the sentence, **inflection**, and **derivational suffixes**.

If we look back at the list of words on page 220, we can see that there are certain words that share the possibility of inflections: for example,

Nouns: lion-**s** bar-**s** rattlesnake-**s** quarterlie-**s**

(Finish the list for yourself. At least two words, which you "feel" should be nouns also, do not seem to inflect. Can you spot them?)

Verbs: bar(r)-**ed** -**s** -**ing** pull-**ed** -**ing** -**s**
see-**ing** -**s** -**n** saw
(Finish the list for yourself.)

Adjectives: noble-**er** -**est** pretty(i)-**er** -**est**

Adverbs: soon-**er** -**est**

We also recognize that many of these words have derivational suffixes or could have them; these suffixes often change them to another part of speech. See the examples in the box below.

N	V	Adj.	Adv.
critic-critic**ism**	critic**ize**	critical	critic**ally**
noble**ness**, nobi**lity**		noble	nob**ly**
Canada	Canadian**ize**	Canadian	
honesty		honest	honest**ly**
lion	lion**ize**		

Do these: **create, impress, develop, illustrate** (all verbs).

Because these four classes of words usually take inflections and often accept derivational suffixes — that is, change their form — they are called **form words**. If we examine an English dictionary, we would find that more than 99.99 per cent of the words are form words and fall into one of these four classes. Indeed, all new words coming into the language are form words, that is, nouns, verbs, adjectives, or adverbs. If we decided to use **lig** as a noun, for instance, we might soon use it as a verb (**to lig**, perhaps **to ligify?**), or an adjective (**liggy, liggier, ligful?**), or an adverb (**liggily, ligfully?**). Form words are **open classes** — open to new items.

> **THE FOUR FORM CLASSES: Nouns, Verbs, Adjectives, Adverbs**
>
> Most of them change form using the devices of
> | inflection
> and | derivational suffixes.
> Form classes are **open sets**—open to new words.

Structure Words: Closed Classes

The following words from our list do not, however, usually change in form:

of into the very between not where which by

These words are **structure words**, a few hundred words repeated over and over to tie together the **form words**. These structure words are **closed classes**, for seldom does a new one come into the language. They can therefore be classified by **listing** each group.

We can think of the **form words** as the bricks of the sentence, making the building, and the **structure words** as the mortar, holding the bricks together.

The FACE of a COUNTRY MAKES a LIVING

AUTOBIOGRAPHY, with the LINES of

HISTORY WRITTEN on it in STONE and

SAND and WATER.

Summary

One way to begin classifying the words of English is by putting them into two large groups:

FORM WORDS

— **open classes** (unlimited; we can add new words to them)

— can usually change their form by inflections and derivational suffixes
— all **nouns, verbs, adjectives, adverbs**

STRUCTURE WORDS

— **closed classes** (limited to a few words; we rarely add a new structure word)
— do not usually change their form

ACTIVITY

Lewis Carroll, the author of *Alice in Wonderland* and other children's books, enjoyed playing with language. He understood that by retaining the structure words he could keep the shape and "feel" of an English sentence.

'TWAS **BRILLIG**, AND THE **SLITHY TOVES**
DID **GYRE** AND **GIMBLE** IN THE **WABE**:
ALL **MIMSY** WERE THE **BOROGOVES**,
AND THE **MOME RATHS OUTGRABE**.

Write your own nonsense poem.

ACTIVITY

What words in the following selection could be replaced by nonsense-words? (They will be form words.)

What words cannot be replaced by nonsense-words? (They will be structure words.)

1. Jean loved to lie in bed and listen to the patter of the rain on the roof.

2. As the plane dived, the pilot leaned forwards and signalled with his hand to the parachuter.

A Closer Look at the Open Classes (Form Words)

Nouns

Identify the nouns in the following nonsense-sentences. Then describe the clues that helped you do so.

A dib is gribbing on the bumption.
Each cantip's tib daged slowly.
Have you teeled my new bellony?
She liffs Dorothy two bittals every lob for her roosh.

Traditionally, nouns have been defined as "the names of persons, places, or things". Though helpful, this definition is incomplete and often confusing. For example, **red** is the "name" of a colour, yet **red** is not a noun in the sentence, "The red ball belongs to Ruth." (We can use: The **redder** ball is mine or The **reddest** ball is mine — that is, the inflections of an adjective.)

A more accurate way to recognize and classify nouns is to use the following clues:

1. Position (word order and patterns with other words)

In the rigid word order of the English sentence, nouns tend to occur in certain positions. Here are a few typical noun positions.

I have found my _____.
Each _____ was given a large _____.
The _____ is interesting.
A _____ was sitting on the _____.

Notice that certain words such as **a**, **an**, **the**, **some**, **each**, **this**, **my**, and others "signal" to the listener or reader that a noun is probably following.

2. Word Form — Inflections

Another clue: most nouns inflect for both number and possession.

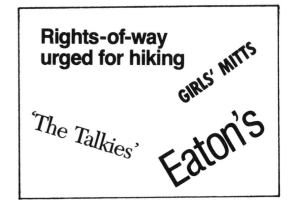

(a) two forms to show **number**:

singular	plural
boy	boys
fox	foxes
church	churches

(b) two forms to show **possessives**:

boy's (singular possessive)
boys' (plural possessive)
fox's (singular possessive)
foxes' (plural possessive)

(Note: marked in **writing** by the apostrophe, but in speech the possessive forms sound like plurals.)

Notice that in **writing**, the plural endings are either -**s** or -**es**. In **speech**, however, there are three possible endings. Make these words plural, and see if you can hear the different endings. (Some add an **s** sound, some a **z** sound, and some an **iz** sound.)

tap   dog   toe   rose   church   kick   fly   speech

The right sounds to these endings come automatically to people who speak English as a native language, but may cause trouble to those learning English as a second language. Each language has its own subtle patterns of sound.

3. Word Form — Derivational Suffixes

Another clue: many English nouns have characteristic derivational suffixes. Although you might not know what the words "bomption" or "pompetence" mean, the suffixes -**tion** or -**ence** suggest that they could be nouns. Here are a few examples of typical noun endings. Add to each list.

-acy	democracy	legacy	accuracy
-er, -eer	engineer	farmer	_____
-ence	reference	_____	_____
-ance	remembrance	_____	_____
-ism	communism	_____	_____

-ity	humility	_____	_____
-ment	arrangement	_____	_____
-ness	cleverness	_____	_____
-ship	friendship	_____	_____
-sion	permission	_____	_____
-(a)tion	attention	_____	_____

OTHER INTERESTING THINGS TO NOTICE ABOUT NOUNS

1. We often construct nouns by compounding different parts of speech. Here are a few examples. Add to each list.

two nouns:
life-jacket   bedroom   airlines   bookshelf
verb and noun:
go-cart   playground   driftwood   pack horse
noun and verb:
nosedive   haircut   shoeshine   heartbreak
adjective and noun:
freeway   hardtop   freshman   lowland
verb and adverb:
drive-in   runabout   turnover   blackout
adverb and verb:
intake   afterthought   bypass   downpour

How many nouns can you make with these as an element?

(a) fire   (b) eye   (c) dead   (d) down   (e) run

2. In English, nouns are often run together in groups. This tendency to compound is a Germanic characteristic. The German language, however, makes one word of the compound (and also marks a noun with a capital letter), as:

the music room — **das Musikzimmer**
the stroke of the clock — **der Glockenschlag** (literally, 'the clock-stroke')
hospital in the tropics — **das Tropenkrankenhaus** (literally, 'the tropic-sick-house')

English has no definite rules about compound nouns. Sometimes the nouns are joined:

flowerbeds floodlight barnyard carhop

sometimes hyphenated:

fighter-bomber hair's-breadth mischief-maker

and sometimes written separately:

Christmas tree	coffee break
life insurance	hockey stick

Notice, too, that English will "string" many nouns together:

Christmas tree ornament counter
circus tent roof
life insurance salesman
fighter-bomber pilot
cottage cheese salad recipe
radio relay stations

THE WAX-ME-NOTS

How do you recognize that **wax-me-not** is a noun?

"Well, what did you expect a watchdog to do?"

ACTIVITY

Read these to find the pattern in the stress. The stress pattern, though it has a few exceptions, is nonetheless important in English speech because we use it to differentiate between groups such as the following. Can you make a general rule?

compound	not a compound noun
a freeway	a free way
a freshman	a fresh man
a hardtop	a hard top
the lowlands	the low lands
a highchair	a high chair
a briefcase	a brief case

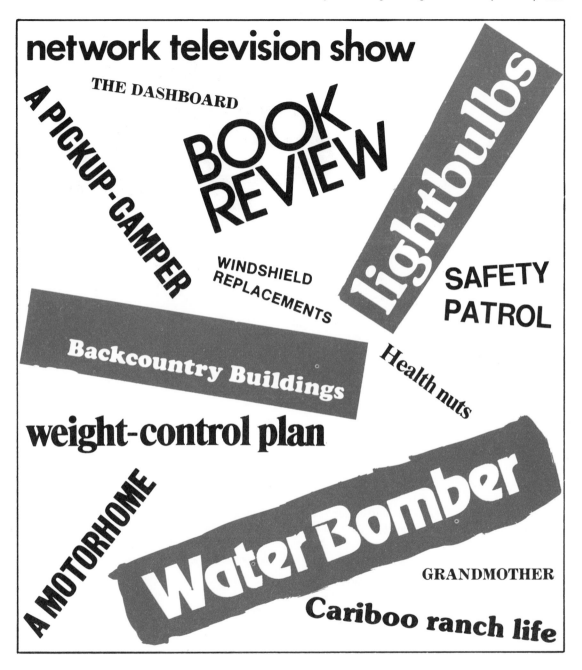

network television show

THE DASHBOARD

A PICKUP-CAMPER

BOOK REVIEW

lightbulbs

WINDSHIELD REPLACEMENTS

SAFETY PATROL

Backcountry Buildings

Health nuts

weight-control plan

A MOTORHOME

Water Bomber

GRANDMOTHER

Cariboo ranch life

ACTIVITY

Collect other examples of compound nouns. Discuss how they are formed.

" Look out, it's . . . God, I'm awful with names!"

ACTIVITY

Nouns name the objects we see and the ideas we have. We must use them precisely. Find all the nouns used in the following paragraph. See how many you can replace with a near-synonym.

In the past twenty years man has virtually completed the huge task of exploring the earth's surface for evidence of mineral deposits. In all the world only a few outcropping ore bodies can have gone undetected; most of the earth's remaining mineral resources lie beneath the surface. The discovery of raw materials has become to a large extent the job of geophysicists. Geophysics has long been important in the search for petroleum; since the end of World War II it has revolutionized mineral prospecting, helping to keep pace with the exponential rise in the demand for new resources. This revolution in exploration involves a number of methods of detecting buried or hidden deposits, but in the end it rests largely on one instrument — the airborne magnetometer — and related techniques that it has brought into use.

—Homer Jensen: "The Airborne Magnetometer"

ACTIVITY

List ten nouns that have come into the language in the past fifty years. Examples are **cortisone** (1949), **radar** (1942), and **nylon** (1932). The latest supplement to the *Oxford English Dictionary* or other large dictionaries will give you the dates.

```
┌─────────────────────────────────────────────┐
│                                             │
│          Summary About Nouns                │
│                                             │
│ 1. You can recognize a noun partly from its:│
│                                             │
│   (a) patterns (What words often signal that│
│       a noun is to come?)                   │
│   (b) inflections (Most nouns are inflected │
│       for _____ and _____.)           │
│   (c) typical derivational suffixes (List   │
│       some.)                                │
│                                             │
│ 2. Nouns are often compounds. (Give six     │
│    examples, two spelled as one word, two as│
│    hyphenated words, two as separate words.)│
│    We often "string" nouns together, for    │
│    example, **election night victory party**.│
│                                             │
└─────────────────────────────────────────────┘
```

Verbs

Find the verbs in the following nonsense-sentences. Tell how you identified them.

1. While he vorted, he disted a gorler sankton.
2. I will vant that gomp tomorrow when the nome korps.
3. "Let's flusterize the accrume," dobed Bill, "before the yarbs can cuttle into the drine."

Traditionally, verbs have been defined as "words expressing action or a state of being". But words like **departure**, **flight**, and **strife** express action, and are not verbs; and words like **happiness**, **dead**, and **beauty** express "a state of being", but are not verbs.

Thus, although the traditional definition may be helpful, other facts about verbs make identification more certain.

How did you recognize the verbs in the sentences above?

What "clue" words and patterns helped you?

What typical inflections and derivational suffixes helped you?

INFLECTIONS OF VERBS

English verbs are classified as **regular** when they have these typical inflections:

Jump can change to jump**s**, jump**ed**, and jump**ing**.
Hate can change to hate**s**, hate**d**, and hat**ing**.
Reach can change to reach**es**, reach**ed**, and reach**ing**.

A regular verb can inflect, then, by adding **-s** (or **-es**), **-d** (or **-ed**), and **-ing**. This makes **three** regular inflections.

ORAL ACTIVITY

Which form of **jump** goes automatically into each of these patterns?

I will _____ over the creek.

I have _____ over the creek.

I _____ over the creek yesterday.

I was _____ over the creek.

I like to _____ over the creek.

I like _____ over the creek.

_____ over the creek is fun.

To _____ over the creek is fun.

He _____ over the creek. (2 possible)

They _____ over the creek. (2 possible)

INFLECTIONS OF IRREGULAR VERBS

The **s** and **ing** forms of all verbs are regular. But about one hundred and forty English verbs are irregular because they do not use the regular **-d** or **-ed** in the past form or in the past participle (the form used after **have**), for example:

I **took**—not, I **taked**
I have **taken**—not, I have **taked**

Here are other examples of irregular verbs:

	Past	Past Participle
I sing.	singing	sang	(have) sung
He sings.			
I bring.	bringing	brought	brought
He brings.			
I sit.	sitting	sat	sat
He sits.			
I give.	giving	gave	given
He gives.			

There is now no easy pattern for learning the standard forms of these old, but frequently used, irregular verbs. The forms for each verb must be learned individually. For some irregular verbs there may be more than one form. Do you say, for example: "**have got**" or "**have gotten**"? "**have forgot**" or "**have forgotten**"? "I **dived** into the water" or "I **dove** into the water"? and would you change the form if speaking of a submarine diving? "I **sneaked** into the room" (regular form) or "I **snuck** into the room"?

Most errors in the use of irregular verbs come from confusing them with regular verbs or wrongly copying the form of a similar verb:

I **knowed** him. — copying the regular pattern.
He **throwed** it.
He **brang** it. — copying the pattern of **sing, sang**.

ACTIVITY

Here is a list of irregular verbs that are sometimes usage problems. Test yourself by writing the standard form of each, as below:

I **sing**	I **sang**	I have **sung**
I **bring**	I **brought**	I have **brought**

flee	fling	shine	wear	hang
creep	cling	shoot	freeze	grow
breed	wring	slide	break	know
pay	lead	win	beat	slay
strike	catch	choose	hide	eat
ring	spin	weave	blow	see
swing	spit	swear	lie	do
give	teach	steal	lay	take

forgive	run	forbid	begin	rise
drink	write	swim	ride	shrink
drive	sink	come	fly	go

Special Irregular Forms

(a) **to be:** be — being — been (a regular pattern)
   am, is — are
   was — were

(b) **verbs that do not have an -ed inflection** for the past or the past participles.

I **cut** the bread now.
I **cut** the bread yesterday.
I have **cut** the bread.

   Others: let, bet, hit, hurt, quit, burst, cast, cost, put, shed, slut, slit, split, thrust

What common features do you notice in these verbs?

ACTIVITY

An English Grammar dated 1762 gives the following verb forms. Which ones are now regular verbs? Give the present-day form for each.

I have **hoven** the rock.
The baby **crope** to the ball.
The boys **clomb** the fence.
I have often **sitten** on the chair.
He has **lien** down.
Mother has **baken** bread.
The child **clang** to its mother.

Look in the King James Bible (1611) for examples of other verb forms that have changed.

DERIVATIONAL SUFFIXES CHARACTERISTIC OF VERBS

English verbs are also made by adding certain derivational suffixes to other parts of speech. Change the following words into their corresponding verbs. Each group illustrates a typical suffix.

1. atom; emphasis; monopoly; apology; colony
2. to make into a **liquid**; to make into a **fort**; to make **clear**; to make **beautiful**
3. **light; dark; fright; height; bright**

Auxiliaries: Structure Words That Go with Verbs

One of the marvels of the English language is the system by which English expresses many subtleties of meaning surrounding an action by using **only three forms of the verb** and a small, closed set of words called **Auxiliaries**. (Because the auxiliaries are a small, closed set that can be listed, they are classified as **structure words**.) Here are the three forms of the verb that are used with auxiliaries:

Base Form   -ing Form   -en, -ed Form
            (present participle)   (past participle)

take   taking   taken
walk   walking   walked

In front of these go the auxiliaries, for example,

can will may do	take

is will be should be has been	taking

has had would have might have been	taken

Can you add to each group?

Which two forms of the verb are **not** used with auxiliaries? (Test with the verbs **give, sing,** and **eat,** then with regular verbs.)

What is the position of the auxiliaries in relation to the verb?

The following are the most commonly used auxiliaries:

1. can — could
   will — would
   shall — should
   may — might
   must — (must)

2. have (has) — had

3. are (is, am) — were (was)
   be, being, been

4. do (does) — did

Understanding the English use of auxiliaries can help us to see how different English is from most other European languages, which depend largely upon numerous inflections to express such subtle meanings. For example, many beginners learning French, Spanish, or German make the error of translating **I am going** or **I did do the dishes** literally, without realizing that these verb constructions are uniquely English. Discuss this with your foreign-language teacher.

AUXILIARIES AND VERBS

Three words — **be, have,** and **do** (and their inflected forms) — can function as auxiliaries **and** as verbs. Can you work out the system from these examples?

VERBS

1. I **am** cold.
2. You are **being** foolish.
3. You have **been** foolish.
4. I **have** a cold.
5. They **had** a holiday.
6. They have **had** a holiday.
7. I **do** homework every night.
8. She **did** the dishes.
9. I do **do** homework every night.

AUXILIARIES

1. I **am** getting a cold.
2. You **are** being foolish.
3. It **has** been eaten.
4. I **have** seen him.
5. They **had** taken a holiday.
6. They **have** had a holiday.
7. I **do** know my history.
8. She **did** do the dishes.
9. I **do** do homework every night.

Which are auxiliaries (structure words) in these:

I **will be having** a party on Saturday.
I **have been doing** my work.
He knew that I **had had** a party.

OTHER VERB COMBINATIONS

Some verbs are commonly used like auxiliaries, giving the English verb even greater versatility. Here are examples:

He **went** skating.   He **kept** skating.
He **went on** skating.   He **wanted** to skate.

How can you tell these groups from auxiliaries? There are two ways in which auxiliaries differ from any other grammatical groups. Use these as tests for auxiliaries.

Test 1. The auxiliaries may add n't. (Note: the test is n't, not **not**.) The **n't** is attached to the first auxiliary if there is a series.

I **do** skate.   I **have** skated.
I **don't** skate.   I **haven't** skated.

I **was** skating.   I **should have** skated.
I **wasn't** skating.   I **shouldn't have** skated.

But — Do we say: He wentn't skating?
He keptn't skating?
He wentn't on skating?

Those that can add n't — **do, have, was, should,** etc. — are auxiliaries.

Those that cannot add n't — **went, went on, kept,** etc. — are verbs or verb groups, not auxiliaries.

Test 2. When a statement becomes a question, the first auxiliary comes before the subject.

He **can** walk.   They **have** gone.
Can he walk?   **Have** they gone?

I **should have** come.
Should I **have** come?

We do not say: **Went** he skating?

Kept he skating?

Wanted he to skate?

How are these made into English question forms?

It is best to treat these other verb combinations as **verb groups**. Here are other examples. Apply the **n't** and question-pattern tests to each to check that it is not an auxiliary.

I **began** to drive.

He **began** driving.

He **stopped** talking.

He **used** to go every day.

I **wanted** to go.

The enemy **ceased** firing.

They **started** to shout.

He **wished** to leave.

He **continued** talking.

He **went on** talking.

VERB TENSE

All mankind exists within time, and all cultures are aware of **present, past,** and **future time.** But each language has its own devices to express these notions of time.

Tense is a technical term in grammar to refer to the **inflectional devices** used with verbs and auxiliaries to express the idea of time. English (and any other Germanic language) has only two clear-cut tenses marked by inflection: the **present tense** and the **past tense.**

PRESENT TENSE	PAST TENSE
walk(s)	walked
take(s)	took
are (is)	were (was)
have (has)	had
may	might
can	could
will	would
etc.	etc.

Notice that the past inflection for all regular verbs and for most of the auxiliaries is -(e)d or -t, and, except for the verb **to be,** there is no -s form for the "singular" of the past tense.

Even without the auxiliaries, either of these two forms — present tense and past tense — may be used to express any of the three natural divisions of time—the present, the past, and the future. There is not a complete one-to-one correspondence.

TENSE (a grammatical category — a change in the verb or auxiliary)	TIME (an "idea" category — a change in our thinking)
PRESENT TENSE	PRESENT I **see** him at the window now. PAST When Napoleon **sees** his troops withdraw, he **knows** he **is** defeated at last. FUTURE I **leave** next Monday for Toronto.
PAST TENSE	PRESENT If I **had** the money, I **would** buy it now. PAST The bird **flew** away. FUTURE If you **paid** us tomorrow, I'd be grateful.

With the use of the auxiliaries, the English language can express not only ideas about "time" but also many other meanings related to the "action". Discuss the meanings added to the verb by the tenses (present and past) and the auxiliaries in the following sequences.

PRESENT TENSE

He **goes** to university.
He **is going** to university.
He **has gone** to university.
He **has been going** to university.
He **will go** to university.
He **may go** to university.
He **will have gone** to university by now.
He **does go** to university.

PAST TENSE

He **went** to university.
He **was going** to university.
He **had gone** to university.
He **had been going** to university.
He **would go** to university.
He **might go** to university.
He **would have gone** to university by now.
He **did go** to university.

INFORMING IDEA

The English grammar system allows the meaning of the "action" expressed by the verb to be changed by two major devices:

1. auxiliaries—a closed set of structure words (**be, have, can, may, shall, will, must, do**)
2. two tenses — an inflection (usually **-(e)d** or **-t**) added to the **present tense** form of the verb or auxiliary to make the **past tense** form.

By combining these two devices in various ways, we can express present, past, and future time, and many other meanings related to the action.

Tense, a grammatical term, is not the same as **time**, but refers to the **inflections** we use to indicate time.

ORAL ACTIVITY

Tense is not the only way to indicate time. We can use expressions of definite time and of comparative time, for example, **soon, tomorrow, December tenth, next month, yesterday, a year from now, before, after**, etc., and we can use various verb groups.

In how many different ways can you express future time (for example, that you will leave for England) without using the auxiliaries **will, shall**, or their past forms **would** and **should**?

—reproduced with permission—Chicago Tribune Syndicate

ACTIVITY

In the poem on page 181, the poet uses verbs to help achieve the effect of stretching out a few moments of time. Study the verbs in the poem. Then try to write something similar, using a series of verbs.

MAKING NOUNS INTO VERBS

Because we continue to make new nouns and verbs, these are **open classes**. Some nouns can be used as verbs without any change in form except, of course, taking on the typical verb inflections and verb positions.

NOUNS	VERBS
The **iron** is hot.	I will **iron** your shirt. (I **ironed**, was **ironing**, etc.)
My **face** was cut.	You must **face** your problem. (You **faced**, were **facing**, etc.)

ORAL ACTIVITY

Use these nouns as verbs, giving short sentences:

line   book   water   surprise
man   cross   note   trail

Mall Cost
Split OK'd

ORAL ACTIVITY

Which of the following nouns could, without changing form, be used as verbs?

typewriter	knowledge	hunt	powder
sugar	return	mutiny	choir
judge	swim	funnel	function
science	mirror	language	verdict
patrol	sentence		

ORAL ACTIVITY

Sometimes there is change in stress or pronunciation when a noun is changed to a verb. Use these words as both nouns and verbs, and see if you can discover what happens in each group:

1. use, house, abuse
(Does your generalization apply also to **refuse** and **excuse**?)
2. contract, record, conduct, present
(Does your generalization also apply to **permit, convict, desert, suspect, convert,** and **rebel**?)

ORAL ACTIVITY

The change from a noun to a verb may be a spelling change, sometimes with a change in pronunciation also. What verbs correspond to these nouns?

advice   device   prophecy

The word **practice** is a noun, and **practise** is a verb, but the differentiation is tending to disappear, as is the difference between **licence** (noun) and **license** (verb).

What verbs correspond to these nouns? What is the pattern?

life   belief   strife   relief   grief   proof

REVIEW ACTIVITY

Write all the possible forms of these verbs:

Examples:

hope—hope, hopes, hoped, hoping (4 forms)
cut—cut, cuts, cutting (3 forms)
drink—drink, drinks, drank, drunk, drinking (5 forms). If you count **drunken** (a drunken sailor) there are 6 forms.

1. swing	2. slip	3. creep
4. become	5. fly	6. dry
7. go	8. rise	9. raise
10. sit	11. set	12. flow
13. lie	14. lie	15. lay (to
(to lie	(to tell	lay some-
down)	a lie)	thing down)

ORAL REVIEW ACTIVITY

English is basically a noun-verb language. The verb is often the "keyword" of the sentence, giving the thought its movement. The good writer chooses his verbs carefully.

Find all the verbs in the selections below. Discuss the effectiveness of the choices made by the authors.

1. Above us the wind whipped and tore at the curtain of flame on the canyon lip, as if protecting the stunted pine clinging there. Red-tongued, the fire plucked the poplars clean of leaves, smashed at the black battalions of spruce, and drove back with glaring light the darkness of coming night.

   —John.R. Barrett: "Red Invader"

2. Plows sliced the black prairie earth, wheat sprouted, cattle nibbled the new bunch grass, oil flowed from the breast of the central plains, miners' drills punctured the northern tundra, last year's crop moved in endless procession of freight trains to the Lakehead, and ships with bellies full of grain wallowed towards the St. Lawrence.

—Bruce Hutchison: *Canada: Tomorrow's Giant*

REVIEW ACTIVITY

What verbs would **you** use in the marked spaces? You must read the whole poem carefully, so that your choices will fit the images of the complete "idea" of the poem.

Your teacher will give you the poet's choices. Discuss how the verbs "fit" the poem.

REVIEW ACTIVITY

WRITING SENTENCES WITH EFFECTIVE VERBS

Write verbs that describe vividly how these move or act:

1. fog spreading over fields or a town

2. a fast river

3. a cat

4. a sailboat

5. wind

6. a crowd

7. skaters

Then write five interesting sentences using some of these verbs.

REVIEW ACTIVITY

Tape a sports broadcast—especially one giving a summary of scores—and comment on the verbs used. For example, how many are clichés? How many are conversions from nouns? How many are verbs of violence, and why are they used?

SNOW

It _____ from Leaden Sieves—
It _____ all the Wood.
It _____ with Alabaster Wool
The Wrinkles of the Road —

It makes an Even Face
Of Mountain, and of Plain —
Unbroken Forehead from the East
Unto the East again —

It _____ to the Fence—
It _____ it Rail by Rail
Till it is lost in Fleeces —
It deals Celestial Vail

To Stump, and Stack — and Stem —
A Summer's empty Room —
Acres of Joints, where Harvests were,
Recordless, but for them —

It _____ Wrists of Posts
As Ankles of a Queen —
Then stills its Artisans — like Ghosts —
Denying they have been —

—Emily Dickinson

Adjectives

Adjectives (like **nouns** and **verbs**) belong to the open classes (form words). Traditionally, an adjective has been defined as a word that modifies a noun. But, what does the word **modify** mean? Dictionaries give the following synonyms: to limit; to restrain; to restrict; to alter; to make partial changes; to qualify; to qualify the sense of; to tone down; to distinguish by investing with specific characteristics; to determine the amount of; to change without altering its essential nature; to qualify the sense of one word by another.

In the grammatical sense, **to modify** means 'to limit , to restrict'. For example, various modifiers can limit or restrict the idea of **car**:

Suppose we witness the "get-away" of some bank robbers, and we tell the police:

They went away in a **car**.

We are not very helpful, as there are thousands of cars. But if we add a modifier to **car**, for example,

They went away in a **green** car.

the modifier **green** limits the possibilities. All other colours are eliminated. Another modifier, for example, a **battered** green car   or

a green car **with a broken windshield**

further limits or restricts the idea of the car. A modifier of a noun is a word or phrase that limits or restricts the idea expressed by the noun.

Similarly, the noun **tree** may arouse many different images in your mind. But the placing of any modifier before **tree** limits the number of images possible.

Examples:

maple tree	**Christmas** tree	**dead** tree
large tree	**nut** tree	**old** tree
this tree	**our** tree	**dying** tree
Tom's tree	**the** tree	**growing** tree

All the words in bold type are **modifiers** of the noun **tree**. Sometimes the modifier follows the noun:

the tree **there**

the tree **outside**

the tree **by the gate**

the tree **with blossoms**

the tree **whose branches are bare**

the tree **growing by the gate**

All the above words or phrases modify the noun **tree**, but can they all be put into one class called "adjectives"? The traditional definition does not clearly separate adjectives from all the other kinds of modifiers of nouns. Yet we "know" that:

a **soapy** dish	is not	a **soap** dish
a **fortunate** hunter	is not	a **fortune** hunter
a **vicious** squad	is not	a **vice** squad
a **handy** book	is not	a **hand** book
a **watchful** man	is not	a **watching** man
a **medical** man	is not	a **medicine** man

By looking at the **form** of adjectives and how they **pattern** with other words, we can identify adjectives more exactly and separate them from all other modifiers of nouns.

INFORMING IDEA

All adjectives can function as modifiers of nouns. But not all modifiers of nouns are adjectives.

What then are the particular characteristics that distinguish adjectives from all other noun modifiers?

Test 1. Inflection

Some adjectives inflect for degree:

POSITIVE DEGREE	COMPARATIVE DEGREE	SUPERLATIVE DEGREE
a **pretty** girl	a **prettier** girl	the **prettiest** girl
a **sad** story	a **sadder** story	the **saddest** story
a **hot** day	a **hotter** day	the **hottest** day
hard work	**harder** work	**hardest** work

Other adjectives (usually longer) use the intensifiers **more** and **most** to indicate degree:

a **beautiful** tree   a **foolish** mistake
a **more beautiful** tree   a **more foolish** mistake
the **most beautiful** tree   the **most foolish** mistake

The words **less** and **least** follow the same pattern as **more** and **most**.

ORAL ACTIVITY

Use the inflection test or **more** or **most** to pick out the true adjectives in the following list:

grandfather clock	**heirloom** clock
ticking clock	**radio** clock
electric clock	**chiming** clock
expensive clock	**beautiful** clock
alarm clock	**accurate** clock
small clock	**white** clock
shiny clock	**Swiss** clock
cuckoo clock	**old** clock

IRREGULAR ADJECTIVES

A few adjectives do not have the regular -er and -est inflections. Here are their forms for degree:

good	better	best
bad	worse	worst
far	farther or further	farthest or furthest
old	older or elder	oldest or eldest
little	less or littler (or, to avoid this, smaller)	least or littlest

Test 2. Pattern with Intensifiers

The intensity of the true adjective can be affected by such words as **very, rather, somewhat, fairly, quite, too, more, most, less, least,** etc. Any word that can be substituted for **very** or **rather** in such patterns as the following is called an **intensifier**.

a **very** pretty tree   a **rather** pretty tree
a **very** beautiful tree   a **rather** beautiful tree

Traditionally, these were called adverbs; the name you give them, however, is not so important as making sure that you understand the structures.

ACTIVITY

Try the two tests for adjectives on the examples below.

(a) Do they inflect for degree (or with **more** or **most**)?
(b) Can they pattern with intensifiers, for example, **very** or **rather**?

(a) a **musical** teacher	(b) a **music** teacher
(c) a **flower** pattern	(d) a **flowery** pattern
(e) a **difficult** test	(f) a **spelling** test
(g) a **youth** group	(h) a **youthful** group
(i) a **young** group	(j) a **football** player
(k) an **intelligent** player	(l) a **record** player
(m) **this** player	(n) **Tom's** teacher

SOME TYPICAL ADJECTIVE SUFFIXES

Change the following words into adjectives. (Try **very** or **rather** before each one, to check if it is an adjective.) Each group illustrates a typical adjective suffix. Find what it is.

A. Nouns to Adjectives

(a) beauty, thought, power, help, doubt

(b) moss, rock, ice, anger, dirt, frost

(c) atom, athlete, nomad, cube

(d) accident, occasion, exception, continent, nature, person.

(e) courage, vigour, fame, marvel, disaster

B. Verbs to Adjectives

(a) possess, represent, explode, digest, construct

(b) perish, obtain, rely, suit, work, drink, read

ACTIVITY

Write sentences that show you understand the meanings of the following adjectives. Each pair illustrates how a different suffix makes a different meaning.

1. judicial — judicious

2. literate — literary

3. luxuriant — luxurious

4. childish — childlike

5. continuous — continual

6. contemptible — contemptuous

7. notable — notorious

8. respectable — respectful — respective

9. sensible — sensitive — sensual — sensuous

10. healthy — healthful

Functional Shift

We have already seen that a word in one form class can shift to another form class (verb to noun to adjective, etc.) by the use of derivational suffixes, for example, **decorate** (verb) — **decoration** (noun) — **decorative** (adjective).

Similarly, many **form words** may move from one class to another without using derivational suffixes. When they do, they take on the inflections typical of that class. This kind of change in function without the use of derivational suffixes is called **functional shift**. Here are examples of adjectives shifting to another form class.

Adjectives:

The **calm** water looked inviting.

He **calmed** the frightened children. (verb)

The **calm** of the water was deceiving. (noun)

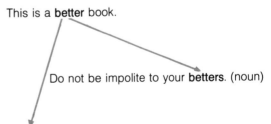

This is a **better** book.

Do not be impolite to your **betters**. (noun)

I **bettered** his score by two points. (verb)

ORAL ACTIVITY

Add an **-s** or an **-es** to these words, generally used as adjectives, and thus see which of them can be used as nouns.

Example: white — whites (Beat the **whites** of the eggs.)

- (a) blue
- (b) red
- (c) high
- (d) narrow
- (e) wide
- (f) western
- (g) strange
- (h) flat
- (i) special
- (j) huge
- (k) spectacular

Which of these can also be used as verbs without adding a derivational suffix?

(Test: Try each in the past tense.)

ACTIVITY

Write sentences in which these words are used as (a) adjectives, (b) nouns, (c) verbs.

1. right
2. yellow
3. equal

HOW WRITERS USE ADJECTIVES

Poor writers tend to use too many adjectives; good writers use adjectives sparingly and choose them with care.

ACTIVITY

In the following sentences a "key" adjective has been omitted. What adjectives would you put in? Discuss in class the authors' choices and yours. (The authors' choices are given on page 242.) What other adjectives are found in these selections?

1. Then he heard the mourning wind. It lashed the house, hard and _____. The house seemed caught inside one great mouth. The wind tried to swallow it, then rushed moaning across the fields like something out of its mind, gathering up the _____ snow, and returning again and again to knock itself out against the windows.

    —Ernest Buckler: *The Mountain and the Valley*

2. There were heavier pigeons, of a dark slate colour, and rotund, _____ partridges, and woodpeckers with _____ orange throats, and many kinds of hawk.

    —Peter Fleming: *Brazilian Adventure*

3. Small, _____ snails move about over rocks that are slippery with the growth of infinitesimal green plants; the snails scraping, scraping, scraping to find food before the surf returns. Smaller patches of green weed, _____ as mermaids' hair, begin to turn white and _____ where the sun has dried them.

    —Rachel Carson: *The Edge of the Sea*

4. To the shadows under the eastern bank a _____ mist still clung. The wind, a little wind which blew in your face from the north all through the middle of the day, had not yet risen, and the tall trees stood gravely inverted in the _____ surface of the water.

    —Peter Fleming: *Brazilian Adventure*

Summary of Adjectives

An adjective may be distinguished from other words that modify nouns by these tests:

1. adjectives inflect for degree (**-er, -est** endings) or take the substitutes **more** and **most** for the inflections.

2. adjectives pattern with intensifiers (very _____, rather _____, somewhat _____).

3. some adjectives have typical derivational suffixes. (List five.)

4. adjectives have typical positions and functions:

   (a) A rather _____ person is a person who is very _____.

   (b) A rather _____ thing is a thing that is very _____.

Remember:

A noun can have many different kinds of modifiers.

An adjective is one specific class of noun modifier.

Other Modifiers of Nouns

In English, adjectives are not the only modifiers of nouns. The language offers a wide range of possibilities. Here are examples of the most common.

1. NOUNS MODIFYING NOUNS

English shares with other Germanic languages the grammatical pattern of nouns strung together. Thus a noun can modify a noun.

> **oak** tree
> **oak tree** branch
> **doghouse** roof
> **typewriter** ribbon
> **study** room
> **wheat harvest** profits

Nouns (and pronouns) and noun groups followed by the possessive can also modify nouns.

> **the dog's** house
> **its** house
> **the man next door's** house
> **the year's** end
> **John's** camera
> **John and Jim's** camera
> **their** camera
> **someone's** camera

2. DETERMINERS

The class called **determiners** includes many words when they are used as noun modifiers. As the name suggests, a determiner signals that a noun will probably follow.

articles	—**the** boys, **a** big boy, **an** apple
demonstratives	—**this** boy, **these** boys, **that** boy, **those** boys
indefinites	—**some** boys, **no** boys, **each** boy
interrogatives	—**which** boys? **what** boys?
numerals	—**two** boys, **a thousand** boys, etc.

Some of these words can stand alone, in which instance they are generally classified as **pronouns**:

These came.   **Some** came.

Which came?   **Two** came.

They came in **twos**.

It is as modifiers of nouns that they may be called **determiners**.

Because **determiners** are a **closed** set, they are classed with the **structure words**.

ORAL ACTIVITY

Put these three types of noun modifiers (adjective, noun, and determiner) before the noun **tree** and formulate the rule for normal English order.

old (adj.), **oak** (noun), **the** (determiner):

———— ———— ———— tree

huge (adj.), **maple** (noun), **this** (determiner):

———— ———— ———— tree

two (determiner), **the** (determiner), **gnarled** (adj.), **cypress** (noun):

———— ———— ———— ———— trees

3. -ING FORM OF THE VERB

The **-ing** form of the verb can be a useful noun modifier because it retains something of the force of the verb. This form is called the **present participle**. Here are examples. What is the base or plain form of each verb?

a **sobbing** child
aching arms
the **leading** car
a **shocking** scene

4. -EN (OR -ED) FORM OF THE VERB

This pattern behaves like the **-ing** modifier, and is called the **past participle**. Sometimes the ending is **-en** (fallen), or **-t** (swept). (Note: This is the form of the verb that is used after **have**; for example, I have **swept** the room, have **taken**, and have **cleaned**.)

the **cleared** fields
a **protected** corner
the **hidden** treasure
cracked and **swollen** lips

5. COMPOUNDS

Interesting modifiers of nouns are often made by compounding various parts of speech. Here are some typical examples. Try to identify the elements in each group of compounds and make similar ones.

1. a **tight-fisted** miser, a **high-waisted** dress, a **blue-eyed** girl, a **golden-haired** girl, a **one-sided** argument, a **quick-witted** boy

2. **well-oiled** disposition, **far-flung** dominions, **under-done** roast, **closely-clipped** hedge, **outspoken** member, **well-lighted** room

3. **wind-swept** hills, **waterproofed** watch, **cellar-stored** apples, **grief-stricken** parents, **tongue-tied** child, **careworn** hands

4. **easygoing** parents, **tight-fitting** suit, **unfinished-looking** houses

5. **bone-dry** sand, **blood-red** ink, **footloose** traveller

Into which of the above groups would you place these:

air-borne,   broad-minded,   deep-laid,   outworn, gold-filled,   knife-sharp,   good-looking, headstrong,   ill-bred,   close-packed

There are hundreds more! Watch for interesting ones.

ORAL ACTIVITY

Here are a few good modifiers of nouns, as used by established writers. Discuss these in class, and make some on the same patterns.

heavy-headed wheat	noon-lazy day
the nervous river	foaming apple orchards
frost-whiskered oxen	small, silver splashes
bleeding sumac	the starch-clean pages
blue-cold snow	a corroded island

ACTIVITY

Write down one modifier for each of the following (a) a cat, (b) a body of water that you know, (c) a person you like, (d) the area in which you live, (e) a book or TV program you like, (f) a book or TV program you dislike.

Make your own collection of noun modifiers.

Summary

Modifiers Before Nouns

English nouns can have many different kinds of modifiers. Among the most common modifiers placed **before** the noun are:

(a) adjectives — **heavy** (**heavier**, **heaviest**) a
    rather **heavy** book
(b) nouns — **library** book **school library** book
    casserole recipe book
    possessives — **Stanley's** book
    — **his** book
    — **someone's** book
(c) determiners (structure words) — **the** book
    — **that** book
    — **any** book
(d) **-ing** form of the verb (present participle) —
    talking book
(e) **-ed** or **-en** form of the verb (past participle)
    — **borrowed** book
    — **stolen** book
(f) many kinds of compounds — **shopworn** book
    out-of-print book

Authors' Choices in Activity on Adjectives, page 238 .

1.   lost, helpless
2.   pompous, splendid
3.   dingy, stringy, crinkly
4.   thin, silken

Modifiers After the Noun

a fun-filled ten-day cruise

>   a cruise **filled with fun**
>   a cruise **of ten days**

a high-quality outdoor jacket

>   **a high-quality** jacket **for outdoors**
>   **an outdoor** jacket **of high quality**
>   a jacket **of high quality for outdoors**

a forest-fire fighter

>   a fighter **of forest fires**

A long list of modifiers before a noun can become unwieldy, for example,

>   **a relaxing fun-filled ten-day ocean** cruise

though of course such a structure can be used for special effects. But usually the distance between the determiner **a** or **the** and the noun is just too much for a listener or reader to hold in his head easily. For this reason the language allows some choices in the placement of modifiers, and long group modifiers are often placed **after** the noun, sometimes with slight changes in structure.

Here are examples of modifiers after the noun:

The apple, **red and juicy**, tempted her.
The child, **sobbing bitterly**, searched in the crowd for its mother.
The car **leading the procession** was gaily decorated with flowers.

The fields, **so carefully cleared by hand**, were now reverting to forest.
We found a quiet corner **protected from the sun.**
His lips, **cracked and swollen by fever**, could scarcely say the words.
His shoes, **far too big for him**, gave him blisters.

Notice that the **whole group** is the modifier. It is not necessary to break it up.

In which of the above sentences could the modifier be placed **before** the noun?

Usage and Modifiers

1. THE POSITION OF MODIFIERS

"Please return this form with tooth attached to your child's teacher."

Modifiers of nouns cannot wander too far from the noun they modify. When a noun modifier opens a sentence, for example, the word it modifies must follow immediately:

This pattern:

Clanging loudly, the bells of the church announced the New Year.
On hearing this, the child burst into tears.
Hidden in the cave, the treasure remained unfound for centuries.

But not this pattern:

Clanging loudly, the New Year was announced by the bells of the church.
On hearing this, tears came into the child's eyes.
Hidden in the cave, centuries went by before the treasure was found.

The reader **expects** the modified noun to follow the modifier.

The pattern is really like this:

The bells of the church | clanged loudly.
The bells of the church | announced the New Year.

Because the first two parts are the same, one can be omitted, to get the structure:

Clanging loudly, the bells of the church . . .

But the listener or reader expects the omitted part to be next.

Try doing this kind of analysis with the other two.

When the right noun does not follow the opening modifier (as in the last three examples), the modifier is said to be a **dangling modifier**. (For further work on dangling modifiers, see Chapter 4, pages 133-5.)

2. AMBIGUITY WITH MODIFIERS OF NOUNS

The writer in English can use many kinds of words as modifiers of nouns. This range of choice makes the language flexible, but increases the danger of giving two meanings (ambiguity). Note the possible meanings of:

The old book salesman

Does **old** modify **book salesman**, "the book salesman who is old", or does **old** modify only **book**, "the salesman of old books"? Here hyphens are necessary to show the groupings of your words:

the old book-salesman   the old-book salesman

There is less trouble if the group is spoken aloud. Many sentences are clear when spoken, but ambiguous when written. For example, why are the following **written** phrases ambiguous?

my last summer job
a French teacher
fresh raspberry ice cream
a light blue dress
a boys' school choir
a plain woman's dress

Sometimes when we write structures such as these, we "hear" the words the way we "mean" them, but the reader may find them confusing — or amusing.

Our pills contain an extra active ingredient.

a wild mink jacket

ORAL ACTIVITY

Find all the modifiers of nouns. Discuss the writer's choices.

I remember the rainy lakeside days, and how, after the rain, great raindrops would cling on to the serrated leaves of brambles like hundreds of minute lenses, through which the sun, emerging in a rinsed sky, would gleam with a new-seeming whiteness. I remember the long black slugs on paths wrinkled by many torrential downpours, and the smell of the earth, and how on our walks we found rock crystals on the stones like lost enjewelled caskets.

—Stephen Spender: *World Within World*

ACTIVITY

Join each group of ideas into one good sentence.

Try various positions of the modifiers until you find the arrangement you like best, and mark that sentence with a star.

Then compare your sentences with those of a partner or of others in your class.

1. The owner of the shop stood at the door. He was little. He was stooped. He had shrewd eyes.
2. The three children rode saddle horses. The children were the oldest. They were aged six, ten, and eleven. They herded the cattle.
3. The sky was clear. It was black. It seemed studded with stars. The stars looked icy. The sky seemed remote. It seemed to be high above the spruce trees. The spruce trees were shaggy.

4. The paintings of Van Gogh are now recognized. They are seen as the work of a genius. In his lifetime, they were overlooked.

ORAL ACTIVITY

The following was a newspaper headline. What part of speech is each word? How do you know?

> # Police Police Police
>
> # Ball

ORAL ACTIVITY

What is the difference in meaning between these two groups? Is there a pattern of difference in stress?

(a) a dancing child
a waiting client
a flying bird
wading birds
playing children
diving birds

(b) a dancing school
a waiting room
a flying field
wading boots
a playing field
diving boards

ACTIVITY

From either advertisements or literature, collect examples of interesting modifiers of nouns. Write a short discussion of why you find them especially interesting.

Adverbs

The fourth open class is called the **adverb** class. Just as the noun may have modifiers clustered around it, so a verb may have modifiers, called adverbs. Here are some types of adverbs:

The children entered **quietly**. (how?) — adverb of manner

The children came **soon**. (when?) — adverb of time

The children ran **away**. (where?) — adverb of place

The children **soon** ran **away quietly**.

POSITION OF ADVERBS

Find all the possible positions for the adverbs in the following sentences. Discuss the resulting changes in emphasis.

The children left **reluctantly**.

The mob had dispersed **quietly**.

You must return **soon**.

The student answered **often rudely**.

Lilacs are blooming **profusely there now**.

Unlike adjectives, which have fairly fixed positions before and after the noun, adverbs can often move freely in the sentence. It is in this sense that "the adverb can be the controlling word in the sentence".

PATTERN OF ADVERBS WITH INTENSIFIERS

Some adverbs can be modified by intensifiers, such as **very, rather, quite,** or **somewhat**. Try adding intensifiers to the adverbs in the sentences above.

FORM OF ADVERBS: A TYPICAL DERIVATIONAL SUFFIX

How are these adjectives made into adverbs of manner?

a **noisy** crowd	The crowd shouted _____.
a **mischievous** boy	The boy grinned _____.
an **unhappy** woman	The woman spoke _____.
a **rude** student	The student spoke _____.
a **playful** puppy	The puppy jumped _____ on me.

Many adverbs—especially adverbs of manner—are formed with the **-ly** derivational suffix added to an adjective. Add to the list above.

ACTIVITY

Try making up some "Tom Swifties"—puns using **-ly** adverbs of manner. Here are some examples:

"Pass the sugar," she said sweetly.
"I work with Xerox machines," he explained repeatedly.
"My pencil is dull," she said pointlessly.
Patiently, she sat waiting in the doctor's office.
"I'll take a chance and pass on the curve," he said finally.
The little boy stretched his hand towards the candy counter, longingly.
She made many errors in the manuscript, typically.
The author of *Gulliver's Travels* wrote swiftly.

Warning: Do not think that all **-ly** words are adverbs! Look at the following pattern:

Noun	Adjective
a **man**	a **manly** act
a **friend**	a **friendly** person
the **heavens**	a **heavenly** blessing
a **ghost**	a **ghostly** appearance

FORM OF ADVERBS: INFLECTION

Do adverbs, like adjectives, inflect for degree? (Try the **-er**, **-est** endings with such short adverbs as **fast** (He ran fast), **soon**, **late**, **near**.

Do longer adverbs, like longer adjectives, use **more** and **most**? Try **quickly**, **mischievously**, **noisily**, **beautifully**.

Do all adverbs inflect for degree? Which of the following can be inflected?

She sings **loudly**.	They talked **quietly**.
He came **yesterday**.	I do it **sometimes**.
We looked **around**.	She laughed **self-consciously**.
Please look **up**.	He walked **away**.

Functions of Adverbs

1. ADVERBS MODIFY ALL FORMS OF VERBS.

-ing form:

the **early** rising birds
Rising **early** is a good habit.
a **quietly** clucking hen
the hen **quietly** clucking to her chicks

-ed or **-en** form:

an **easily** constructed house
well-cooked eggs
newly chosen treasurer
the work **never** finished
prunes **slowly** cooked in water
the chairperson **newly** chosen by the company

infinitive form (**to** + verb):

To see you **again** is a pleasure.
I want you to stop **soon**.
It is better to wait **awhile**.
There is nothing to fear **now**.

2. ADVERBS MODIFY ADJECTIVES.

her **quietly** insistent demands

her **sadly** beautiful face

his **unusually** quiet manner

his **always** ready smile

These are different from intensifiers such as **very**, **somewhat**, and **rather**, as the words can themselves be adverbs modifying verbs. (We would not, for example, say: he ran **very**, he coughed **somewhat**, he laughed **rather**, but we can say he coughed **quietly**.)

3. ADVERBS MODIFY OTHER ADVERBS.

The child speaks **amazingly** well.

We moved **far** away.

As in the group above, these are adverbs rather than intensifiers, as they can also be used with verbs.

However, this distinction is not important, as the whole group **amazingly well** or **far away** is the modifier of the verb.

4. ADVERBS MODIFY WHOLE SENTENCES.

Slowly and quietly, he got out of bed.

Truthfully, I didn't do it.

Adverbs are a problem for grammarians. Sometimes an adverb seems to modify the whole statement. The first example above means almost the same as:

He was slow and quiet as he got out of bed.

Usually (but not always) such sentence modifiers come first in the sentence. Sometimes they are marked off by commas, but the punctuation depends upon the emphasis and rhythm the writer wants. Here are examples of adverbs used as sentence modifiers. Try reading these aloud with and without commas to "hear" the difference.

Obviously he has been to a party.

Meanwhile, somebody found the puppy.

Surely you will study tonight!

Unfortunately, nothing happened.

Nothing, **unfortunately**, happened.

Nothing happened, **unfortunately**.

Some grammarians also include with sentence-modifying adverbs such words as:

Yes, I'll go tonight.

Never, I could not do it.

Perhaps, but I'm busy now.

These are really connectives, referring to the previous statement.

Also included may be such explicit connectives as **however, nevertheless, moreover, therefore, hence, furthermore, secondly, consequently**, used to relate the ideas of two sentences or statements. Like adverbs, they may move around within the sentence, and are therefore usually set off by commas. Note the punctuation.

He looked very ill. **However**, he did go to school.

He looked very ill; **however**, he did go to school.

He looked very ill; he did, **however**, go to school.

(usually considered the best placement)

He looked very ill. He did go to school, **however**.

Nouns as Adverbs or Adverbial Groups

He comes **Mondays** to clean.

He comes **every day**.

He'll be here **Monday**.

We waited **a long while**.

We waited **two hours**.

Every summer we go to camp.

All summer it rained.

Do it **this way**.

They arrived **two days ago.**
He fell **ten feet.**
We waited **two hours more.**
We went **home.** (Compare: We went **there.**)
Day after day it rained.

Very common in English are nouns or noun groups used as adverbs. Just call these **adverbial groups.**

Note: Although adverbs may often move to various positions in the sentence, each change in position can change the meaning of the sentence.

Tom borrowed **only** a dime from me.

Only Tom borrowed a dime from me.

Tom **only** borrowed a dime from me.

Tom borrowed a dime from **only** me.

When speaking, we need not be so careful, as the intonation of our voice suggests the right meaning. In writing, however, we place the modifier carefully. Notice how our voice can give this written sentence two possible meanings:

Tom borrowed a dime **only** from me.

Adverb or Adjective?

Some of the short adverbs without the **-ly** ending can be used as either adverbs or adjectives. Which are adverbs in the following?

He worked **hard.**
Hard work will not hurt you.
The candy is too **hard.**

He ran **fast.**
A **fast** runner could catch him.

Early fishermen catch the fish.
You must get up **early** to catch fish.

I worked **longer** than you did.
A **longer** string is necessary.

Summary of Adverbs

1. Some adverbs inflect for degree.
2. Many adverbs end in the derivational suffix -ly.
3. Some adverbs may be intensified by such words as **very, rather, scarcely,** and **too.**
4. Adverbs may modify verbs, adjectives, adverbs, or whole sentences.
5. Some adverbs are movable, and thus can give various meanings and emphases to the sentence.

ACTIVITY

The following sentences are based on sentences used by Charles G. D. Roberts to describe a mink. Find the adverbs or adverbial groups, and tell what each modifies. Discuss in class the author's choices.

1. His pointed, sinister, quietly savage face and head **were** set on a long but heavily-muscled neck.

2. His legs were ridiculously short.

3. This he probably adopted for the fun of it, for his hunting tactics were usually those of stealthy advance.

   —"When the Tide Came over the Marshes"

The following sentences, based on sentences used by Roberts, describe the actions of a blue heron. Find the adverbs. Discuss the author's choices.

4. Then, for no apparent reason, the long neck uncoiled violently like a loosed crossbow, and the javelin beak shot downward.

5. Deep into the weeds and water it darted,—to return with a small, silvery chub securely transfixed.

6. He was also fishing for some extraordinarily hungry nestlings in the cedar swamp.

7. Having hidden the frog, the heron raised his head and steadily surveyed the shores.

8. Assured that no peril was lurking near, he winnowed slowly along the shore, his legs trailing ludicrously.

9. Suddenly he unlimbered, and went stalking gravely up along the sloppy mud.

    —"The Heron in the Reeds"

Summary

Four open classes (the form classes):
1. Nouns
2. Verbs
3. Adjectives
4. Adverbs

These are recognized by a speaker of English by various "clues":

1. word form
   - inflections
   - derivational suffixes

2. patterning with other words — for example, nouns with determiners (structure words)
   adj. and adv. with intensifiers (structure words)

3. meaning and function — for example, adj. and adv. function as modifiers

No one test is usually enough for identification. But the speaker of English recognizes the classes from these various clues.

An ippy ip ipped ippily.
Can you classify each word?

The Main Classes of Structure Words (Closed Classes)

Because there are only a few hundred structure words in English and they are closed classes, we can define them by **listing** them, and showing how they function in a sentence. Most of them can be classified into smaller groups. We have already looked at two classes of structure words: **determiners** (**the, a, these, two**, etc.) which pattern with nouns; and **intensifiers** (**very, rather, too, more, most**, etc.) which pattern with adjectives and adverbs. The other main classes are: **Pronouns, Prepositions, Conjunctions** (co-ordinate and subordinate), and **Interjections**.

Pronouns

> The truth is that our English pronouns are a disorderly and drunken lot. We no sooner straighten them up on one side than they fall over on the other.

—Stephen Leacock

No one would write the following sentence (except to illustrate a point):

Martha's father said that Martha's father would punish Martha if Martha stayed out later than the time Martha's father had set.

To avoid repetition of nouns, we use pronouns (**pro-** 'acting for' **nouns**):

Martha's father said that **he** would punish **her** if **she** stayed out later than the time **he** had set.

It is not difficult to recognize pronouns; they are a closed class, and we can list them. Here are the words commonly used as pronouns, arranged according to kind.

1. PERSONAL PRONOUNS

SUBJECT FORMS		OBJECT FORMS	
singular	plural	singular	plural
I	we	me	us
you	you	you	you
he		him	
she	they	her	them
it		it	

POSSESSIVE FORMS	
singular	plural
my, mine	our, ours
your, yours	your, yours
his	
her, hers	their, theirs
its	

To Note:

The personal pronouns inflect for:

1. number (Which one does not?)

2. person (first person, **I, me, us**, etc.; second person, **you, your**, etc.; third person, **he, she, it, they, them**, etc.)

3. gender — to refer to sex (In which person only? Does the plural inflect for gender?)

4. case — according to the function of the pronoun in a sentence (Which one does not contrast subject and object forms?)
   — There are two possessive forms; one is a modifier of a noun:
   my book   **her** desk   **their** pencil (etc.)
   the other is used when it stands alone:
   It is **mine**. **Hers** is over there. Give me **theirs**.

Note — The possessive forms of the personal pronouns do **not** use an apostrophe.

2. REFLEXIVE PRONOUNS

myself — ourselves
yourself — yourselves
himself — herself — itself — themselves

Do they inflect for number? (Which part changes?)

Do they inflect for person? (Which part changes?)
Do they inflect for gender?
Do they inflect for case? (Try them in various places within sentences; do they change form?)

These eight are the **only** standard forms; the expressions **hisself**, **theirselves**, and **theirself** do not exist in standard English.

3. OTHER PRONOUNS

The pronouns **this** and **that** have plural forms, **these** and **those**:

This is mine.	**These** are mine.
Give me **that**.	Give me **those**.

This, **that**, **these**, and **those** are called the **demonstrative** pronouns.

The pronoun **who** may inflect for case (with forms parallel to **him** and **his**): **who whom** (objective)   **whose** (possessive).

Some pronouns that do not inflect are: **which**, **what**, **whichever**, **whatever**, and **that** (when it is not a demonstrative).

All these **wh-** pronouns are used as question-words (interrogatives):

Who is it?

Whose is it?

What do you want?

Whatever does he want?

All these may also be used as connectives, and will be discussed later with Conjunctions.

I know **who** it is.
I'll take **whatever** you have.
The one **that** I want is gone.

4. INDEFINITE PRONOUNS

This is a large class of pronouns, some singular, some plural, and some either singular or plural. They are called **indefinites** because of their meaning. Here are the most common indefinite pronouns:

any	some	nobody else
anybody	somebody	somebody else
anyone	someone	someone else
anything	something	something else
none	each	other(s)
nobody	everybody	another
no one	everyone	each other
nothing	everything	one another
many	one(s)	**All** is fine.
both	all	**All** were right.
much	either	
most	neither	**Few** came.
few		**Neither** came.

Bring a big **one**.	**Most** of it is green.
Bring only big **ones**.	**Most** of them are green.

Many of the indefinite pronouns inflect for possessives. Notice that, unlike other pronouns, the indefinites use an apostrophe (like nouns) for the possessive form.

anybody's guess
somebody else's coat
no one's responsibility

The indefinite pronouns may also have a modifier. Compare the **position** of these modifiers with that of modifiers of nouns:

Something **soft** was in the box.

Someone **honest** will return it.

(But: Bring **the two biggest** ones.)

PRONOUNS AND DETERMINERS

The two word classes, pronouns and determiners, overlap; that is, many may occur by themselves (in regular noun positions) and may also occur as modifiers before nouns. It is perhaps simplest to call them **pronouns** when they occur by themselves, and **determiners** when they modify nouns.

PRONOUNS	DETERMINERS
Each costs ten cents.	**Each** book costs ten cents.
Each of the books costs ten cents.	
Few of the parents came.	**Few** parents came.
Some left early.	**Some** guests left early.
Give me **some** of the apples, please.	Give me **some** apples, please.

PRONOUNS AND USAGE

1. Case — Johnny and I? **or** Johnny and me? He and she? **or** Him and her?

A helpful rule is to try one pronoun only, and your own language sense will tell you the correct form; for example:

Johnny and **I** went to the movies. (**I** went to the movies.)

She asked Johnny and **me** to the party. (She asked **me** to the party.)

2. Spelling of Possessives — Remember that the personal pronouns (**hers, his, its, theirs, yours,** etc.) and the forms of **who** never take an apostrophe for the possessive.

The book is **yours.**   The bird is in **its** nest. **Whose** book is it?

Any form with the apostrophe must be a contraction, for example:

it's = **it is** or **it has.**   **It's** in the nest. **It's** been a long, long time.

who's = **who is** or **who has.**   **Who's** there? **Who's** taken my book?

For more about pronouns and usage, see Chapter 8, page 306.

Summary of Pronouns

Pronouns are a closed set, so are classified as structure words.

Some pronouns have inflections for number, case, and a few use grammatical gender for sex-reference (**he — she — it**, etc.).

There are various kinds of pronouns: personal, reflexive, demonstrative, indefinite, and others.

Some words can function as pronouns (by themselves) or as determiners (as modifiers of nouns).

ORAL ACTIVITY

Find all the pronouns in the following excerpts. Discuss what kind each is, and its use.

1. Perhaps the most valuable result of all education is the ability to make yourself do the thing you have to do, when it ought to be done, whether you like it or not; . . . however early a man's training begins, it is probably the last lesson that he learns thoroughly.

   —Thomas H. Huxley

2. Our map shows all those that can be seen in this telescope. Others, of course, can be seen in one with stronger lenses.
3. One of the inns was taken over by the soldiers, for, although it looked like nothing at all from the outside, it was warm and comfortable inside. This remained their headquarters for several months.
4. I could easily see what some of the signs stood for: one with a huge spool was for a dry-goods store; another, with a bottle, was the wine-merchant's; one that puzzled me was a huge golden ram, but this, I discovered, was the name of the local restaurant. Who, I wondered, would know that unless he were acquainted with the village?

CAN YOU DO THIS?

1. English personal pronouns are very old, and have kept many of their _____ .
2. The pronoun **who** inflects for _____ only.
3. Unlike nouns, personal pronouns in the possessive case have no _____ .
4. The expression **it's** always means _____ or _____ .

ACTIVITY

In how many ways can you interpret this newspaper headline? For each interpretation, mark the parts of speech you are recognizing.

To save space, newspaper editors omit from headlines all unnecessary words, particularly the structure words.

Put the determiners **a** or **the** into your various interpretations. What do you discover?

COMMITTEE TOLD

Content chief concern of CBC

Prepositions

"What did you bring that book I don't like to be read aloud to out of from up for?"

THE NAUGHTY PREPOSITION

I lately lost a preposition;
  It hid, I thought, beneath my chair;
And angrily I cried, "Perdition!
  Up from out of in under there!"

Correctness is my vade mecum,[1]
  And straggling phrases I abhor,
And yet I wondered, "What should he come
  Up from out of in under for?"

—Morris Bishop

In the following selection, all prepositions have been omitted. Reading this shows us how important prepositions are, and why they are called "structure words".

_____ the morning I watched the geese _____ the door _____ the mist, sailing _____ the middle _____ the pond, fifty rods off, so large and tumultuous that Walden appeared _____ an artificial pond _____ their amusement. But when I stood _____ the shore they _____ once rose up _____ a great flapping _____ wings _____ the signal _____ their commander, and when they had got _____ rank circled _____ _____ my head, twenty-nine _____ them, and then steered straight _____ Canada, _____ a regular honk _____ the leader _____ intervals, trusting to break their fast _____ muddier pools.

—Thoreau: *Walden*

---

[1]Guide, or manual.

Many prepositions are very old words. We have about seventy prepositions, and most of them have been used for centuries. Here are the most common ones. Note that prepositions have no inflections. They belong to a limited and closed set.

about	inside
above	into
across	like
after	near
against	of
along	off
among	no
around	out
at	over
before	past
behind	since
below	through
beside	throughout
between	to
beyond	toward
by	under
concerning	underneath
despite	until
down	up
during	upon
except	with
for	within
from	without
in	

There are also compound and group prepositions, such as:

> alongside
> out of
> ahead of
> by way of
> on account of
> by means of
> in front of
> in place of

> owing to
> because of
> instead of
> in spite of
> in accordance with

Eight prepositions—**at, by, for, from, in, of, to,** and **with**—are used again and again. (Check by looking at a few pages of prose.)

Prepositions are not used alone, but make tight groups with other words; these groups are called **prepositional phrases**.

> on the street
> to school
> near the gates
> towards our house
> without any food or water
> throughout the year
> ahead of the wagon
> in spite of the weather

They are called **adjectival phrases** if they modify a noun or pronoun:

> the car **on the street**
> the way **to school**
> the house **near the gates**
> the plans **of the house**
> the time **without food or water**
> the weather **throughout the year**
> somebody **ahead of the wagon**
> the weakness **of the plan**

What is their position in relation to the nouns they modify?

They are called **adverbial phrases** if they modify a verb:

> Drive **on the street.**
> He went **to school.**
> We lived **without food or water.**
> He walked **ahead of the wagon.**

PREPOSITIONAL PHRASES IN GROUPS

We often find prepositional phrases in groups. Frequently an **of** phrase is part of the group:

1. He opened it **with a smile of anticipation.**

2. I found his name **in the list of students in first year.**

3. **In my search for the book,** I found an interesting letter **from an uncle of mine.**

4. We will walk **from here to there.**

In sentence 1, treat the whole group **with a smile of anticipation** as an adverbial phrase modifying the verb **opened.** The phrase **of anticipation** is adjectival, modifying the noun **smile,** but there is little point in breaking up the whole natural adverbial group.

Adverbial phrases, like adverbs, are "movables" in the sentence. We may change their position to get sentence variety and a change of emphasis. It is not always possible to say exactly what the phrase does modify.

His father waited **near the gates.**

Near the gates waited his father.

Near the gates, his father waited.

His father was **near the gates.**

Near the gates was his father.

OBJECT OF THE PREPOSITION

Most prepositional phrases have a noun at the end; such a noun is said to be "object of the preposition". If a pronoun replaces the noun, it is in the objective case form:

He came with **John.**
He came with **him.**

He came with **Margaret.**
He came with **her.**

With **whom** did you come? (formal)
Who did you come with? (informal)
(Note the position of the preposition.)

FUNCTIONAL SHIFT: ADVERB OR PREPOSITION?

Most of the prepositions in our list may also be used as adverbs. They are **adverbs** if used **alone,** as modifiers of verbs. They are **prepositions** if they are **structure words,** that is, beginning a prepositional phrase:

ADVERBS
Someone walked **past.**
He fell **down.**
The dog ran **about** wildly.
Look **above** and see the stars!

PREPOSITIONAL PHRASES
Someone walked **past me.**
He fell **down the stairs.**
He talked **about his plans for the factory.**
Look **above the word** and find its synonym.

ACTIVITY

Try patterns similar to the above with **before, after, around, aboard,** and **across.**

Leave off the **OFF**, and take out the **OUT**. What happens?

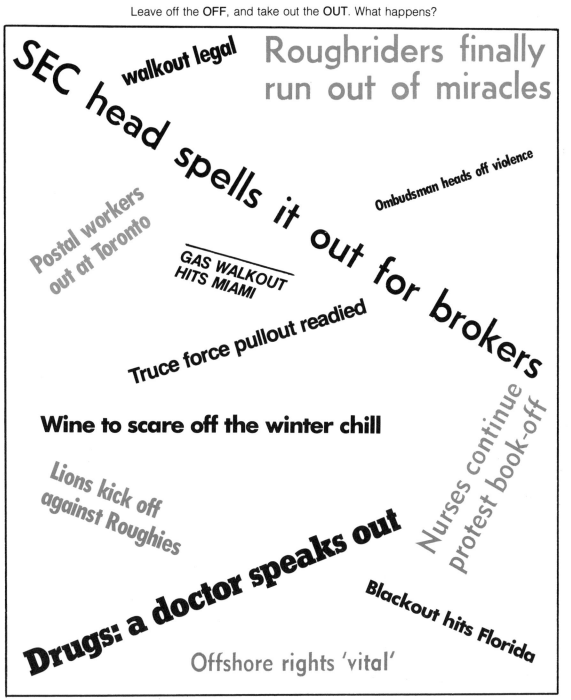

SEC head spells it out for brokers

walkout legal

Roughriders finally run out of miracles

Ombudsman heads off violence

Postal workers out at Toronto

GAS WALKOUT HITS MIAMI

Truce force pullout readied

Wine to scare off the winter chill

Nurses continue protest book-off

Lions kick off against Roughies

Drugs: a doctor speaks out

Blackout hits Florida

Offshore rights 'vital'

PHRASAL VERBS

Some of the short words that belong to both the adverb and the preposition classes — uninflected words such as **in**, **out**, **by**, **to**, **up**, **down**, **off**, and **on**— can be so closely related to a verb that they are really part of the verb.

Here are a few examples of such "phrasal verbs". Add to each group.

give in	get in	take on	put on
give up	get up	take in	put up
give out	get on	take up	put up with
set up	set down	send off	make for
set off	set apart	send up	make up

run on (about)	do for
run up against	do away with
run out of	do in

Thus in the sentences:

> Mother **put up** seven quarts of fruit.
> I will not **put up with** your nonsense.
> I must **get in** some wood.
> I must **do away with** these old jars.

the groups act like units. In sentence 1, for example, **seven quarts of fruit** is direct object of **put up**. Listen for the natural groupings.

FUNCTIONAL SHIFT WITH PHRASAL VERBS

When phrasal verbs are converted into nouns or modifiers (as is characteristic of English), the combination remains a unit:

a good **send-off**	an actor's **make-up**
a bad **setback**	a **put-up** job
the spring **run-off**	a **run-down** clock
a **runaway** horse	a **come-back**
the plane's **take-off**	

Note the order of these: **outlet, input,** a **downpour.** What combinations does your dictionary give with **come,** and **keep?**

ORAL ACTIVITY

Suggest the situations that would give rise to these sentences. Then discuss how the meaning of the verb **took** may be affected by what follows it. Try to replace **took, took up,** etc. with another verb.

1. I took up the drawing.
2. I took up drawing.
3. I took the drawing.
4. I took the job.
5. I took over the job.
6. I took on the job.
7. I took to the job.
8. He took in the chairs.
9. He took in what I said.

"Wouldn't you feel **put out** if you were **evicted?**"

ORAL ACTIVITY

In the previous Activity, replace each noun group after the verb with the pronoun **it** or **them.** What do you discover about word order?

ACTIVITY

What phrasal verb could you use to replace these single verbs?

Examples: erase — rub out, or rub off
   enter — go in, or come in

1. return	2. insert	3. inspect
4. approach	5. rehearse	6. advance
7. adopt	8. discover	9. pursue
10. detach		

ACTIVITY

In a dictionary, look up all the meanings of the preposition **with**. How many do you find? Make sentences using the various meanings. Others in the class may do similar work with **by, of, to, at,** and **for.**

ACTIVITY

Find all the prepositional groups in the following excerpt.

> I broke off work to walk on the terrace on the roof of my apartment building in Montreal. It was nine-thirty in the evening. Cars were streaming down the slope of Côte des Neiges in a steady cascade. Less than a mile away, on a lower level, the lights in the Sun Life Building showed that cleaners were at work in the empty offices. Across the St. Lawrence an undulating bracelet of light marked the line of the farther shore. The smoke shrouding the acres of slums near the left bank of the river glowed and smouldered in the lights striking through it.

— Hugh MacLennan: "The Tyranny of the Sunday Suit"

ACTIVITY

Write five sentences beginning with a prepositional phrase. Use different prepositions.

PREPOSITIONS AND USAGE

1. Choice

WHAT'S THE DIFFERENCE?	
I believe him.	He reached him.
I believe in him.	He reached toward him.
a concern for his patients	
a concern of his patients	
I walked in the room	I talked to him.
I walked into the room.	I talked with him.
I walked to the room.	I talked at him.

Preposition usage depends on custom rather than rule. We must learn the preposition when we learn a new expression. It is "English" to say, for example:

full **of** water   yet   filled **with** water

He was angry **with** me.   yet
He was angry **at** my behaviour.

In other words, the use of prepositions is really a vocabulary problem. If in doubt, consult a dictionary.

2. Preposition at the End

In certain structures involving the **wh-** "question words" (see page 111), we put the preposition at the end of the sentence, separated from the rest of its group:

What are you talking **about**? (about what)

I don't know **what** you are talking **about**.
(about what)

Which car are you riding **in**? (in which car)

I'm not sure **which car** to ride **in**. (in which car)

I do not care **where** you are **from**. (from where)

I know **which city** he is **from**. (from which city)

It is sometimes said that we should not end a sentence with a preposition. Certainly it is a good policy to save for the final position of a sentence a strong word — and a preposition is only a structure word. Nevertheless, the idiom sometimes demands a preposition at the end, and it is better to use one than to write something awkward.

Churchill once made fun of a proof-reader who worked by the rule rather than by ear. Churchill wrote beside the awkward sentence, "This is the kind of English up with which I can not put."

For further work on Prepositions and Usage, see Chapter 8, page 311.

Conjunctions

What two kinds of words or groups are joined by the word in bold type:

The river was swift **and** deep.
The river was swift; **yet** we decided to cross.
Here the river runs slowly **but** treacherously.
The river was swift; **so** we decided not to cross.
The river runs past our house **and** around a big bend.
The river is **neither** swift, **nor** treacherous.
The creek, **as well as** the river, is deep.

Check: Can you change the position of the joining words?

CO-ORDINATE CONJUNCTIONS

Conjunctions are structure words that connect words or groups of words. All the above conjunctions are **co-ordinate conjunctions**, because they connect two words or two groups that are **co-ordinate**, or of equivalent grammatical value. The most common co-ordinate conjunctions are:

and or nor but

Sometimes **for yet as well as** work as co-ordinate conjunctions.

Co-ordinate Conjunctions in Pairs: Correlatives

Co-ordinate conjunctions sometimes work in pairs called **correlatives**. Find the words or groups joined by the following correlatives. Are they equal grammatically?

The river is **neither** deep **nor** treacherous.
You must **either** swim **or** drown.
The river is **not only** deep, **but also** treacherous.
Both the river **and** the creek are deep.

ACTIVITY

Write sentences using co-ordinate conjunctions joining:

(a) the nouns **bicycles, cars**

(b) the verbs **listen, believe**

(c) the prepositional phrases **into the air, over the treetops**

(d) the adverbs **selfishly, foolishly**

(e) the **-ing** groups **denying** . . . , **refusing** . . .

(f) the prepositions **in, out**

(g) two sentences

Parallelism

Co-ordinate conjunctions make it possible to shorten sentences. Rather than repeat the whole statement, as:

I like to skate and **I like to ski.**

we can eliminate one of the repeated parts **I like** or **I like to** and list the other elements as a series:

I like | to skate.

I like | to ski.

I like **to skate** and **to ski.**

I like to | skate.

I like to | ski.

I like to **skate** and **ski.**

Notice that the elements joined are grammatically alike — or **parallel** — in structure. When joining two structures with correlatives, we must be careful that the two are parallel, for example,

either _____ or _____
either **swimming** or **boating**
(**not**: either **swimming** or **to boat**)

not only _____ but also _____
not only **to make money** but also **to help others**
(**not**: not only **to make money** but also **helping others**)

For further work, see Parallelism, Chapter 4, pages 135-9.

ACTIVITY

Diagram the following sentences to show the parallel elements. (Use one of the methods shown above.) First find the co-ordinate conjunctions. Discuss how parallelism improves the sentences.

1. He was tired of living but afraid of dying.
2. We must hope that the war will be brief, that the victory will be ours, and that justice will prevail afterwards.
3. I did not know where I was or how I got there.
4. I knew neither where I was nor how I got there.
5. The letter is not only untidy but also poorly spelled.
6. He is not only a good athlete but also a first-class student.
7. People either like this program, or hate it.

ACTIVITY

Compose sentences in which you use parallelism to stress ideas about:

1. a television program
2: compact cars
3. jazz
4. a good _____ player
5. Christmas
6. the wind

Ambiguity with Co-ordinate Conjunctions

ORAL ACTIVITY

Explain why the following written sentences are ambiguous:

1. A young, tired-looking woman carrying a small child and her husband entered the store.
2. I was excited, for it was the day before the concert and my birthday.
3. We had fresh bread, fruit, and milk.

ORAL ACTIVITY

Find all the **and**s in the following paragraph. Then tell what type of structure each joins. Discuss the writer's use of parallelism.

Up the valleys and down the plains, over mountain-tops and across rivers, the storms came striding towards us. Those lovely smaller lakes of the highlands of Kenya, whose deep-blue waters are so heavily burdened with sunlight and cloud and pink flamingos along their shores; those snow-capped towers of Mount Kenya; those snug homesteads and blood-red roads going from nowhere to nowhere through bush and plain, were now all hidden from view as completely as if it had been night. Bumping and driving hard through heavy rain, we hardly saw land again until some hours later we climbed with relief out of the plane at Nairobi.

—Laurens van der Post: *Venture to the Interior*

Conjunctions and Meaning: "Signal" Devices

Conjunctions do more than "join". What different meanings do these conjunctions give to the two statements?

He is a young man, **and** I'll vote for him.
He is a young man, **but** I'll vote for him.

He's very generous, **and**...
He's very generous, **but**...

SUBORDINATE CONJUNCTIONS

Co-ordinate conjunctions are used to join two (or more) **equal** ideas.

The car went through a stop sign.
The police arrested the driver.

If we join these two sentences with the co-ordinate conjunction **and**, we are adding one idea to another:

The car went through a stop sign
and the police arrested the driver.

If we use the co-ordinate conjunction **but**, we are contrasting one idea with another, or expressing some idea of qualification.

The car went through a stop sign
but it did not hit anything.

The co-ordinate conjunctions **or** and **nor** separate alternatives:

You must stop at the sign
or the police will arrest you.

Subordinate conjunctions express more subtle relationships:

Because the car went through a stop sign, the police arrested the driver.

After the car went through a stop sign, the police arrested the driver.

Although the car went through the stop sign, it did not hit anything.

Unless you stop at the sign, the police will arrest you.

The precise use of subordinate conjunctions is one mark of the skilful writer.

The most common subordinate conjunctions are:

although	as	so that	where(ever)
though	as soon as	in order that	when(ever)
because	as though	until	while
unless	as if	before	which(ever)
if	whereas	since	who(ever)
even if	that	after	

Because the subordinate conjunction introduces a full sentence group (a **clause**), the whole group is called a **subordinate clause**.

The car went through a stop sign.
When the car went through the stop sign, the police arrested the driver.
Even if the car goes through the stop sign, the police cannot arrest him.
Until the car goes through the stop sign, the police cannot arrest him.

The wh- Words as Subordinate Conjunctions

A small, closed set of words—often called the **wh-words** — is used to ask questions in English:

1. The following group may occur by themselves, and be called **Pronouns**:

who (whom, whose) what which
whoever whatever whichever

This group can also modify nouns, and be called **Determiners**:

What man called out? **Which** book do you prefer?

2. Another small group may act as **Adverbs**:

where when why how wherever whenever

Where is he? **When** did he leave? **Why** did you do it? **How** did he do it?

It is but a simple step to use these **wh-** words to introduce a clause subordinated to a main clause, for example:

He is the man **who rented us the cottage**.
There is the cottage **which we rented last summer**.
Here is the cottage **where we stayed last summer**.
I'll go **whenever you are ready**.
I wonder   what he wants.
       which he likes.
       why he chose this one.
       how he made it.
I know   which he likes.
      whatever he knows.
      when you came in last night.
      where you put it.

Often **that** is used in the same way to connect and subordinate a clause:

I know | that | I know a book | that you will find interesting. |

| You can do it. | | You will find it interesting. |

All these words are: **connectives**—**conjunctions** that tie one clause to another,

and **subordinators** — that subordinate the clause that they are in,

thus: **subordinate conjunctions.**

ACTIVITY

Join the following statements by subordinating one statement to the other. Use as many different subordinate conjunctions as possible. (Refer to the list.) Try various combinations and star the one you prefer.

1. I did not enjoy the voyage. I was dreadfully seasick.
2. He failed the examination. He decided to look for a job.
3. The boat was damaged in the storm. Ted had built the boat.
4. I decided to call Dr. Johnson. His office was not far away.
5. Jake told me stories about his grandfather. His grandfather had been a pioneer in Alberta.
6. The farmer had to do some of the field work himself. He could not afford more hired help.
7. The town was destroyed by a flood. The flood arose overnight.
8. The priest lived in a small house at the end of the street. He was well known to my friend.
9. His proudest possession is a model schooner. His grandfather had made it for him.

Interjections

Oh, I'd never do that!
Heavens, who let you in?
Oh no! I have forgotten my key.

These words or expressions have no grammatical relation to the rest of the sentence in which they are found; they are expressions of emotion or feeling. Sometimes interjections are expanded and become exclamatory sentences.

Heaven help us! What will we do?
Shame on you!
What a beautiful day!

Swear words are often interjections. Interjections belong mainly to oral language.

Review of the Parts of Speech

Form Words (open classes)—defined mainly by **characteristic changes of form**

Nouns
—inflect for number (**-s** or **-es**) and possession (**'s**, **'**)

Verbs
—inflect for number (**-s** or **-es**) and tense (**-d** or **-ed**), and when with auxiliaries (**-ing**, **-ed**, or **-en**).

Adjectives
—some inflect for degree (**-er**, **-est**)
—can be intensified (by **very**, **somewhat**, etc.)
—accompany a noun

Adverbs
—often inflect for degree (**-er**, **-est**)
—often can be intensified (by **very**, **rather**, etc.)
—often are "movables"

Structure Words (closed classes)—each group is small, so can be classified by listing

Pronouns
—reference words or "substitution" words
—personal pronouns retain some old inflections of number, gender, person, case, and two possessives
—**who** inflects for case
—some others inflect for number or possessives
—but each type of pronoun can be listed (limited sets)

Auxiliaries
—**be**, **have**, **do** are most common, and inflect
—others such as **will**, **shall**, **may**, etc. have past forms only
—used before the verb to express complex ideas about the "action"
—can be listed (a limited set of words)

Determiners
—fixed positions before nouns (pattern like **the**, **this**, **two**, etc.)

Intensifiers
—fixed positions before adjectives and adverbs (pattern like **very** or **rather**)

Prepositions —begin phrases that usually end in a noun, and make patterns such as: **to the house, from the windows**. These phrases are nearly always modifiers.

Conjunctions —connective words
—co-ordinate conjunctions join grammatically equal words or groups (**and, but, or,** etc.)
—subordinate conjunctions begin and "tie" subordinated clauses (**because, if, where, after, that, who,** etc.)

REVIEW ACTIVITY: TO RE-VIEW FORM AND STRUCTURE WORDS

Here is a message for a telegram. Write it out in "telegraphese". See what **kinds** of words you have omitted. What kinds could you **not** omit?

My suitcase has been lost and I need money to buy some clothes. Send the money to the Bank of Commerce, Winnipeg.

Scientists who study information and how it is sent would tell us that form words are "high in information value", whereas structure words mark relationships.

Look at advertisements, want ads, headlines, telegrams, and report on the **kinds** of words that are usually omitted. Try writing some of these styles of English.

REVIEW ACTIVITY: WHAT DIFFERENCE DOES A LITTLE ARTICLE MAKE?

Sometimes a great deal. When Neil Armstrong became the first man to step on the surface of the moon, in July 1969, he said:

That's one small step for a man, one giant leap for mankind.

This was reported, however, as:

That's one small step for man, one giant leap for mankind.

What difference in meaning did the article **a**

make? Try making similar pairs that differ in the article only. Here are some examples:

I'll have a coffee, if you please.
I'll have coffee, if you please.

He gave her a red and a white rose.
He gave her a red and white rose.

There are separate schools for the boys and the girls.
There are separate schools for the boys and girls.

He is fighting for women's rights.
He is fighting for the women's rights.

He is married to Ann Winchester, the actress.
He is married to Ann Winchester, an actress.

> Do you see two meanings?
> He likes amusing guests.
> Put in **the**. What happens?

REVIEW ACTIVITY: FUNCTIONAL SHIFT

English words can be used as many parts of speech. Identify the part of speech represented by each word in bold type. Be prepared to tell how you identified each.

1. She had a **run** in her stocking.
2. The children **run** along the beach.

3. The **buildings** were tall.
4. They are **building** a new school.
5. You use too many **and**'s.
6. Look **inside** the trunk.
7. Look **inside**.
8. The **inside** was lined with silk.
9. He **sided** with the linesman in the argument.
10. **Some** of the men were asleep.
11. Will you **chair** the meeting?
12. **Yellow** is my favourite colour.
13. Age has **yellowed** the cloth.
14. The ladies **oh** and **ah** as they look at the dress.
15. **Oh**, isn't it beautiful!
16. She came **after**.
17. She came **after** me.
18. She came **after** I had gone.
19. **This** is mine.
20. **This** book is mine.

REVIEW ACTIVITY: FUNCTIONAL SHIFT IN A POEM

Here is a poem of one sentence whose Subject is **sunset** and whose Predicate consists of a series of verbs. Many of these verbs have been made from other parts of speech. Read the poem. Then find all the verbs and discuss their effectiveness.

ORNAMENTAL SKETCH WITH VERBS

Sunset runs in a ream
over the brows of buildings
 dropping west to the river,
turns the street to a gilded stagger,
makes the girl on skates,
 the man with the block of ice,
 the basement landlady calling her cat
creatures in a dream,

scales with salamander-red
 the window-pitted walls,
hairs the gutters with brindled light,
helmets cars and boys on bikes
and double-dazzles
 the policeman's portly coat,
halos the coal truck where
 nuggets race from a golden sled,

festoons lampposts to fantastic trees,
lacquers sooty roofs and pavements,
floats in every puddle
 pinks of cloud,
flamingos all the pigeons,
grands all dogs to chows,
enchants the ash cans into urns
 and fire-escapes to Orleans balconies.

—May Swenson

REVIEW ACTIVITY

Write sentences using:

1. **colour** as a verb

2. **head** as a verb

3. **like** as a preposition

4. **touch** as a noun

5. **reason** as a verb

6. **hard** as an adjective

7. **herd** as a verb

8. **ideal** as an adjective

9. **ideal** as a noun

10. **last** as a noun

11. **serve** as a noun

12. **about** as a preposition

13. **about** as an adverb

14. **until** as a preposition

15. **until** as a subordinate conjunction

16. **by** as an adverb

17. **by** as a preposition

18. **where** as a subordinate conjunction

19. **indeed** as an interjection

20. **quite** as an intensifier

REVIEW ACTIVITY : TEST ON THE PARTS OF SPEECH

Identify the part of speech of each italicized word.

Noun	Pronoun	Subordinate Conjunction
Verb	Determiner	Co-ordinate Conjunction
Adjective	Preposition	Auxiliary
Adverb	Intensifier	Interjection

As the morning broke *they* saw the traces of his fall. It *seems* impossible he *could* have uttered *a* sound. He had slipped *eastward* towards the *unknown* side *of* the mountain; far below he had struck a *steep* slope of snow, *and* ploughed his way down *it* in the midst of a *snow* avalanche. His track *went* straight to the *edge* of a frightful precipice, and *beyond* that *everything* was hidden. Far, far *below*, and hazy with *distance*, they could see trees *rising* out of a *narrow*, shut-in valley —the lost Country of the Blind.

"He *speaks*," said the *third* man. "*Certainly* he *is* a man."

"*Ugh!*" said Pedro, at the *roughness* of his coat.

"And you *have* come *into* the world?" *asked* Pedro.

"Out of the world. *Over* mountains *and* glaciers; right over above there, half-way *to* the *sun*. Out of the great big world *that* goes *down*, twelve days' *journey* to *the* sea."

—H. G. Wells: *The Country of the Blind*

The ability to see familiar facts in a new light is equivalent to acquiring a new sense.

—Francis Dineen, Preface to *An Introduction to General Linguistics*

And the words slide into the slots ordained by syntax, and glitter as with atmospheric dust, with those impurities which we call meaning.

—Anthony Burgess: *Enderby*

The English Grammar System

Sentence Patterns

Part Two

**COMMISSION ATTACKS INVALID
SAYS SENATOR**

Stable farm output, prices
aired at Ottawa meeting

BUILDING BOOMS
IN YUKON

Teacher quits
job to fight
drugs and drink

Some of the above headlines carry two possible meanings. How is it that we can understand these messages, even though many of the structure words have been purposely omitted, and how is it that we can do something as sophisticated as seeing ambiguities?

Part of our understanding of the messages comes from knowing the meanings of words. But even if we do not know the meanings of all the words, as in:

The two rodans urped brittily to the carbetion.
or What are those planths doing in my riggy kelbig?

we do receive some meaning from the pattern of the sentence.

What meanings do you receive from the above sentences?

Grammar is more than the study of categories of words (parts of speech); it is also the analysis of how thought is expressed in units or groups of words. The basic unit is the sentence. English sentences are built upon a few simple patterns.

A knowledge of the basic sentence patterns and of how sentences are built upon these patterns is interesting in itself; it also helps us to appreciate English prose, and that mysterious thing called "style" This section will investigate seven basic patterns of the English sentence.

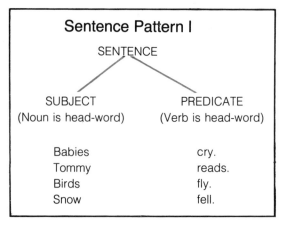

Sentence Pattern I

SENTENCE

SUBJECT (Noun is head-word)   PREDICATE (Verb is head-word)

Babies	cry.
Tommy	reads.
Birds	fly.
Snow	fell.

The English sentence has two basic parts, called the subject and predicate. The head-word of the subject (the **bare subject**) is usually a noun. The head-word of the predicate (**bare predicate**) is always a verb. This noun-verb combination is the simplest pattern of a statement sentence.

We can expand this basic pattern by adding modifiers to the noun:

The two **babies cry.**
The two little **babies** in the crib **cry.**
The two little **babies** who are lying in the crib **cry.**

and by adding modifiers and auxiliaries to the verb:

Babies cry loudly.
Babies cry loudly when they are hungry.
Babies will always **cry** loudly if they are frightened.

and by adding modifiers to the whole sentence:

Every morning at five, the two **babies** were **crying** loudly for their food.

But the basic structure or "skeleton" of the sentence is the same.

ORAL ACTIVITY

Expand these basic patterns into interesting sentences by adding modifiers. You may use auxiliaries but be sure to keep the two given words as the main or "key" words.

1. car travels
2. cat sleeps
3. wood burns
4. team cheered
5. Carl walked
6. sheep grazed

Think of how many nouns there are in the language.

Think of how many verbs there are in the language.

How many sentences do you think can be made by using pattern I — even without modifiers?

ACTIVITY

Find the noun — verb "skeleton" (that is, bare subject and bare predicate) of each of the following sentences:

1. A loud explosion came from the direction of the refinery.
2. Six months later, without any warning, the young man disappeared.
3. The news of the child's death spread rapidly through the town.
4. On coming out of the station, the boys walked towards the bustling shopping area.
5. Every Sunday, the small group gathered there for a short service.
6. David, an old friend since school days, lived in a small apartment in the northeast part of the city.

SUPPLYING A SUBJECT

Because the English language follows a subject-predicate pattern, some sentences that really have no subject begin with the structure word **it**. The **it** is a "starter word" or a "filler word", supplying the necessary subject. Here are examples:

It rained all day.
It is late.
It is seven o'clock.
It was Tuesday.

AGREEMENT

Notice changes in the verb forms below. Try to account for these changes.

Baby **cries**.
Babies **cry**.

The wind **blows**.
The winds **blow**.

The water **rises**.
The waters **rise**.

In an English sentence, the bare subject governs the form of the verb. This principle is called **agreement**. When is the **-s** form used?

Put the above sentences into the past tense. What happens?

Isn't it strange that the English system uses **-s** as an inflection to mark "plural" for a noun, yet also uses **-s** to mark "singular" in a verb? Many people learning English as a second language find this fact difficult to understand, yet little children learning English as their first language use this part of the system when quite young and without being aware that they have learned it!

WHAT IS GOING ON?

CHILD: May I have a kleenek, please?
ADULT: You mean "kleenex", don't you?
CHILD: One will do, thank you.

The baby **may cry**.
The babies **may cry**.

The baby **will cry**.
The babies **will cry**.

Which of the following can be full sentences? How do you know?

BEE STING
BEES STING
A BEE STING
A BEE STINGS

The principle of agreement applies to all the sentence patterns of English. Remember that agreement depends upon the **bare subject** (the headword), not upon its modifiers. Don't let group modifiers (for example, prepositional groups and clauses) confuse you.

One of the dogs **was barking**. (**One was barking**.)

Several of the dogs **were barking**. (**Several were barking**.)

A huge **bouquet** of white flowers **was** at the door.

The **reason** for his many absences from school **has been discovered**.

Each of the two boys who work in the drug store **plans** to go to university.

The two **boys** who work in the drugstore **plan** to go to university.

Be wary of inverted sentences, that is, those that begin with an adverbial group:

Near the gate **stands** a **monument** to the men who died in the war.

Near the gate **stand** several old **monuments**.

AGREEMENT WITH AUXILIARIES

What happens if the verb has an auxiliary, or several auxiliaries? Here are examples from which we may formulate a generalization:

The baby **is crying**.
The babies **are crying**.

The baby **does not cry**.
The babies **do not cry**.

The baby **has been crying**.
The babies **have been crying**.

Remember that some auxiliaries, such as **may**, **will**, **shall**, **must**, and **can**, have no **-s** form, so do not change for agreement in number.

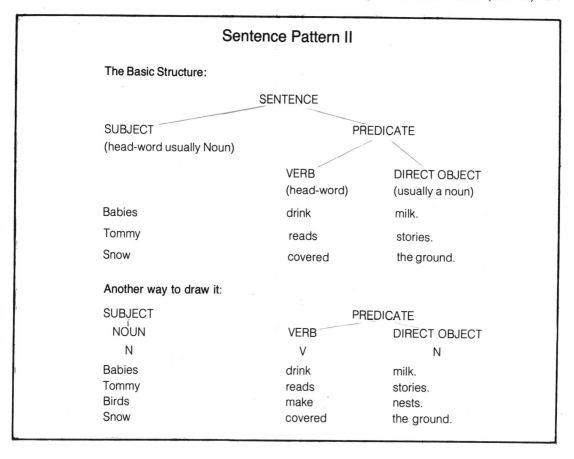

Sentence Pattern II

The Basic Structure:

SENTENCE

SUBJECT
(head-word usually Noun)

PREDICATE

VERB
(head-word)

DIRECT OBJECT
(usually a noun)

Babies	drink	milk.
Tommy	reads	stories.
Snow	covered	the ground.

Another way to draw it:

SUBJECT NOUN N	PREDICATE VERB V	DIRECT OBJECT N
Babies	drink	milk.
Tommy	reads	stories.
Birds	make	nests.
Snow	covered	the ground.

This is the most common sentence pattern in English. As the two diagrams show, the sentence (like all English sentences) has two parts: the **subject** and the **predicate**. The part of speech (that is, the class of words) that usually fits into the subject "slot" is the **noun**. The predicate of this pattern, however, is further divided into the **verb** and a second noun, called the **direct object**. The direct object "slot" is usually filled from the noun class. Modifiers can be added to any of the words to extend the sentence.

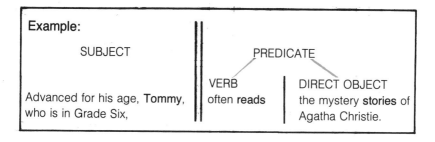

Example:

SUBJECT	PREDICATE	
	VERB	DIRECT OBJECT
Advanced for his age, **Tommy**, who is in Grade Six,	often **reads**	the mystery **stories** of Agatha Christie.

A useful test of the direct object is to ask the question "what?" or "whom?" after the verb; for example, Babies drink (what?) **milk.**

Birds make (what?) **nests.**

A Reminder:

Terms like **noun, verb, adjective, preposition,** etc. refer to the categories into which **words** are classified.

Terms like **subject, predicate,** and **direct object** refer to certain "slots" or "positions" in the sentence. Into these slots, certain classes of words typically fit.

WHAT DOES "SUBJECT" AND "DIRECT OBJECT" MEAN?

Words or word-groups within certain "position-slots" in the basic sentence patterns seem to carry out certain functions. Generally, and rather vaguely, the words in the subject position-slot seem to have the function of "doer" of the action of the verb: **The dog** chased the cat; **The cat** scratched the dog; etc.

All the words in the direct object slot seem to be "receivers" of the action. But these "meanings" are general, and not always accurate. Some verbs seem to allow various noun-groups in the subject-slot that are not necessarily the "doers" of the "action".

Example:

verb: **bake**   nouns: **Grandmother**
good bread
this old oven

Notice the sentences possible:

Grandmother	bakes	good bread in this old oven.
This old oven	bakes	good bread.
Good bread	bakes	in this old oven.

It is probably more useful to think of "subject" or "direct object" as the noun (or the equivalent word or word-group) in certain position-slots in a sentence pattern, rather than as "doers or receivers of the action".

"My monkey did it."

ACTIVITY

Expand these "skeleton" sentences of Pattern II (N V N) by adding modifiers to each of the three parts:

(a) boys pitched tent

(b) people collected money

(c) girls felt remorse

(d) lady prepared lunch

(e) cat catches birds

ACTIVITY

Find the "skeleton" (bare subject, verb, direct object) of the following sentences:

1. The carpenters found a packet of money under the floorboards.

2. The weary travellers ordered a huge pitcher of cold lemonade.

3. The boys soon constructed a seaworthy craft from some old planks and an empty barrel.

4. Soon, through the trees, we saw smoke from a group of white houses.

5. Very carefully the nurse bound his torn and swollen hand.

6. Every Saturday the boys of my class play football with the boys of a neighbouring school.

ACTIVITY

Write six sentences in Pattern II (N V N). Exchange with a partner and check.

ACTIVE AND PASSIVE CONSTRUCTIONS

Nearly any sentence written in Pattern II (N V N) may be reworded so that the object becomes the subject. (Remember: **Subject** refers to the **position** of the noun in a sentence.)

A
The sailor cut **the rope**.
The birds have made **a nest**.
Father will paint **the house**.
The car hit **me**.

B
The rope was cut (by the sailor).
A nest has been made (by the birds).
The house will be painted (by father).
I was hit (by the car).

The Direct Object of the basic sentence (A) moves into the Subject "slot" (as in B). The former Subject becomes part of a prepositional phrase beginning with **by**, and can be omitted (for example, one can say **I was hit**, as well as **I was hit by the car**).

What happens to the form of the verb? Note how the form of the verb **signals** to the listener or reader whether the subject refers to the "doer" or to the "receiver" of the action:

The sailor cut _____.
The sailor was cut.

Father will paint _____.
Father will be painted.

The basic sentence pattern is called **active**. The verb is said to be in the **active voice**.

The second type, in which the former object is now in the subject "slot" or position, is called **passive**. The verb is said to be in the **passive voice**.

The verb group in a passive construction always contains a form of the verb **to be**, and ends with the past participle (with the forms **-ed**, **-en**, etc.) of the verb.

ACTIVE VOICE

The child **took** the cookie.

The dog **bit** Tom.

The police **investigated** the crime.

I **will stop** him.

The dog **ate** the biscuit.

The dog **has eaten** the biscuit.

The dog **was eating** the biscuit.

The dog **must have eaten** the biscuit.

PASSIVE VOICE

The cookie **was taken** (by the child).

Tom **was bitten** (by the dog).

The crime **was investigated** (by the police).

He **will be stopped** (by me).

The biscuit **was eaten** (by the dog).

The biscuit **has been eaten** (by the dog).

The biscuit **was being eaten** (by the dog).

The biscuit **must have been eaten** (by the dog).

This kind of change from a basic structure to a different structure is called by some grammarians a **transformation**. Notice that the **passive transformation** works in a regular pattern.

ACTIVITY

Change these sentences of Pattern II (N V N) so that the verb is in the passive voice.

Remember to find the direct object, and to make it the new subject. Keep the same tense. (Examine the examples above to see the auxiliary patterns.)

1. Our club sent six delegates to the conference.
2. Cultivated forage crops have replaced the native prairie grass.
3. The farmer sends the milk to the co-operative cheese factory.
4. Since the Second World War, the government has supervised the wheat market.
5. The late spring delayed crops in many sections of the country.
6. The farmer will harvest the wheat in September.
7. The cat is watching the mouse-hole.

ACTIVITY

Write four sentences based on the pattern N V N. Use modifiers and auxiliaries.

Then transform each sentence so that the verb is in the passive voice.

Uses and Effects of the Passive

A sentence in the active construction seems to have more direct movement than its counterpart in the passive and, for this reason, is usually stronger.

Active: Everyone had a good time.
Passive: A good time was had by everyone.

Active: In the last ten yards, John passed the other runners.
Passive: The other runners were passed by John in the last ten yards.

A passive construction is useful and appropriate if:

the "doer" is unknown:

The jewellery was stolen last night.
The farmhouse was torn down years ago.

the "doer" is vague:

She was knocked down in the rush.
The roadway was flooded.
The book was published first in 1901.
These cars are imported from France.

the "doer" is less important than the "receiver":

I was bitten by the cat.
I was bitten in three places.

The effect we want and the rhythm of the whole paragraph will govern our choice.

Notice the use of the structure word **it** to make a passive — often to **avoid** mentioning the "doer":

It has been suggested that the building should be sold.

It is said that he drinks too much.

It has been decided that you cannot go.

ACTIVITY

If the verb is passive, put **P** beside the sentence. If the verb is active, put **A** beside the sentence. Rewrite the sentence in the opposite construction. Then put a tick beside the construction you prefer. (If they are equally effective, use two ticks.) Defend your preferences.

1. The company closed down its two branch offices.
2. Two mysteries are written every year by W. H. Kerfoot.
3. The war was lost by the loyalists because of poor equipment.
4. The book describes in detail the social revolution sweeping the country.
5. The sergeant, fearful for his life, contrived a story to explain his escape.
6. This exciting book is boldly and colourfully illustrated by Clark Wilder.
7. It is felt by the Students' Council that better school spirit would be built up by these free dances.
8. These songs were sung by bards in the chieftain's hall.

ACTIVITY: THE PASSIVE VOICE IN HEADLINES

The following are examples of the use of the passive voice in newspaper headlines. Write each one out as a full sentence. What words, if any, have been omitted? Then write each sentence in the active voice, and reduce that to a headline. Discuss the differences in effect on the reader. Why has the passive rather than the active form been used for the original headlines?

ACTIVITY

Make a collection of headlines from your own newspaper. What proportion of passive verbs has the editor used? Do you find any difference related to **content**, for example, sports, social news, etc.?

Royal Bank building sold

TROOPS HIT BY AVALANCHE

Woman killed in collision

Montreal pair slain, cab driver wounded

BATTLE WITH GRIZZLY RECALLED

DAM STILL OPPOSED

DRUG LINKED TO DEFORMITY

U.S. EMBASSY PICKETED

$80 MILLION PACT SIGNED WITH RUSSIA

UNION FINED $127,500

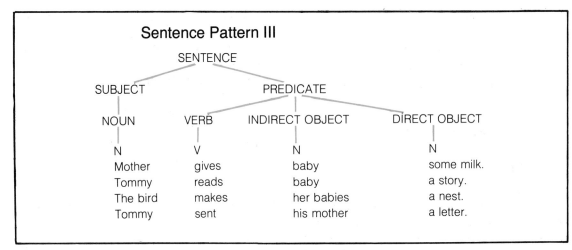

Sentence Pattern III

SUBJECT	PREDICATE		
NOUN	VERB	INDIRECT OBJECT	DIRECT OBJECT
N	V	N	N
Mother	gives	baby	some milk.
Tommy	reads	baby	a story.
The bird	makes	her babies	a nest.
Tommy	sent	his mother	a letter.

Check: Can you change the order of the two nouns in the predicate without changing the essential meaning of the sentence?

Only a small subset of English verbs can fit into Pattern III (N V N N), but they are among the most frequently used verbs.

The verbs most commonly used in this pattern are:

give	ask	bring	owe	offer	tell
send	sell	pay	teach	take	find
buy	read	make	lend	show	promise

If we wish to get away from the rigid word order of this kind of predicate, we can "mark" the indirect object with the preposition **to** or **for** and thus be able to move its position. For example, the basic sentence pattern:

N	V	N	N
The bird	makes	her babies	a nest.

can be transformed into:

The bird makes a nest **for her babies**.
For her babies the bird makes a nest.
The bird makes **for her babies** a nest of soft leaves.

The structure word **to** or **for**, rather than position, now "signals" the indirect object, and allows the indirect object to become a "movable". The basic meaning is the same, but the transformation allows a different emphasis and rhythm.

Now transform the other three examples above.

ACTIVITY

Expand these sentences of Pattern III (N V N N) by adding modifiers to any or all of the basic parts. Make the sentences interesting.

N	V	N	N
The druggist	offered	the boy	a job.
The father	bought	the boys	suits.
The fair	brought	the stores	business.
The girls	took	the children	gifts.
The salesman	sold	the boys	a car.

Then transform one of your sentences into the **to** or **for** structure in several ways.

ACTIVITY

Find the "skeleton" pattern of the following sentences.

1. The teacher handed the students their examination papers.

2. Finally the man bought all of the children ice cream and candy.

3. Small children can teach adults many fundamental truths.

4. Every passenger must show the immigration inspectors his passport.

5. Every week their father gave the boys two dollars for pocket money.

ACTIVITY

Write four sentences in Pattern III. Have another student check them by finding the "skeleton" structure N V N N.

THE PASSIVE OF PATTERN III (N V N N)

Can we transform a Pattern III sentence to the passive voice? Experiment with the following, and discuss your conclusions.

The postman handed Mother the letter.
Uncle Joe bought the boys ice-cream cones.
The woman paid the clerk the money.
The politician promised the public lower taxes.

As with Pattern II (N V N), the direct object of Pattern III (N V N N) may become the subject:

The letter was handed (to) mother (by the postman).[1]

Sometimes you can put the indirect object in the subject "slot":

Mother was handed the letter (by the postman).

But often the indirect object in the subject position is awkward:

The boys were bought ice-cream cones (by Uncle Joe).

Whichever structure we choose, the other object can be kept or **retained** after the verb.

---

[1]The parentheses are symbols to show that these words or structures may be omitted.

ACTIVITY

Transform these Pattern III sentences so that the verbs are in the passive voice. Try both the Direct Object and the Indirect Object in the Subject "slot". Then discuss the "transformation" you prefer for each.

1. The class sent the Korean student books and money.

2. My aunt always gives me a tie for Christmas.

3. The owners gave Mr. Jackson no reason for his dismissal.

4. Marion sent every girl in the class an invitation to the party.

5. The town councillors gave the prisoner a fair trial.

6. Our teacher frequently tells us exciting stories about the war.

7. The first-aid instructor showed the class a film on water safety.

8. The police asked the boys many questions about the money.

9. This delay at the customs caused the travellers much trouble.

10. We paid the taxi driver two dollars.

REVIEW OF THE THREE PATTERNS

Here are the three basic sentence patterns we have learned.
I.   Tom reads. (N V)
II. Tom reads mysteries. (N V N)
III. Tom reads baby a story. (N V N N)

ACTIVITY

What is the pattern of each of the following sentences?

1. A committee of students decorated the floats.

2. The boys brought the committee baskets of flowers.

3. The committee worked hard.
4. The judges gave this float the first prize.
5. The money will provide a scholarship to university.
6. The money will give some student a scholarship.
7. The mayor sent the committee a letter of congratulation.
8. The principal congratulated all the students.
9. The Students' Council voted the committee fifty dollars for expenses.

ORAL ACTIVITY

Does a change in pattern signal a change in meaning? Study the following sentences.

1. The merchant left for China.
2. The merchant left his wife and family.
3. The merchant left his wife and family much money.
4. Every week-end the father brought his daughter to her grandparents' farm.
5. Every week-end the father brought his daughter a present.
6. The soldiers charged.
7. The soldiers charged the civilians.
8. The soldiers charged the civilians outrageous prices for the sugar.
9. The minister called.
10. The minister called my parents.
11. The minister told my parents the story of my escapade.

12. You should pass.
13. You should pass that truck.
14. You should pass Susan the cake.

Sentence Pattern IV

Discuss the differences in these two groups of sentences:

PATTERN II (N V N)
Ted met my friend.
The puppy chased the terrier.
The birds chased the robins.
Tom hit the sailor.

PATTERN IV
Ted is my friend.
The puppy is a terrier.
The birds are robins.
Tom became a sailor.

In Pattern II, the two nouns do not refer to the same thing. In Pattern IV, **Ted** and **friend** are the same person, and **puppy** and **terrier** refer to the same dog.

The verbs in Pattern IV sentences are called **linking** (or **copula**) **verbs**, because they link two nouns that have the same referent (that is, they refer to the same person, thing, or idea). Pattern IV is thus symbolized usually as:

N	LV	N
SUBJECT	LINKING VERB	COMPLEMENT
Ted	is	my friend.
The puppy	is	a terrier.
The birds	are	robins.
Tom	became	a sailor.
Honesty	is	our policy.

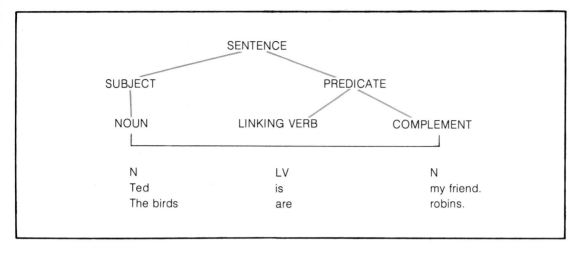

The spelling of **complement** is derived from the word **complete**. Why do you think this grammatical structure was named **complement**?

The most common copula verb is the verb **to be**; some others that *may* be used as copula verbs are **become, remain, seem, appear, look, taste,** and **smell.**

ORAL ACTIVITY

Find the "skeleton" (or basic pattern) of the following Pattern IV (N̄ LV N̄) sentences:

1. Alcohol is poison to many people.

2. This wood is teak from India.

3. Little brothers can be a great nuisance.

4. The premier was obviously master of the situation.

5. Bill became an outstanding speaker.

6. Soon John and his brother became leaders of a gang.

7. His first venture into business was a complete failure.

8. After a little practice, Tom became a good goalkeeper.

9. The man looked a soldier in every way.

ORAL ACTIVITY

Name the pattern of each sentence (Pattern II (N V N) or Pattern IV (N̄ LV N̄)).

1. Jane pressed the dress carefully.

2. The material is red silk.

3. The two boys remained friends for years.

4. The two boys soon found new friends of their own age.

5. The thieves stole a famous picture from the Louvre.

6. The picture is a copy of a famous picture in the Louvre.

7. The thieves were two art students.

8. This quiet student later became a famous author.

ACTIVITY

Write four basic sentences in Pattern IV (N̄ LV N̄). Then expand them by adding modifiers to the main parts.

Sentence Pattern V

How are the following two groups of sentences alike? How are they different? What is the basic pattern of the second group of sentences?

PATTERN IV (N̄ LV N̄)	PATTERN V
Tom is a student.	Tom is studious.
The birds are robins.	The birds are hungry.
The boys remained friends.	The boys remained friendly.
Nelson became an admiral.	Nelson became ill.

Pattern V is like Pattern IV, except that the complement is an adjective. So we write Pattern V as N̄ LV Adj.

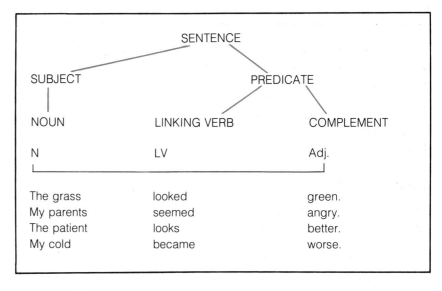

NOUN	LINKING VERB	COMPLEMENT
N	LV	Adj.
The grass	looked	green.
My parents	seemed	angry.
The patient	looks	better.
My cold	became	worse.

Do the subject and complement have the same referent? Can the verb be replaced by a form of **to be** or **become**?

ORAL ACTIVITY

Add suitable adjectives as complements. Then expand the sentences to make them interesting:

1. The students are _____.

2. The children looked _____.

3. This book seems _____.

4. The weather became _____.

5. The emigrants felt _____.

A problem: How shall we classify the pattern below?

N	V	Adv.
The man	is	here.
A woman	appeared	at the doorway.
The girl	remained	at home for several days.
A cottage	was	in the garden.

The verbs are those that appear in the Linking Verb + Complement patterns (N LV N and N LV Adj.), but the adverb in the third "slot" does not function in quite the same way as do the other two kinds of complements. This pattern is also like Pattern I (NV) because we can use both linking and non-linking verbs in the verb slot. We can say:

> The man **is** here.
and > The man **walked** here.

> The woman **was** at the doorway.
and > The woman **stood** at the doorway.

Therefore we will classify this kind of sentence with Pattern I.

ACTIVITY: A REVIEW

(a) Many English verbs can work in more than one sentence pattern. Here are examples.

1. The tree grew. (Pattern I — N V)
2. The farmer grew corn. (Pattern II — N V N)
3. The patient grew weaker. (Pattern V — N LV Adj.)
4. The man turned. (Pattern I — N V)
5. The man turned the heavy wheel. (Pattern II — N V N)
6. The man turned traitor. (Pattern IV — N LV N)
7. The man turned pale. (Pattern V — N LV Adj.)

(b) Give the pattern of each of the following sentences; for example, I like doughnuts. N V N

1. The doughnuts taste good.
2. The boys tasted the doughnuts.
3. Mother made the boys a plateful of doughnuts.
4. Doughnuts were on the table.
5. The blind man felt my face.
6. The blind man felt helpless.
7. The prisoner looked sad.
8. The prisoner looked wistfully out of the window.
9. The butter smells rancid.
10. The butter is in the refrigerator.
11. I smelled the butter.
12. Certainly this butter is not fresh.
13. He grows sweet peas as a hobby.
14. Sweet peas grow well in this soil.
15. In the garden grew sweet peas, nasturtiums, and red roses.
16. My uncle has grown old and grey.
17. Large department stores in the downtown area are becoming more numerous.
18. That policeman is becoming angry.
19. Suddenly two policemen appeared at the door.
20. The two policemen appeared worried.

Sentence Pattern VI

Compare these two patterns. How are they alike? How are they different?

PATTERN III

N	V	N	N
SUBJECT	VERB	INDIRECT OBJECT	DIRECT OBJECT
The parents	gave	the child	a toy.
The mayor	sent	my father	money.

PATTERN VI

N	V	N———————N	
The parents	named	the child	Peter.
The mayor	appointed	my father	guardian.

Both Patterns III and VI are N V N N.

Pattern III deals with three nouns, all referring to different things. In Pattern VI, however, the last two nouns refer to the same thing. The speaker of English knows that the meaning is: "The child is Peter", "My father is guardian". There are only a few verbs which go into this pattern.

Compare the following:

The parents named the child. (Pattern II — N V N)

The parents named the child Peter. (Pattern VI — N V N̄ N)

The mayor appointed my father. (Pattern II — N V N)

The mayor appointed my father guardian. (Pattern VI — N V N̄ N)

The final noun (**Peter**, or **guardian**) refers to the same person as the second noun (**child**, or **my father**). Because the final noun seems to complete the meaning of the object and of the verb, it is usually called the **objective complement**. The basic pattern is thus:

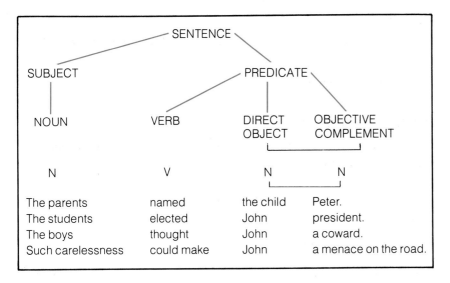

The parents	named	the child	Peter.
The students	elected	John	president.
The boys	thought	John	a coward.
Such carelessness	could make	John	a menace on the road.

ORAL ACTIVITY

Tell whether each sentence is:
Pattern III: N V N N
or Pattern VI: N V N̄ N.

1. The teacher's advice made our play a success.
2. The teacher gave our drama club some excellent advice.
3. The students thought the teacher a helpful adviser.
4. The king sent his prime minister an urgent message.
5. My grandfather made me a flat-bottomed boat for the lake.
6. My grandfather made the garden a show-place of the neighbourhood.
7. The teacher considered this essay my best piece of writing this term.
8. My father kept my new bicycle a secret until my birthday.

ACTIVITY

Expand the following by adding modifiers, but keep the basic pattern (Pattern VI — N V N̄ N).

1. boys	consider	the man	a bore
2. event	made	the child	a coward
3. fear	made	soldier	traitor
4. workers	voted	Jones	delegate
5. teacher	appointed	girls	leaders

ACTIVITY

Write three interesting sentences in Pattern VI (N V N̄ N), using three of these verbs:

call   appoint   choose   name   elect   consider

Sentence Pattern VII

Compare sentences of Pattern VI (N V N̄ N) with those of Pattern VII. How are they alike? How are they different?

PATTERN VI

N	V	N	N
The visitor	thought	the child	a boy.
The thieves	found	the cave	a trap.
The experience	made	the soldier	a braver man.

PATTERN VII

The visitor	thought	the child	beautiful.
The thieves	found	the cave	empty.
The experience	made	the soldier	braver.

Pattern VII is exactly like Pattern VI except that an adjective rather than a noun is the objective complement. The basic pattern is thus:

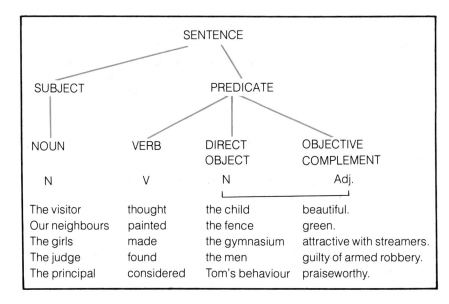

SUBJECT		PREDICATE	
NOUN	VERB	DIRECT OBJECT	OBJECTIVE COMPLEMENT
N	V	N	Adj.
The visitor	thought	the child	beautiful.
Our neighbours	painted	the fence	green.
The girls	made	the gymnasium	attractive with streamers.
The judge	found	the men	guilty of armed robbery.
The principal	considered	Tom's behaviour	praiseworthy.

ACTIVITY

Build interesting sentences of Pattern VII (N V N̄ Adj.) with the following:

1. boys	found	book	dull
2. teacher	thought	answer	amusing
3. news	made	people	uneasy
4. speaker	cut	talk	short
5. girls	scrubbed	room	clean
6. thieves	found	safe	empty

ACTIVITY.

Find the basic pattern, and state whether it is Pattern VI (N V N̄ N) or Pattern VII (N V N̄ Adj.).

1. The exaggerated newspaper reports made the sailor a great hero.

2. The fireplace certainly makes the room cosy.

3. A plastic cover will keep the fruit fresh and moist.

4. Within a few years the company appointed Mr. James the head salesman.

5. I always considered Jane a good sport.

6. Students must keep their lockers clean and tidy.

7. Electronics will make mail-handling procedures much more efficient.

ORAL ACTIVITY

Discuss the differences in meaning of each group of sentences. Use grammatical terms in your discussion.

1. (a) He called me a taxi.
   (b) He called me a juvenile delinquent.

2. (a) He made the children toys.
   (b) He made the children thieves.
   (c) He made the children nervous.
   (d) He made children's toys.

THE PASSIVE TRANSFORMS OF PATTERNS VI AND VII

Both Patterns VI and VII can be transformed so that the verb is in the passive voice. Try various sentences from the last Activity on page 285 (in both patterns). What becomes the new subject? What is retained?

ACTIVE: The parents named the baby Peter.
PASSIVE: The baby was named Peter (by the parents).

ACTIVE: The parents painted the crib blue.
PASSIVE: The crib was painted blue (by the parents).

ORAL ACTIVITY

Make the active voice pattern of these:

1. The two girls were made full members (by the vote).

2. The boy is considered a genius (by his teachers).

3. The dough is kept cool (in the refrigerator).

4. The basement was pumped dry (by the workmen).

5. The door was blown open (by a sudden gust of wind).

6. Camels have been called "the ships of the desert" (by many writers).

7. The song has been named the hit of the month (by a radio survey).

8. After a spirited campaign, Alex was voted class president (by the students).

Review of Sentence Patterns

The seven sentence patterns we have studied are not the only ones possible in English, but are the most common. By adding modifiers and by combining sentences, we can make an almost unlimited number of sentences.

Here, for quick reference, are the seven patterns. Make up a set of similar examples, using any other noun as the subject. Then expand your sentences by adding various types of modifiers.

Pattern I	N V	Money talks.
Pattern II	N V N	Money buys food.
Pattern III	N V N N	Money gives people power.
Pattern IV	N LV N	Money is legal tender.
Pattern V	N LV Adj.	Money is desirable.
Pattern VI	N V N N	Money makes some people penny pinchers.
Pattern VII	N V N Adj.	Money makes people wealthy.

Which of the patterns may be transformed to the passive voice?

When a sentence fits into two patterns, it carries two messages, one for each pattern. Confusion caused by ambiguity is less frequent in speech, because the intonation of the voice signals which pattern is being used. But ambiguity can occur in writing because the voice is absent.

ACTIVITY

Each of the following sentences is ambiguous because it can fit two basic sentence patterns. For each, show the two conflicting patterns.

Example: He called me a friend. (Patterns N V N N and N V N̂ N)

1. University students are revolting.
2. She showed the baby snapshots.
3. This office will issue the student visas.
4. He found Mrs. Mackay a good teacher.
5. You can't name me a witness.
6. They are reading lessons.
7. The woodcutter left the forest bare.
8. He gave her dog biscuits (3 ways?)

Joining the Sentence Patterns

Any two or more sentence patterns may be joined by a co-ordinate conjunction (**and, but, or, for, yet, nor, either-or, neither-nor, both-and**). A sentence made up of two or more complete sentence patterns joined co-ordinately is called a **compound sentence**.

Thunder Bay lies twenty-four hundred kilometres from tidewater but **the St. Lawrence Seaway has made this city a seaport.** (Patterns I — N V and VI — N V N̂ N)

A sentence with one or more subordinated clauses and one main clause is called a **complex sentence**.

Although **Thunder Bay lies twenty-four hundred kilometres from tidewater, the St. Lawrence Seaway has made this city a seaport**.

Some sentences are made up of **two** or more **main** clauses co-ordinated, and **one** or more **subordinated** clauses; such sentences are called **compound-complex sentences**. Find the two co-ordinated main clauses and the one subordinated clause in the following compound-complex sentence:

Thunder Bay, which lies twenty-four hundred kilometres from tidewater, is a Great Lakes port, but it has been made a seaport by the St. Lawrence Seaway.

The ability to handle the complex (or compound-complex) sentence is one marker of growth in writing ability. This is not to say, however, that a simple or compound sentence is necessarily weaker than the complex. Each type has its use. But the good writer is aware of the choices available, and therefore can choose wisely.

ACTIVITY

Examine the sentences in one of your own compositions. List the sentences as **simple** (one clause), **compound** (co-ordinated main clauses only), **complex**, or **compound-complex**.

What sentences in your composition could be improved by a different method of joining?

Substitutions for Nouns

We have discovered that English is mainly a noun-verb language, with nouns as subjects, objects, and complements. In any of the places where nouns usually occur, we may use other kinds of words and groups. The basic sentence pattern remains the same; the word or group merely substitutes for the noun. Here are examples of various structures replacing the noun as subject:

1. a pronoun, or a pronoun with modifiers:
   Someone must do the job.
   Someone strong could lift the box.
   Someone who is strong could lift the box.
   Nobody in his right mind would go there.

2. **-ing** verb or **-ing** group:
   Fishing is forbidden.
   Fishing in this lake is forbidden.
   Fishing after the season has closed is forbidden.

3. an infinitive or infinitive group:
   To walk is pleasant.
   To walk so near the park is pleasant.
   To walk before you run is natural.

4. a clause:
   What you say is foolish.
   Where you are going does not concern me.

5. a prepositional phrase:
   Beyond that fence is out of bounds.

ORAL ACTIVITY

What type of structure replaces the noun as subject in the following sentences? What is the pattern of the whole sentence?

1. Running away will not solve your problems.

2. To run away would seem cowardly.

3. They greeted their friends affectionately.

4. Someone who knows the road should go first.

5. Planning the party is part of the fun.

6. Where I went is a mystery.

7. To be a doctor is her great ambition.

8. Buying a new hat always makes Mother happy.

9. To copy someone else's work is dishonest.

10. He took the patient a huge basket of fruit.

11. For you to go on a long trip now would be unwise.

SUBSTITUTES FOR NOUNS IN OTHER POSITIONS

Similarly, other structures can be substituted for nouns that are direct objects, indirect objects, complements of copula verbs, and objective complements; for example,

as direct object:

I like | **to play hockey.** (infinitive group)
playing hockey. (-ing group)
whatever he likes. (clause)
anyone who enjoys the outdoors. (pronoun and modifiers)

as indirect object:

Mr. Shaw gave **everyone in the class** a detention. (pronoun with modifiers)

as complement of a copula verb:

My hobby is **playing hockey.** (-ing group)
My ambition is **to be a professional player.** (infinitive group)

as objective complement:

We will call the baby **whatever my wife decides.** (clause)

ACTIVITY

What type of structure is substituted for a noun in each of the following patterns:

Pattern I N V
What he fears will never happen.

Pattern II N V N
Judy enjoys **teasing her little brother.**

Pattern III N V N N
You must not tell John **what you have discovered.**

Pattern IV N LV N
His ambition was **to win a scholarship.**

Pattern V N LV Adj.
To leave now would seem odd.

Pattern VI N V N N
We must elect **someone** captain.

Pattern VII N V N Adj.
The news made **everyone in the city** rather uneasy.

ACTIVITY

1. Substitute a pronoun for **that book** in the sentence:
   I want that book.

2. Substitute an infinitive group for **a trip** in the sentence:
   Our family is planning a trip next July.

3. Substitute an **-ing** group for **vintage cars** in the sentence:
   His hobby is vintage cars.

4. Substitute a pronoun and modifiers for **his neighbours** in the sentence:
   He gave his neighbours the fish he had caught.

5. Substitute an **-ing** group for **this disturbance** in the sentence:
   This disturbance terrified the children.

6. Substitute a noun clause for **a favour** in the sentence:
   In a quavering voice, the old woman asked the governor a favour.

7. Substitute an infinitive group for **speaking before a group** in the sentence:
   Speaking before a group always terrifies me.

8. Substitute an -ing group for **this chore** in the sentence:
   Sydney hates this chore.

TRANSFORMS TO DELAY THE SUBJECT

We have already seen that the structure word **it** can fill the Subject "slot" in expressions about time and weather:

It is ten o'clock. **It** is raining.

The structure word **there** may be used somewhat similarly to open a sentence. Note that the Subject comes **after** the verb:

There was no sense to his argument.
There are several reasons for his withdrawal.

The structure words **it** and **there** may also be used to **delay** the subject, holding the real **subject** for a more emphatic position:

It is a pity **that he can't come.**
(Compare: **That he can't come** is a pity.)

It is pitiful **to watch him try.**
(Compare: **To watch him try** is pitiful.)

There came **three wise men, bearing gifts.**

There once lived in a huge palace **a beautiful princess.**

Is **there a school** in this district?

The transformation moves the Subject to a position after the predicate, and fills the Subject slot with the structure word **it** or **there**.

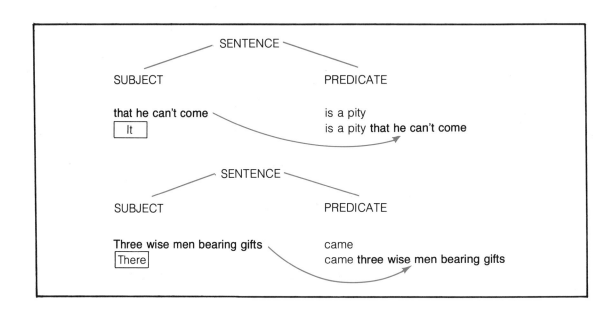

SENTENCE

SUBJECT   PREDICATE

that he can't come   is a pity
It   is a pity **that he can't come**

SENTENCE

SUBJECT   PREDICATE

Three wise men bearing gifts   came
There   came **three wise men bearing gifts**

Note: You can "hear" the difference between the adverb **there** and the structure word **there**. Which is more heavily stressed?

Thére he is! (adverb)

There is a school in our district. (structure word)

There is a school over **thére**. (structure word, adverb)

Is **there** a school over **thére**? (structure word, adverb)

Another way of delaying the subject is to begin with an adverb or adverbial group:

Then came three wise men. (Three wise men came then.)

In the garden lived an old toad. (An old toad lived in the garden.)

Over the fence went the ball.

Over the fence and straight towards Mr. Brand's window sailed the ball.

In this land where it was always afternoon Ulysses lingered.

Notice that the subject and predicate may be merely delayed (**Ulysses lingered**) or may be reversed (**sailed the ball**).

ORAL ACTIVITY

Discuss in class the uses of structural **it** and **there** in the following sentences. Try rewriting the sentences without **it** or **there**. If you can rewrite the sentences, what changes in rhythm or emphasis occur?

1. There was nothing to say.

2. There is nothing dramatic in the world, nothing pathetic, except in human relations.

3. It was against this that I was butting my head.

4. There had been granted me one second of respite.

5. As every pilot knows, there are secret little quiverings that foretell your real storm.

6. It was not I who moved towards those zones of relative calm, those almost green oases clearly painted on the sea, but they that flowed towards me.

7. Towering over the round hills on which the winds have left a residue of stony gravel, there rises a chain of prow-shaped, saw-toothed, razor-edged mountains stripped by the elements down to the bare rock.

—all from Antoine de Saint-Exupéry: *Wind, Sand and Stars*

Using Sentence Structures

Knowledge of the various sentence patterns helps us to revise our compositions: to choose the groupings we want; to improve emphasis and rhythm.

Here is an exercise that shows how we can, by following the directions, combine short, jerky sentences into more interesting patterns. The suggested groupings are not the only possible ones nor necessarily the best ones. But practice of this kind can help us to become more aware of structure when we revise our own compositions.

ACTIVITY

Combine the short sentences according to the directions. Make only those changes in wording made necessary by the changes in structure. The sentences are numbered for convenience.

(a) 1. The *Aeneid* tells the story of the Trojan Aeneas.
    2. Aeneas was the son of Aphrodite.

Combine sentences 1 and 2 by making 2 into a modifying group.

(b) 1. He escaped from burning Troy.
    2. He wandered for many years.
    3. He settled in Italy.
    4. He founded the Roman race and nation.

Make 1 and 2 subordinate **-ing** groups and join them co-ordinately, and join 3 and 4 co-ordinately.

(c) 1. Fiddleheads grow along the St. John River in New Brunswick.
    2. Fiddleheads are the tiny new shoots of a fern.

3. They are sold on the market.
4. They are canned.
5. They are even frozen.

Reverse 1 so that the sentence begins with the adverbial group. Subordinate 2 to 1. Join 3, 4, and 5 to one another by compounding the verbs.

(d) 1. The Stevens family left their home in Ontario.
    2. They set out for a farm on the prairies.
    3. They took only a few supplies.
    4. They travelled in a second-hand wagon.

Join 1 and 2 by compounding the predicates. Join 3 to them by expressing the idea as an **-ing** group. Join 4 to them by using only the adverbial phrase.

(e) 1. Tyrone Guthrie was a famous director.
    2. He was the great-grandson of the famous Irish actor Tyrone Power.
    3. He started out in the theatre as an actor.
    4. He soon decided that he preferred to direct.

Join 1 and 2 by making part of 1 a modifier. Join 3 and 4 co-ordinately, omitting the subject of 4.

(f) 1. Agenor was the king of Tyre.
    2. He had a daughter.
    3. She was named Europa.
    4. Europa was very beautiful.
    5. He loved Europa dearly.

Join 1 and 2 by making part of 1 a modifier. Join 3 and 4 to these by reducing them to modifiers. Join 5 to them by making it a subordinate clause.

ACTIVITY

Join the ideas expressed in the following sentences to make **one** or **two** good sentences, subordinating the less important ideas. Try various patterns, and then put a check beside the one you prefer.

Remember: To subordinate ideas, we use modifiers of all kinds, including **-ing** and **-ed** groups and subordinate clauses.

1. The Appalachian Mountains in Canada are very old. Erosion has planed the mountains down. The highest peak is only 1260 metres. Glacial action has deposited silt in the valleys. The valleys are very fertile.

2. The painter El Greco was born on the island of Crete. He studied art in the studio of Tintoretto. Tintoretto was a great Venetian painter. El Greco's finest pictures are on the walls of a church. It is an obscure church in Toledo, Spain.

3. In 1513 Balboa reached the western ocean. He did this by an overland journey across the Isthmus of Panama. He called the ocean the South Seas. He thought that he was now close to the southern coast of India.

4. In 1728 Bering found a strait. This strait proved that America was not connected with Asia. Fifty years later, Captain James Cook named the strait after Bering.

5. Each spring the ice went out of the St. Lawrence. Then great brigades of canoes left Montreal. They were bound for the West. There they would trade with the Indians.

6. The ladybird lays about fifteen hundred eggs. They are orange-coloured. She lays them near a supply of food. Their chief food is aphids. The aphid is also known as the green-fly.

Structural Economy

The same — or almost the same — idea may often be expressed in many different ways. For example, a clause may often be reduced to a phrase or to a single word modifier:

A man **who is honest** would return the money.

A man **of honesty** would return the money.

An **honest** man would return the money.

An opening clause that has the same subject as the main clause may be shortened or changed to an **-ing** or **-ed** group:

When I was a small boy, I longed to see a circus.

When a small boy, I longed to see a circus.

While Gail was hurrying to class, she dropped a book.

While hurrying to class, Gail dropped a book.

If you are finished, you may do your homework.

If finished, you may do your homework.

Our choice of structure — clause, phrase, or word — depends upon the emphasis we want and the rhythm of the whole passage. A good general rule, however, is to be as concise as possible.

ACTIVITY

Reduce the italicized part of each sentence to a shorter construction.

1. *After he has checked every instrument carefully*, the scientist writes the measurements in his notebook.
2. *If you are in doubt*, you should ask a policeman.
3. The Alcan Highway, *which is now called the Alaska Highway*, runs from Dawson Creek to Fairbanks, Alaska.
4. Each of the plans *that have been suggested* has its advantages and *has its disadvantages*.
5. *Although I was tired from the swim*, I felt relaxed.
6. She read all the books *that she had borrowed from the library*, and then the old magazines *that she found about the house*.
7. *I paid the porter, and* then I settled down in a corner seat *so that I could read the morning paper*.
8. *After we had crossed the border*, we found ourselves in a country *that was very flat and empty*.
9. *When we were camping in Jasper Park*, we often got up early *in order that we might watch the sun as it rose behind the peaks*.
10. *You should arrange your time better and then you could get your homework done and you could have more time to practise.*

Anything that can be learned has structure and can ultimately be analyzed and described.

—Edward T. Hall, *American Anthropologist*

. . . in form of speech there is great change within a thousand years, and some words then that had great value, now seem queer and strange to us; and yet they spake them so and sped as well in love as men do now.

—Chaucer, about 1385 (rendered here in more recent English)

Chapter 8

Language in Use

Varieties of English

Language Usage Is Always Changing

Change in Time

There are hundreds of words that were once in common use but over the years have dropped out of the language. Many were strong, matter-of-fact words, as commonplace in their day as words like **hamburger, car,** and **traffic** are in ours. Some are still in use but with entirely different meanings. Others look like English words but have lost their meaning for all but the scholars familiar with the time that produced them.

Examples of the first are words like **pile** meaning 'to plunder' and **leer** meaning 'cheek'. Words like **thring, threep, cantel,** and **swink** still look English but have lost their meaning for us and, when used, sound like nonsense:

I gave a threep a thring because a threep is harder to thole than swink.

(I gave a scold a push because a scold is harder to endure than drudgery.)

Here are some other examples of obsolete words:

Then	Now
adawed	awake
derne	secret
fremde (still used in German)	foreign
lemes	flames
wanhope	despair
wode	mad, insane

Try making a few sentences using these old words.

Pronunciation Changes

— **tea** once rhymed with **obey** (Alexander Pope, 1712)
— **July** was pronounced to rhyme with **truly** (Wordsworth, 1798)

— **home** — when the Saxons were still on the continent, sounded like **hime** (to rhyme with **time**)
   — by 1200, like **hawm**
   — by 1500, like our **home**

Change in Place

Do you pronounce the first vowel of **economics** with the vowel of **see** or of **set**?

Do you fry food in a **spider**? or a **creeper**? or a **fry pan**? or a **frying pan**?

Do you drive on a **freeway**? a **motorway**? an **expressway**? a **turnpike**? a **parkway**?

Do you say, "The cat wants out"?

These expressions are regional, heard in some areas but not in others.

Change for Audience and Situation

ORAL ACTIVITY

In the following, what does the language reveal about the relationship between the speaker, the audience, and the situation? What are the clues within the language that lead you to your judgments?

1. "I agree. I mean exercise is wonderful. I mean it builds the body and everything."
2. "In *this* school, I do any punishing that's got to be done. Nobody else."
3. "I seen that game today, Mister, and you ain't got no ball team. What you got there, Mister, is a side show."
4. "Thank you for your very kind offer of a home for my eldest boy in the event of my sending him to Toronto for schooling."
5. "The ages of some of the beaches in the Arctic have been determined from radiocarbon dating of marine shells and driftwood, so that the gen-

eral pattern of uplift of the land can now be sketched in for the past ten thousand years."

6. "I solemnly swear to exercise in all loyalty and conscience the duties entrusted to me as the president of this organization."

7. "I'm beginning to feel that some of the guys down at the shop are beginning to get wise to me, and I think I'd better go easy for a while."

8. "Oh, lay off. I don't feel like talking about it. Let's skip it for now. It's not important anyway."

9. "He's still dining, I believe. But I shall inquire."

ORAL ACTIVITY

The ability to respond to different situations with the appropriate language is the mark of the skilful and tactful user of English. Here are a number of commonplace situations:

1. saying good-bye
2. calling someone to sit down to dinner
3. asking for a favour
4. thanking for a favour
5. introducing a friend

What words would you use in each situation, when speaking:

1. to your mother
2. to an adult stranger
3. to a small child
4. to your teacher
5. to an elderly friend of the family
6. to a friend your own age
7. to someone who doesn't speak English

What, Then, Is "Good English"?

. . . the English that is most effective in a particular time and place, the English that says most precisely just what we want to say, with the proper emotional overtones and with grace, and force and beauty.

—Bergen Evans: *Comfortable Words*

FOR DISCUSSION

What place have the following in learning to play a game like hockey or basketball?

Observing
Listening
Practising
Reading the rule book

How do these four activities apply in learning to use "good English" as Bergen Evans defines it? Which activities are most likely to help you to improve? Why?

> The question of usage is always: Which word or expression gives the effect we want?

—© 1976, Archie Comic Publications, Inc.

To learn to use habitually, freely, and comfortably the language that educated people speak and write is one of the reasons for the study of English. The surest sign of membership in the community of educated speakers is the mastery and use of the dialect called "Standard English". There are no absolute rules about "correct and incorrect" English. "Standard English" is a loose term, ranging from the language of books, literature, complex ideas, to the language of small talk used by educated people. Our choice of an expression depends upon our sensitivity to what is appropriate in each situation.

> Standard English is . . . "normal": that . . . which draws least attention to itself over the widest area and through the widest range of usage.
>
> —Randolph Quirk: *The Use of English*

What Is the "Right" Expression?

I regret that I cannot attend.
I'm sorry that I can't be there.
Nope, I ain't gonna go.

All these expressions are "English"; they follow English grammatical patterns, and "are true to the language as it is"; their meaning is unmistakable to anyone who knows English. If their differences are not grammatical, how then do they differ and for what reasons do we prefer one to the others? We choose the one

1. that fits the social situation and the degree of formality we want, and
2. that suits our cultural and educational background, and sometimes that of our listener — in other words, what is "comfortable".

When we use such terms as **formal**, **informal**, and **colloquial**, we must avoid thinking that one is "better" than another. These terms simply classify all good usage according to the social context. To use formal language in informal situations is to display as much insensitivity as to use colloquial language in the formal context of the written essay or an examination.

The Problem of Slang

Although slang is often vivid and colourful, it has its limitations.

The life of most slang words is short, sometimes only a month or two; the slang of another generation is either unintelligible or quaint. (Ask your parents about the slang of their youth.) Slang is limited in time and in place, an example of "fashion" rather than "style". It lies outside Standard English, the most widely understood variety of the language.

ACTIVITY

A study of present-day slang can give much information about the nature of language, especially of change in meaning, regional differences, and the relationships between language and attitudes.

Make a dictionary, complete with meanings and pronunciations, of the slang in your school.

You might compare your usages with either those of another school or those of your parents and grandparents.

Common Usage Problems

The following glossary contains some of the most common usage problems. Not all will be problems to everyone. Check through them quickly to find the ones that are problems for you.

> We are all prisoners of language. Even the most skilled user of language finds that he cannot quite say what he means. But we can push out the boundaries. To develop new habits of speech and writing means to **add to**, not necessarily take away from, one's world of language. It means to have new choices and to know when to use what. When we are not aware of the choices available in the language, we are truly imprisoned in too small a world of words.

affect — effect
The word **affect** is a verb, meaning 'to influence':
> Einstein's work has **affected** the course of civilization.

The word **effect** can function as a noun and a verb. The verb means 'to make, to bring about', or 'to accomplish':
> The commission was set up by the government to **effect** a reconciliation.

But **effect** is more commonly a noun, meaning 'consequence' or 'result':
> The **effects** of radiation are frightening.

ain't
Originally, **ain't** was an accepted contraction of **am not**. Today it is frowned upon, even though we have no good replacement, especially for the "tag" question. The British use **aren't I?** and in Scotland and Ireland **amn't I?** is common. **Aren't I?**, however, is grammatically inconsistent, and **amn't I?** is difficult to pronounce. We are left with the formal **am I not?** The form **aren't I?** is commonly used in Canada. For example, I'm invited, aren't I?

all together — altogether
Altogether as one word is used only when it is a synonym for **entirely** or **on the whole**.
> You are **altogether** wrong.

Otherwise, use two words as in
> Not one at a time, please, but **all together**.

among — between
Generally, **between** refers to only two items, for example,
> **between** you and me
> **between** Canada and Cuba

Among is generally used to refer to more than two items, for example,

The six thieves divided the loot **among** themselves.

Sometimes **between** is used when one item is individually related to all the others, for example,

between the provinces and the federal government

between Canada and the other countries of the Commonwealth

anyways, anywheres, anyplace, nowheres, somewheres

Use **anyway, anywhere, nowhere, somewhere**.

bad — badly

Standard usage is **bad** after the copula verb (**to be, to feel, to smell, to taste,** etc.):

He felt **bad** when he hit the child.

The fruit smelled **bad**.

The adverb is **badly**, as in:

He played **badly** last night.

balance

This is a book-keeping term. In most other situations, **rest** or **remainder** is more acceptable.

Leave the **remainder** (or **rest**) of the dishes for me.

being as — being as how

Use **since** or **because**.

Because I was tired, I stayed home.

between you and I

Though heard often, this expression is not accepted as standard. Use:

between you and me

between Harry and me

(See also Case of Pronouns, page 306 of this chapter.)

can — may

In formal English, the difference between **can** (able to act) and **may** (permitted to act) is made. The distinction is disappearing in spoken English.

contractions

Contractions such as **can't, don't,** and **shouldn't** are acceptable standard spoken English, but less frequently used in formal writing. Some writers, however, prefer the contracted form.

double negatives

I haven't no money and I didn't say nothing to him and I can't hardly see are clear communication, but the extra negative is not considered standard.

Use: I haven't any money, or I have no money.

Scarcely, hardly, and barely are also treated as negatives.

Use: I can hardly see rather than I can't hardly see.

farther — further

This distinction is breaking down. Generally, farther is reserved for distance, and further for extension.

We shall speak further on this business.

Tempt me no further.

Let's drive no farther today.

fewer — less

Standard English usage distinguishes between less and fewer, and uses less to refer to an amount, and fewer to refer to a number (that is, to a count noun).

Use: I have less money than you.

I have fewer books than you.

have — of

When have is not stressed in such expressions as:

I may have done it.

I should have gone.

He must have done it.

the have often sounds very much like of, but the word of cannot be an auxiliary. Therefore, use have.

imply — infer

The sender of a suggestion or hint implies; the receiver of this suggestion infers. The distinction is a useful one when precise thinking is involved.

Do you imply that I am not telling the truth, or am I to infer that you are joking?

(That is, an implication is what the speaker suggests or puts into his words; an inference is the conclusion drawn by the hearer or reader from these words.)

learn — teach

That will learn him a lesson and He learned me to skate are non-standard. Use teach and taught instead.

like — as (as if, as though)

In American speech, **like** is commonly used as a conjunction, but it is still considered non-standard in Canada, though the distinction is tending to disappear. We do not write:

It tastes like it is overcooked. But the sentence **It looks like it's going to rain** is often heard.

Use **as, as if,** or **as though.**

It tastes as though it is overcooked. It looks as if it is overcooked.

lie — lay

Non-standard English tends to use only the verb **lay,** perhaps because it is regular in its forms (lay, laid, have laid).

Standard English distinguishes between:

lie, (lay, have lain) — 'to recline'
lay (laid, have laid) — 'to put down, to set down'
I must **lie** down.
Yesterday I **lay** in bed until ten.
I have **lain** in bed all day.
I will **lay** it here.
The hens **laid** two eggs.
I have **laid** the table.

loose — lose

Remember that the double **o** suggests the sibilant or "hissing" **s,** as in **moose, noose,** and **goose.** The verb **lose,** like **lost,** has only one **o.** This is a spelling problem rather than a usage problem.

of

People often add an unnecessary **of** to such prepositions as **inside, outside,** and **off.** This older form is sometimes heard in informal speech. But the **of** should be dispensed with in formal speech and in writing.

These are now standard:

inside the house
off the table

(See also **have — of.**)

raise — rise

Something **rises** by itself, but **raises** something else:

The moon **rises.**
I **rose** at nine.
The store has **raised** my wages.
(In England, one gets a **rise** in salary.)

I **raise** vegetables.
They **raised** the children.
The sun has **risen.**

real

The use of **real** as a substitute for **very** is considered non-standard in Canada. If you must use the word as an intensifier, use the adverbial form, **really**. (**I am really tired**.)

shall — will

As auxiliaries, these two words used to have separate meanings, but prevailing usage is **will**. That is, **will** is used except when, in rare instances, it is confusing, for example,

Shall we adjourn for lunch? Shall we go now?

which is different in intent from

Will we adjourn for lunch? Will we go now?

In other words, **will** has the sanction of good authors and of convenience.

swell

Swell, and such other adjectives as **nice, lovely, lousy**, and **fine** (unless used precisely) are lazy choices and should be avoided.

theirselves, theirself, themself, hisself, ourself

These forms do not exist in standard speech or writing. Use **themselves, himself**, and **ourselves**.

"the reason is because"

This expression almost always signals a wordy, roundabout structure. Cure: rephrase.

Not: The reason I was absent is because I was ill.

But: I was absent because I was ill.

these kind — those kind

Although these expressions are often heard colloquially, **this kind** or **that kind** emphasizes the singular idea, and is preferable. In writing, only agreement in number is standard.

this kind of bread

that kind of apple

these kinds of bread

this here — that there

This double form of "pointing" is not necessary; use **that book** or **this book**.

Special Usage Problems in Which a Knowledge of Grammar Helps

I. Case of Pronouns

The main problems occur in the following patterns:

1. When the pronoun is grouped with a noun and you are not sure which form of the pronoun to use, drop the noun and use whichever pronoun form comes naturally:

John and **I** are going.
(**I** am going.)

He gave it to John and **me**.
(He gave it to **me**.)

He took **him** and Jim for a ride.
(He took **him** for a ride.)

The real culprits, John and **I**, went free.
(**I** went free.)

They overlooked the real culprits, John and **me**.
(They overlooked **me**.)

We boys are going.
(**We** are going.)

He gave it to **us** boys.
(He gave it to **us**.)

2. The sentences **It was me** or **It was him** are usually spoken only, and are acceptable. If, however, a clause follows, the forms **I, she, he,** and **they** are standard in spoken and written English:

It was **I** who did it.
It was **she** who first thought of it.

3. **He was taller than I** is considered a shortened form of **He was taller than I was.**
Thus the standard pattern is:

She was stronger than Kathy or **I.**
They think they are better than **we.**

4. **Who** or **whom**?
There is no doubt that **whom** is moving out of the language. Nevertheless, in some expressions of very formal language, differentiation is still made. If this pronoun is at the beginning of a sentence or clause, the force of the English sentence pattern with subject first has made **who** standard.

Who were you talking to?
I know **who** you will give it to.
Who are you with?
You may invite **whoever** you wish.
Whoever shall we invite?

Note that **whomever** has practically disappeared from the language.

In very formal language and in some set expressions, **whom** is used when it is with its preposition or is object of a verb:

With **whom** are you going?
The letter was addressed, "To **whom** it may concern".
She is a woman **whom** (or **who**) we trust.

If in doubt, substitute **he** or **him**; **who** corresponds to **he**, and **whom** to **him** — or use **who**, which is usually acceptable. The major error is the use of **whom** where **who** is standard. The following are correct:

Who do you think will be chosen? (**He** will be chosen.)
She is a girl **who** we know will succeed. (**She** will succeed.)
The man **who** everyone thought was guilty proved to be innocent. (Everyone thought **he** was guilty.)

II. Agreement of Subject and Verb

Most people automatically change the form of the verb or of the auxiliary to "agree" with the subject:

I **go**	I **am** going
He **goes**	He **is** going
They **go**	They **are** going
I **have** gone	I **do** go there
He **has** gone	He **does** go there
They **have** gone	They **do** go there

The following are the main "trouble spots" of agreement.

1. When the subject is compounded with **and** , treat it as plural:

> John and I **are** going.
> The tram and bus **are** leaving.

A natural combination or anything thought of as a unit is treated as singular:

> This bread and butter **tastes** good.
> Ten cents **is** too much to pay.

But an **or** or **nor** separates items. The verb follows the nearer item:

> Neither the train nor the bus **is** leaving.
> The train or the bus **is** leaving soon.
> The train or the buses **are** leaving soon.
> Either two girls or one boy **is** to go.

2. The bare subject, not a modifying group, governs the verb. Watch especially for prepositional groups that are modifiers only.

> This **bunch** of grapes **costs** only ten cents.
> The **list** of the students who passed **is** on the bulletin board.
> **German**, as well as French and Russian, **is** taught at our school.

Watch especially for the singular pronouns **one, everyone, anyone, each, each one, neither,** either, etc. The use of the singular verb form continues and emphasizes the singular idea.

> **One** of the modern languages **is** to be taken in the first year.
> **Neither** of the boys **is** well enough to go.
> **Each** of the essays **is** to be entered in the national contest.
> **Either** of the answers **is** acceptable.

Notice how the singular idea of **every** governs the verb in the following sentence:

And every twig and every bough, every branch and every limb, every trunk and every crack even in the bark *was* furred with it [snow].

—Frederick P. Grove: *Over Prairie Trails*

(For a full discussion of this point, and of the agreement of pronouns, see pages 132-3 of Chapter 4.)

Notice that usage varies with **none**. Generally, if the idea is singular (**not one**, or **no part**), use a singular verb; if the idea is **not any**, you may prefer the plural verb. The choice is yours.

> None of the apple **is** ripe.
> None of the apples **are** ripe.
> None of the suggestions **was** acceptable. (or **were**)
> None of the boxes **have** been opened. (or **has**)

3. Treat collectives (that is, nouns that refer to groups) as you think of them — singular if one group or unit, and plural if the items are thought of individually.

> The jury **is** bringing in the verdict now.
> The jury **have** disagreed and will be discharged.

Above all, be consistent! Do **not** write such mixed patterns as:

> The jury **is** bringing in **their** verdict now.

4. Inverted sentences and "there" sentences sometimes give trouble.

> Through the window **shines** the moonlight.
> Across the water **shine** the lights of the pavilion.
> There **is** a pencil on the desk.
> There **are** several pencils on the desk.

The form **there is** is often used when what follows is enumerated or is thought of as a unit:

> There is a pen and pencil on the desk. (or **are**)
> There is my wife and four children to consider. (or **are**)
> There is roast beef and Yorkshire pudding for dinner.

5. **"one of those who"**

If puzzled by sentences with this construction, see which noun or pronoun the **who** refers to.

> She is the only one of the girls who **sings** well.
> (The natural grouping is "the only one who sings well".)
> She is one of those who **sing** well without training.
> (The natural grouping is "those who sing well without training".)

Here are other examples:

> She is one of those women who **are** always gossiping.
> She is the one woman of the group who **is** always gossiping.
> He is the only one of the boys who **has** passed the test.
> He is one of the boys who **have** passed the test.

III. Incomplete or Inaccurate Comparisons

1. It is standard practice to use the **comparative** degree when **two** things are compared; the comparative form helps to emphasize the idea of "two".

> Both the sisters are popular, but Jane is the **more** likeable.
> Of the two materials, the **more** expensive is the **better** buy.

2. It is logical to compare only those things that can be compared. The following are examples of **illogical comparisons**:

> The exports from Australia are greater than New Zealand.
> The sports program at Delbrook High School is better than our school.

Make the comparisons logical, as:

> The exports from Australia are greater than those from New Zealand.

or

> The exports from Australia are greater than New Zealand's.
> The sports program at Delbrook High School is better than ours.

3. Beware of the **incomplete comparison**, a device of some advertisers.

> This soap is **better, purer,** and **cheaper.** (Better than what?)
> Buy it because it's **better!**

IV. Verb Forms

Most English verbs are "regular"; that is, their past form and past participle form are **-d** or **-ed** (walk, walk**ed**, have walk**ed**).

Irregular verbs are sometimes usage problems.

1. Some verbs change the vowel in the past forms:

I **lead**	I **led**	I have **led**
I **creep**	I **crept**	I have **crept**

Write the past forms of the following verbs, and check with your dictionary if in doubt:

dig, bring, seek, swing, sit, sling, wring, fling, spin, string, teach

Notice that **hang** has two past forms, used differently:

hanged is generally reserved for one meaning:
The man was **hanged** at dawn.
hung is used in all other instances:
I **hung** out the washing.
The lamp **hung** from the ceiling.

2. Some verbs have no separate past forms:

I **cut** my finger every time.
I **cut** my finger yesterday.
I have **cut** my finger.

Others are: hit, hurt, quit, burst, cast, cost, let, put, shed, shut, split, thrust. (What do you notice about the form of these verbs?)

3. Some verbs change the vowel to form the past, and then add **-n** or **-en** to the stem of this past form to make the past participle:

I **choose** a book.	I **tear** a book.
I **chose** a book.	I **tore** a book.
I have **chosen** a book.	I have **torn** a book.
A well-**chosen** book.	A badly **torn** book.

Others are: weave, swear, steal, speak, wear, freeze, break.

4. Some change the vowel for the past form, but

revert to the vowel of the present form and add -n or -en to form the past participle:

grow	grew	have grown
eat	ate	have eaten
forbid	forbade (băd)	have forbidden

Others are: know, throw, draw, see, fall, give, forgive, take, overtake.

In some verbs, though the same letter is used for the vowel, it is pronounced differently, as in:

rise	(rose)	has risen
do	(did)	has done

Do these orally: write, ride, smite, drive, go.

Note also:

run	(ran)	have run
come	(came)	have come
become	(became)	have become

5. A few verbs change the vowel sound for each form:

begin	began	have begun

The verbs drink, ring, swim, sing, shrink, sink, all follow the i - a - u pattern of **begin**.
The verb **fly** is unique: fly, flew, has flown.
The verb **flow** is regular: flow, flowed, has flowed.
Some English verbs retain the -n form when used as modifiers, but do not when used with **have**. You will also find the old -n forms in certain set phrases.

The ship has **sunk**.
A **sunken** ship

I have **shaved**.
A clean-**shaven** face

Famine had **struck**.
A **stricken** family

Both **has proved** and **has proven** are used; the regular -d form is the more common. What past form of these verbs would you use: **spell, dream, leap, knit, kneel, light, burn**? Check with your dictionaries (Canadian, British, and American).

ORAL ACTIVITY

Supply the correct form of the verb.

1. Not many people have (swim) across Lake Ontario.
2. When Mr. Jones (see) the bear, he (shrink) back in fear.
3. We certainly would have (choose) Margot had we (know) her record.
4. When the whistle (blow), Tom (spring) to his feet and (sling) his axe aside.
5. All the books we have ordered have (come).
6. The bell had (ring) twice before we had (go) back to our classrooms.
7. Mary would have been on time if she had not (take) so much time to fuss with her hair.
8. My sweater must have (shrink) when I washed it.
9. I'm sure I (drink) a litre of water after the hike.
10. The book has (lie) on the shelf for years.
11. The boys have (sneak) into the cloakroom and (steal) the refreshments.
12. He has (quit) his job many times.

TENSE SHIFT

If you begin a story in the present tense, do not confuse your reader by changing suddenly to the past. Be consistent, and avoid awkward shifts.
Here are examples of such awkward tense shifts. Correct them:

1. When the prince **saw** that the shoe fitted perfectly, he **was** puzzled, and he **thinks** to himself, "How could such a poor girl become my wife?"
2. Never **had** the Indians **seen** such a boat, and they **wonder** even more as they **see** the white men

disembark. When one sailor **shot** his gun, some of the timid natives **ran** for the safety of the woods, but a few, though afraid, **stand** their ground.

3. The duties of a baby-sitter **are** not always simple. For example, I **was expected** to wash all the dinner dishes! Sometimes mothers even **ask** me to prepare supper for three or four children.

4. While I **was working** at my homework, who **saunters** in but my classmate Bob Roper. He **asked** me why I **am working** so hard.

   "Why, there's a test in French tomorrow," I **answered**, "and don't forget the science quiz on Friday."

   "Humph!" **replies** Bob. "You'll pass those easily. I know a much better way to spend your time."

Troublesome Prepositions

The correct use of prepositions is not a matter of logic, but of **idiom**. An idiom (from the Greek word meaning 'peculiar') is a piece of language that does not always make sense when translated literally or logically. An idiom must be learned as a unit. All languages have idioms. In English, the most troublesome idioms involve prepositions. For example:

We die **of** age, **by** violence, **through** neglect, **in** battle, **from** wounds, and **for** a cause. To be dying **from** drink is not the same as to be dying **for** a drink.

Can you write sentences using the following expressions idiomatically?

accompanied **by, with**
agree **with, to, on**
angry **at, with**
annoyed **at, with, by**
anxious **for, about**
blame **for, on**
borrow **from**
compare **to, with**
conclude **by, with, from**

contrast **to, with**
differ **from, with**
different **from** (see Fowler's *A Dictionary of Modern English Usage* about **than** and **to**)
wait **on, for**

Learning accepted usage is a matter, not merely of rules, but of exposure to good writing and speech. Even the "rules" are established by what the best writers and speakers do. The following illustrates the confusion that results when the rules are not understood. If you find these items humorous, you have gained some understanding of your language.

GRAMMAR AS WROTE: LETTER FROM A TRIPLE-THREAT GRAMMARIAN

Dear Sir: you never past me in grammar because you was prejudiced but I got this here athaletic scholarship any way. Well, the other day I finely got to writing the rule's down so I can always study it if they ever slip my mind.

1. Each pronoun agrees with their antecedent.
2. Just between you and I, case is important.
3. Verbs has to agree with their subjects.
4. Watch out for irregular verbs which have cropt into our language.
5. Don't use no double negatives.
6. A writer mustn't shift your point of view.
7. When dangling, don't use participles.
8. Join clauses good, like a conjunction should.
9. Don't write a run-on sentence you got to punctuate it.
10. About sentence fragments.
11. In letters themes reports articles and stuff like that we use commas to keep a string of items apart.
12. Don't use commas, which are unnecessary.
13. Its important to use apostrophe's right.
14. Don't abbrev.
15. Check to see if you any words out.

—George W. Feinstein: *College English*

A TEST ON USAGE

Write **S** if the sentence is acceptable as formal standard English. Otherwise write the conventional form of the word or phrase.

1. Are you the man whom advertised for an apprentice?
2. Don't either of you own a car?
3. Aunt Susan sent Mary and I an invitation to her wedding.
4. I was no more to blame than she.
5. He promised not to sell it to anyone except Bob or I.
6. Joan and I are going to Sarah's party.
7. Let's keep it a secret between us three girls.
8. After my cat has washed its face and feet, it lays on the rug and watches the fire.
9. May I lend your pen for a few minutes, please?
10. The fog was so thick that we couldn't hardly see the road.
11. You have fewer errors than me.
12. Had I studied, I could have passed that exam.
13. This is one of the best books that has appeared on the subject.
14. These kind of mistakes are not made by educated people.
15. Every nick-nack on Miss Davidson's crowded shelves have an appointed place.
16. Of course, us students did not know about his illness.
17. He had swum into a dangerous current and had been drownded.
18. The first of the two stories is the best because it has more action.
19. I felt like I had committed a terrible crime.
20. The path was so steep that I couldn't hardly reach the top.
21. The work of the secretary is more demanding than the treasurer.
22. The ball landed in back of the shed and rolled into the neighbour's yard.
23. She is always borrowing off of her friends.
24. In his speech he inferred that the town council had been wasting money.
25. Buy this car, as it uses less gasoline.

Punctuation

> If ideas that are difficult to understand are properly separated, they become clearer.
>
> — Aldus Manutius (1566)

Most of us are so accustomed to reading a written, typewritten, or printed page that we take for granted the punctuation marks that help us to comprehend the meaning. We know how to "read" these visual devices. But when we write our messages for others, we must become conscious of the system that helps the reader to hear our "voices". Reading punctuation is like interpreting a map; writing punctuation is like drawing the map — a much harder task.

No punctuation system can replace or "map" all the possibilities of the human voice and "body language". A written system must be kept simple, limited to a few marks. In English, eleven symbols replace all the variations of tone, stress, pause, and gesture possible in giving an oral message. As well as these eleven, there are four other symbols that either separate or highlight language units.

These are the eleven basic punctuation marks:

3 final marks: . period   ? question mark   ! exclamation mark

4 internal marks: , comma   ; semicolon   : colon   — dash

3 enclosure marks: ( ) parentheses   [ ] brackets   " " quotation marks

1 signal to printer to change type-style: <u>underlining</u> (in print, a style called italics, like *this*)

With these are the four other punctuation signals:

   space

   capital letters

and **two marks that relate to words**:   - hyphen   ' apostrophe

End Punctuation — Three Final Marks

The Period is the most common signal at the end of a sentence:

   He arrived yesterday. (Statement)
   He asked me if I had seen Mary. (Indirect question)

   Please, come again. (Imperative, and mild expression of feeling)

The Question Mark signals a direct question:

   When do you expect your friends to arrive?
   You are Tom, aren't you?

Occasionally, the question mark is not a terminal mark. It is used within a sentence to indicate a series of questions:

   Have you checked the doors?   the windows? the lights?

The Exclamation Mark is used for a command or the expression of strong feeling.

Overuse of the exclamation mark weakens its effectiveness. Often a period is sufficient. Notice the difference in the degree of feeling expressed between:

   Let's go! and Let's go.

   Don't worry! and Don't worry.

   Act now! and Act now.

Because the exclamation mark is a terminal mark, a capital letter is used after it.

   Lights! Action! Camera!

Four Internal Marks

(Marks Within a Sentence)

THE COMMA,

Of the four internal punctuation marks, the comma is the most frequently used. Because it deals with the most subtle intonations, the comma is also the most troublesome. But if we think of the comma as having two major functions:

(1) to group words or phrases for easier and faster reading, and
(2) to make the meaning clearer to the reader

we are closer to mastering its uses.

Custom has made the first function conventional, and standard practice tells us when it must be used. For example, which of the following is easier to read?

(a) 2511 Wallace Crescent Vancouver B.C.
                        or
    2511 Wallace Crescent, Vancouver, B.C.
(b) Yes he came.   or   Yes, he came.

Before the metric system was adopted, long strings of figures were grouped in threes by commas (for example, 14,000,000). Now figures containing more than four digits are separated by spaces rather than commas. The sentence:

My annual salary amounts to $8,900.

is now printed

My annual salary amounts to $8900.

and the sentence:

The provincial budget amounted to $357,000,000.

is now printed

The provincial budget amounted to $357 000 000.

The second function of the comma is to control meaning. The writer must decide whether or not the comma signals his meaning clearly and without ambiguity to the reader. Note the difference in meaning the comma makes in the following examples. Read them aloud to **hear** the difference.

He brought five guests more than we had expected.
He brought five guests, more than we had expected.

Often the comma signals the grouping and prevents misreading:

After the patient eats his dishes should be sterilized. (No signal)
After the patient eats, his dishes should be sterilized. (Correctly signalled)

Only two hours before we had left the house. (No signal)
Only two hours before, we had left the house. (Correctly signalled)

Sometimes the use of the comma is optional, that is, the choice is up to the writer rather than determined by convention or meaning. For example, which do you prefer?

After supper, we played Scrabble.
                        or
After supper we played Scrabble.

In general, if the introductory elements are long, the use of the comma is conventional:

After we finished supper in the dining-room, we played Scrabble in the den.

Other Obligatory Uses: established by convention and needed to clarify meaning.

— to separate items in a series:
    We bought apples, bananas, and oranges.

— to mark off insertions into a sentence:
    Tom, of course, knows what he wants.
    Tom knows what he wants, of course.
    We must, I suppose, do as he asks.

—to mark off the name of a person being spoken
to:

Tom, come here!
Come here, Tom!

THE SEMICOLON;

1. The semicolon can replace the period between sentences closely related in thought:

The Canadians have their hockey; the English
have their cricket.

2. The semicolon can replace the period between sentences linked by explicit connectives,
such as **however, thus, therefore, moreover,** etc.
(see page 174 for a list):

I am tired and cold; nevertheless, I am determined
to go on.

Note: The semicolons above can be used to separate **only elements that can stand alone as full sentences.**

3. The semicolon can be used in a series to separate larger groups in which commas already separate smaller groups:

For the past three years he attended schools in
Edmonton, Alberta; Kitimat, British Columbia; and
Toronto, Ontario.

THE COLON:

The uses of the colon are conventional and not in
any way related to the semicolon. The colon is a
mark which serves the following purposes:

—after a salutation in a formal letter:

Gentlemen:
Dear Sir:

—to introduce an appositive series:

My shopping list included the following items:
bread, milk, soap, and stationery.
But: My shopping list included bread, milk, soap,
and stationery.

—to introduce a lengthy quotation:

Many people could profit from the folk-saying:
"Not knowing ain't nearly so dangerous as knowing so much that ain't so."

—to elaborate on or explain what goes before:

To be or not to be: that is the question.
All of us remember the game: we had ten goals
scored against us and managed only one of our
own.

Often the explanation or elaboration is a subtitle
after a title:

Words: How to Know Them
Abraham Lincoln: The Great Emancipator

Note: It is conventional to use the colon in expressions of time such as:

I must catch the 4:15 ferry.
I usually get up at 7:45.

With the adoption of the metric system in Canada,
however, and with the increasing use of the twenty-
four-hour clock, the following forms have become
accepted practice, particularly when printed or
typewritten:

I must catch the 16 15 ferry.
I usually get up at 07 45.

THE DASH —

The dash can be an effective punctuation mark if
its limitations are understood and strictly observed.
In formal writing it serves the following purposes:

—to signal an abrupt shift in thought or to separate
from the main thought any material "thrown in" as
an afterthought:

I must tell you about my trip—but let me first hear about what you have been doing.

—to signal a summary or restatement:

His education, his interest in economics, his business experience — all his background had prepared him for this difficult task.

—to mark off a climactic statement (a pair of dashes):

I believe—and always will — in the ability of people to govern themselves.

—to set off internal appositives or modifiers when these contain commas:

My friends — Ron, Jim, and Harry — are sure to support me.

Three Enclosure Marks

PARENTHESES ( )

—used to insert extra material:

Our tour ended in Istanbul (previously known as Constantinople).

BRACKETS [ ]

—used mainly in academic writing and to mark material inserted into a quotation:

"I reported to the principal that he [Mr. Ledingham] had given me permission to attend the game."

QUOTATION MARKS "   "— to set off material quoted exactly

—the exact words of a speaker:

Tom said, "No matter what happens, I won't go."

— a word or word group being quoted or used in a special way (especially useful for words or phrases of specialized language):

In the language of drug addicts, a "pusher" is someone who sells drugs illegally.
Bertrand Russell talks of the importance of "useless" knowledge.

For quotes within quotes, use double quotation marks for the outer set, and single quotation marks for the contained set.

Tom said, "I can never remember who said, 'The twentieth century is Canada's.' "

— titles of single poems, magazine articles, and short stories:

I like Phyllis Webb's poem "Sitting".

Underlining: A Signal to the Printer to Use Italic Type

When a manuscript is in writing or typewriting, italic print is signalled to the printer by underlining. Thus a typescript that looks like this:

Shakespeare's <u>Hamlet</u>

will be printed like this:

Shakespeare's *Hamlet*.

Italics are commonly used for:

—the title of a book, play, magazine, painting, or ship:

We sailed on the *Oriana* to Australia.

— a word highly emphasized or quoted as a special example:

Of *course* he doesn't see it, because he's *trained* not to see it.
Our word *pasteurize* was made from the name of Louis Pasteur, the scientist who devised this method of sterilizing milk.

— a foreign word or phrase:

The Maoris of New Zealand call white people *pakehas*.

Marking Symbols

The following symbols will help you to understand your teacher's marking and also help you to identify your errors and discuss them intelligently.

Major Faults

ROS   Run-on sentence. You have run-together sentences that should be separated or punctuated differently. See pages 126-7 of Chapter 4.

Agr   Faulty agreement. Your verb does not agree with the bare subject, or your pronoun does not agree with its antecedent. See pages 307-8 of this chapter and pages 131-3 of Chapter 4.

Frag   A sentence fragment. Whenever you use formal statement sentences, be sure they are complete. See pages 120-7 of Chapter 4.

Awk   The sentence needs restructuring.

Serious Faults

Mod   Your modifier is either dangling (give it the right word to modify) or placed ambiguously (see pages 134-5 of Chapter 4).

Ref   Faulty or vague reference of pronouns. See pages 131-3 of Chapter 4.

M?   The meaning is not clear. Reword.

Comp   This is an illogical or incomplete comparison. See pages 308-9 of this chapter.

Om   You have omitted a word or phrase.

Case	Case errors of pronouns. See page 306 of this chapter.
II	Faulty parallelism. See pages 135-8 of Chapter 4.
W	Wordy. Shorten this. Say it simply.
Vb	A verb error. Inconsistent tense (see pages 310-11 of this chapter), or wrong form (see pages 309-10 of this chapter).

Faults

Ap	Apostrophe missing or wrongly used.
Sp	A spelling error. Check with your dictionary.
P	Faulty punctuation.
D	Diction. Find a better word.
Cl	A cliché. Find a better expression.
Par	Check your paragraphing.
Rep	The repetition jars.

Your own particular weakness in language always comes under the category of a major error. For instance, if you are a good speller, the occasionally misspelled word can be considered as a minor error, but if you are a poor speller, repeated misspellings indicate a major difficulty. Make a list of your own major errors, the mistakes **you** tend to repeat in your compositions. Conquer these.

You have now finished working with this book. Probably the most valuable thing that you can take away with you is a continuing interest in the following questions — questions which still engage the minds of all serious students of language.

1. What is language?
2. How do we acquire language?
3. How does language influence the way we live?
4. How does the way we live influence language?
5. How do experiences (work, play, etc.) influence language?
6. How do we make words? What are the ways in which words come into a language?
7. What part do geography and history play in forming dialects?
8. What are verbal "taboos"? Why do all societies have them?
9. What non-verbal language (silent language) accompanies the process of communication?

CONCLUDING ACTIVITY

Reread Muir's poem "The Animals" on page 9 and discuss the ideas in the poem. Do you see more in this poem than when you first read it?

Index of Quoted Materials

Subject Index